SHAKESPEARE, JONSON, MOLIERE
THE COMIC CONTRACT

By the same author

SYNGE: A Critical Study of the Plays

Shakespeare, Jonson, Molière

The Comic Contract

Nicholas Grene

BARNES & NOBLE BOOKS
TOTOWA, NEW JERSEY

First published in the U.S.A. 1980 by
BARNES & NOBLE BOOKS
81, Adams Drive, Totowa,
New Jersey, 07512
ISBN 0–389–20093–X

Printed in Hong Kong

To the memory of Daniel

Contents

Acknowledgements

I would like to acknowledge gratefully a term's study leave from the University of Liverpool which made it possible for me to complete research for this book in Paris.

I want to thank my colleagues Philip Edwards and Sarah Kay, my mother Marjorie Grene and my wife Eleanor Grene, all of whom read my manuscript at various stages in its preparation and made very helpful comments and criticisms. I am also grateful to Joan Welford, Catherine Rees, and Annette Butler for their excellent team-typing.

Some of the material in the first chapter of this book has already appeared in *Themes in Drama* and is included by permission of Cambridge University Press.

N. G.

Note on Texts and Translations

The texts used for the Shakespeare plays discussed in this book are those of the New Arden series, except in the case of *A Midsummer Night's Dream* (Penguin) and *Troilus and Cressida* (Cambridge) where New Arden editions are not yet available. All quotations from Jonson are taken from the individual editions of the Yale Ben Jonson. The Molière used is the two–volume Garnier *Oeuvres Complètes* edited by Robert Jouannay.

As this study is intended primarily for English-speaking readers, some of whom may not read French, it seemed important to include translations of the frequent quotations from Molière. Where these are no more than a line or two, a translation or paraphrase has been incorporated into the body of the text. In the case of longer quotations, the translations appear in a separate section at the end of the book. The versions are substantially my own; they have no claim to literary merit whatever but are intended solely to help the non-French-speaking reader follow the meaning of the lines quoted. For similar reasons I have given in translation the occasional passages quoted from French critics of Molière.

Introduction

The purpose of this book is to pursue an idea about the relation of the comedian to his audience through the comparison of individual works by the three outstanding comic playwrights of the seventeenth century. What is planned is hopefully something more than a series of essays on Shakespeare, Jonson and Molière, though certainly less than a general theory of comedy. In fact, one starting point for this study was a sense of dissatisfaction with comprehensive theories of comedy as such, which tend so often to be monolithic and inflexible, belying the variousness and complexity of the comic experience. Therefore, instead of beginning with a definition of comedy or discrimination between the several sub-species of the comic, I have largely set aside formal distinctions in my synoptic approach to Shakespeare, Jonson and Molière. The net is thrown wide to include anything which has claims to be called comedy, however loosely: a brief farce (*Les Précieuses Ridicules*), a satire (*Volpone*), a Shakespearean romance (*The Tempest*). I have even included plays with more dubious titles to be considered within the comic genre (*Dom Juan, Troilus and Cressida*). The result may at times seem arbitrary in its selection of examples and eccentric in their juxtaposition. There is, however, a design which I hope will emerge in the course of the book as a whole. After an introductory analysis of comic structure in *Bartholomew Fair* (Chapter One), each chapter will involve the comparison of two or more plays to illustrate a variety of different patterns of comic structure and meaning. These will range from the essentially optimistic view of man in society usually associated with romantic comedy (Chapters Two and Three), through the more satiric stance of what may be roughly categorised as comedies of manners (Chapters Four, Five and Six), to a radical scepticism found in plays bordering on other dramatic genres.

The juxtaposition of apparently odd bedfellows can, I believe, result in new insights into the individual plays compared and their authors; I hope that this book may be of some value to people primarily interested in any one of the three comedians. However, it is mainly intended as an exploratory method to find terms of reference sufficiently open to include the different sorts of comedy with which Shakespeare, Jonson and Molière are identified. All three are major comic playwrights who lived and worked within seventy years of each other, and their plays are central to that continuous European tradition of comedy which runs from Machiavelli in sixteenth century Italy through to, say, Beaumarchais in eighteenth century France.[1] Yet they are seldom if ever compared. Romantic comedy represented by Shakespeare, the moral satiric comedy of Jonson, Molière's neo-classical social comedy, are considered as quite separate phenomena. If Shakespeare is compared with Jonson it is nearly always for the purposes of blank contrast, often to Jonson's disadvantage.[2] Molière has very occasionally been compared with Shakespeare, but without much conviction that such an approach is of value except as an analysis of dissimilarity.[3] Jonson and Molière have been considered together even more rarely, partly no doubt because Jonson is not particularly widely known or highly thought of outside the English-speaking world.[4] As far as I am aware, this is the first critical study to be centrally concerned with a comparison of all three.

Very different assumptions about the nature of comedy underlie modern criticism of Shakespeare, Jonson and Molière, so different that the term comedy itself used to denote a common genre almost ceases to have meaning. What comedy is, what comedy does, what comedy means, the answers to these questions change radically depending on whether they are answered by the critic of Shakespeare, Jonson, or Molière. With titles such as *Much Ado About Nothing*, *As You Like It*, *What You Will*, Shakespeare seems to offer his comedies as pure entertainment, untroubled by neo-classical notions of didacticism. Critics have tended, therefore, to try to locate the meaning of Shakespearean comedy in the form of the comic action itself rather than in an identifiable moral lesson to be drawn from it. Northrop Frye, for instance, relates the comic rhythm to its origins in ritual and defines the pattern of Shakespearean comedy as the progress from an 'anti-comic society, a social organisation blocking and opposed to the comic drive' through a Saturnalian period of sexual licence or confusion, to the discovery of identity in a new comic society represented in the celebration of marriage.[5] This connection between comedy and festivity is given detailed historical substance in the work of C. L. Barber and others who have shown in Shakespeare's comedies the development of patterns characteristic of traditional holiday sports and pastimes.[6] From this point of view, the release of a temporary period of allowed misrule leads to the deeper and more secure social order of the ending. The new society created by the dénouement even has transcendental significance for some critics who concentrate on Shakespeare's pastoral comedy and its idyllic images of paradise.[7] Still another way of finding meaning in the comic form is to analyse the ironic multiplicity of different sorts of experience in the plays. The very heterogeneousness of Shakespeare's comedies, their mixture of the fantastic and the realistic, the romantic and anti-romantic, to which Jonson so much objected, contributes to a deliberate effect of enlarging the imagination both of characters and audience. To critics with this view of Shakespearean comedy, it is the constant shift in dramatic mode, rather than a single period of licensed disorder and confusion, which brings the characters through a beneficial alienation to a deeper understanding of themselves and their situation.[8]

Jonsonian criticism has understandably remained much closer to the neo-classical concept of comedy, and has generally been concerned to justify Jonson's own claim for the moral effect of his work. Beginning with L. C. Knights's study, *Drama and Society in the Age of Jonson*,[9] much of the best and most illuminating analysis of the plays has been devoted to the relation between comic technique and moral vision. Jonson, it has been argued, upholds a high ideal of order and truth, traditional and conservative, by the elaborate ridicule of its opposite.[10] Though at an individual level we may not be taught by *The Alchemist* to avoid the excesses of Sir Epicure Mammon, we are confirmed in the general principles by which Mammon is condemned. This moral view of Jonson may be said to represent critical orthodoxy, but several writers have questioned whether he is as monolithic as the moralists would suggest. Jonas Barish, among others, has argued that Jonson moved away from the stern didacticism of his earlier plays, towards a less austere, in some ways more Shakespearean, form of comedy.[11] In John J. Enck's view, Jonson's whole career represents a continuing series of experiments in the development of all available varieties of comic form.[12]

The criticism of Molière illustrates most strikingly of all the debate on comic structure and meaning. A longstanding critical tradition identified the significance of Molière's plays in terms of the ideas of his time. For some he was a radical, associated with the tradition of seventeenth-century freethinking and a rationalist 'philosophy of nature';[13] for others his comedies illustrated a vaguer and more moderate ideal of the 'juste milieu'.[14] Paul Benichou argued for a Molière committed to the aristocratic values of the court;[15] John Cairncross proposed on the contrary a 'Molière bourgeois et libertin'.[16] However, in the last thirty years there has been what Molièristes still think of as a revolution in criticism, started by the work of W. G. Moore and René Bray.[17] They attempted to liberate Molière from association with one ideological position or another, to remind us that he was first of all a man of the theatre, and that his comedies are best analysed in terms of dramatic technique rather than moral or philosophical statement. Though the historical tradition of ideological interpretation has continued, the concern with comic structure has dominated Molière studies since the Second World War.[18] The significance of the comic structure, however, is as much a matter

for debate as ever. W. G. Moore was inclined to see a general theatrical
exploitation of the gap between social mask and human reality. Other
critics, most outstandingly Jacques Guicharnaud, have suggested that the
irrationalism of Molière's comic characters reveals an even more basic
absurdity in the human situation which takes us beyond what we normally
understand by comedy. [19]

Modern critics of Shakespeare, Jonson and Molière share a concern with
the relation of comic meaning and structure; there are interesting parallels
betweeen the controversy over Molière as man of the theatre or as man of
ideas and the debate in Jonson criticism between those who stress his
sustained moral attitude and those who see him as a varying comic
playwright. Yet the terms of analysis used, the basic approach to any of the
three authors, could scarcely be transferred to the other two. In looking for a
concept of comedy sufficiently flexible to accommodate all three, however,
my aim is not to discover a single pattern of comic meaning, nor yet a
rhythm or structure of comic action applicable alike to Shakespeare, Jonson
and Molière. In fact, it is a main thesis of my argument that no such
comprehensive view of the form and meaning of comedy is possible.
General theorists have often found it necessary to attempt some cosmic
explanation, whether psychological, social, philosophical, or anthropological for the significance of comedy. Yet, although complicated taxonomies
of the comic are demonstrated, in many cases it would seem that the general
theory has really one main tradition of comedy, or even one author, at its
centre. Thus Meredith's definition of the comic spirit would allow only
Aristophanes, Menander, and Molière to be pure comedians. [20] Although
Bergson's concept of the mechanical as the source of the comic is ingeniously
extended to a wide range of different forms of comedy, it seems to apply most appropriately to farce and the comedy of situation. [21] For
Northrop Frye, even in *The Anatomy of Criticism* where he analyses a
spectrum of comic form from satire to romance, the basic archetypes
deriving from Roman and Greek New Comedy are most centrally
represented by Shakespeare. [22]

There can be no doubt that comic structures and themes are traditional,
yet they may vary radically not only from one playwright to another,
but from play to play within the works of a single comedian. What remains
constant, I would argue, is not any basic structure of meaning but rather the
relationship between the comedian and his audience. The audience at a
comedy agree to see things in a certain light, agree to accept the terms of
reference which the comic structure establishes and which is frequently
recognised as traditional. But this view of the comic world is not fixed and
universal. It is not always, for instance, socially conservative and reactionary,

as some comic theorists would suggest who insist on the conformist effect of comedy.[23] Nor, on the other hand, need it be progressive or anti-reactionary, as another school of thought would have it.[24] It is not to be identified with the attitude which one or other class or creed of the audience might normally be expected to adopt outside the theatre. Rather it is a hypothetical agreement of comedian and audience to share assumptions for the duration of the comedy which they might well not share at any other time. It is to illustrate this agreement and its varying forms that the present study is designed.

One final caution is necessary to avoid misconception. I need to explain what I mean by the audience of comedy, or rather what I do not mean. I do not mean the audience in the theatre for whom the play was first written and before whom it was first performed, nor yet the succession of various audiences who have seen it since. If there is such a thing as the Platonic form of an audience of which any and every actual audience is an imitation, then it is with such an ideal audience that this book is concerned. That sounds very much like a literary rather than a dramatic point of view. 'Theatres of the mind', so common in earlier criticism of drama, have come to be suspected as an attempt by the literary critic to amplify his or her opinions about a printed text into the reaction of a whole auditorium. No-one is now likely to forget that Shakespeare, Jonson, and Molière were all three men of the theatre, working under the pressures of a demanding practical profession. Throughout this book I have tried where possible to take into account theatrical considerations which may have shaped the comedies discussed and to make use of what information is available about their original staging. My views have clearly often been influenced by productions of the plays I have seen myself. Yet a dramatic structure, above all a comedy, does imply an audience which is something other than the assortment of spectators it happens to meet with in a given theatre. Any serious playwright writes not only with his actual public in mind — a joke for the groundlings here, a literary allusion for the gentlemen there — but also for a notional audience (to avoid the ambiguous term 'ideal') to whom the aesthetic design of the whole might be apparent. It is the shared and agreed response which the comedian seems to expect from his notional audience that I shall be concerned to define.

1 The Comic Contract

The comedian who is, personally or politically, a staunch upholder of the principle of law and order, yet in his comedies seems to celebrate the forces of anarchy and licence — the paradox is so familiar to us that it scarcely registers as a paradox. No one is likely to be startled by the gap between Aristophanes' social conservatism and the exploded image of society which his plays present. Central to 'festive comedy' is the period of allowed misrule which, like the holiday or feast-day of which it is an image, serves only to strengthen the normal social fabric. Ben Jonson, however, has such a formidable reputation as doctrinaire moralist that it is still possible to be puzzled by his festive comedy, *Bartholomew Fair*, where he appears to abdicate from the position of high authority which he occupied in earlier plays. Critics have interpreted this abdication in different ways. Some, already mentioned in the Introduction, have traced a gradual mellowing through the years away from the heavily didactic 'comical satires' towards a more genial and permissive comedy of which *Bartholomew Fair* is the final achievement. Jonas Barish, for example, concludes his persuasive analysis: 'One might suggest, finally, that with this play, in which reformers are reformed by the fools, Jonson confesses his own frailty and his own flesh and blood.'[1] Other critics, however, will not admit that Jonson the moralist has abdicated, but argue that he has simply gone underground. Although there is no explicit figure of authority, no Jonson surrogate in the play with whom we are to identify, the point of view may be no less satiric or judicial.[2] Indeed, if it is seen in this light, it may be construed, not as Jonson's most genial and light-hearted, but as one of his darkest and most pessimistic comedies, for in it no character, no action, redeems the picture of humanity as a tangle of animal appetites rather than a community of social or spiritual beings.

The attempt to place the tone and attitudes of *Bartholomew Fair* between the poles of judicial satire and indulgent comedy has been the main concern of the critics of the play. Jonson, it would seem, must either be asking us to join in the spirit of the fair, or expressing his ultimate disapproval of it. These must necessarily be the alternative readings of the play if we are trying to define its meaning in terms of a definitive authorial position. But our engagement with comedy is more complicated, less direct than this approach would imply. It is not a matter of identifying and responding to Jonson's own moral attitude, whether indulgent or critical, but of entering into the special agreement which he sets up with his audience for the purposes of this particular comedy. In the Induction, this agreement is written out as an explicit comic contract and provides us with a striking instance of the formalised frame of author-audience relationship. This chapter will be concerned ultimately with what that contract represents and how it affects the understanding of the play. But first it is necessary to look in detail at what the audience at the Hope theatre on 31 October 1614, and King James's court on the following night, were asked to watch.

For the modern generation of critics, accustomed to finding hidden principles of unity, *Bartholomew Fair* has obvious attractions. For many years condemned for its sprawling plotlessness and its lack of conformity to the rules of classical decorum, it has naturally found twentieth-century apologists to discover criteria of construction by which it succeeds. The revisionist critics who want to do away with the image of Jonson the classical formalist take it as a major talking-point. [3] An even more ingenious school of opinion argues that *Bartholomew Fair* in fact fulfils the demands of classical precept liberally interpreted. [4] More commonly recent Jonson critics have focussed attention on individual words or concepts which recur in the play as its organic centres. [5] By now it is probably quite unnecessary to defend the play against charges of a chaotic lack of organisation. It is, however, worth analysing the structure of *Bartholomew Fair* not simply in order to show that it exists, but because the meaning of the play emerges only from the apprehension of its structure.

The oftener one re-reads the play the less *Bartholomew Fair* appears formless. Certainly no audience would be likely to miss its dramatic rhythms, for the action of the play is governed by certain basic theatrical dynamics which are easy to understand. We start with the movement towards the fair, the first act being taken up with establishing the various groups of visitors and giving them motives for visiting Smithfield. The fair itself, when we get there, has its own time-scale. There are casual references to the time of day from the first purchases of morning to Justice Overdo's invitation home to supper, and the sorts of activity change with the changing hours. Early on we have the fancy-goods stalls, hobby-horses and ginger-bread, accompanied by preparation of the roast pigs. As the crowds thicken, the purse-cutting and the quarrelling start. [6] By late afternoon some serious drinking has been done, and a tent-load of staggering fair-goers are in their 'vapours'. Finally, but for the interruption of Overdo, the puppets would be a prelude to the whores that Ursula was so anxious to provide for the evening entertainment of Edgworth and his friends.

Against this basic background rhythm there are several progressive theatrical sequences. The stripping of Cokes is one of the most obvious. Bartholomew Cokes heads for the fair, complete with his entourage – Humphrey Wasp his 'governor', Mistress Overdo, Mistress Grace his fiancée, and the marriage licence which we have seen drawn for him by John Littlewit at the beginning of the play. At the fair he is not only separated from all his companions and the licence, but he is in turn stripped of his two purses – small change and sovereigns – his hat, sword and cloak. He is such an easy mark that the cut-purses lament that he has no more to steal:

> Nightingale. Would he had another purse to cut, 'Zekiel.
> Edgworth. Purse? a man might cut out his kidneys, I think, and he never
> feel'em, he is so earnest at the sport.   IV ii 38–40

He appears finally at the puppet-show in the naked simplicity of his doublet and hose, oblivious to losses, absorbed in the action of the puppets. One way in which we mark the development of the fair is by the stages in Cokes's progress to this ultimate natural state.

A more complicated and more important pattern in *Bartholomew Fair* can be summed up as 'justice in the stocks'. It has been frequently remarked that the three characters who are placed in the stocks, Busy, Wasp, and Overdo, are the pretenders to authority, the 'serious asses' of the play. They are, of course, the kill-joys of the fair, each one preaching against its enormities, its distractions or its devilment. It is therefore appropriate to the poetic justice of comedy that the fair should take its revenge upon them. But they are, besides, all tyrannous abusers of their authority – Wasp who bullies unmercifully anyone who will allow himself to be bullied, Busy who has a self-imposed mission to denounce all and sundry, and Justice Overdo who must go seek his enormities himself rather than sit in his court of Pie-powders and wait for them to be brought before him. All three are marked from the start for punishment and the audience is not disappointed. Apart from the ritual moment in which they appear in the stocks together, they are visited with other sorts of discomfiture. When Cokes learns that his governor has been in the stocks and has been robbed of the marriage licence, Wasp has lost his moral authority over his ward for ever. Busy not only misses his chance of the rich Widow Purecraft, but is defeated ignominiously in dispute by a puppet. For Justice Overdo, the biggest fool of the three, is reserved the hardest fall. Having endured beatings, revilings, and every other sort of humiliation, he has the ground of his magnificent moment of revelation cut from under him by the discovery of his wife as one of the whores in his audience. One of the most basic and simplest types of comedy, the putting down of the mighty from their seats, or more often the removal of the seat from under the mighty, is centrally represented in *Bartholomew Fair*.

Yet even this movement which culminates with justice in the stocks is not, as some critics would argue, the main driving-force of the play.[7] It, along with similar sequences such as the stripping of Cokes, is integrated into a larger pattern which takes in all the characters and which comprehends the whole image of the fair. In order to understand this larger pattern it is necessary to trace the way in which the visitors to the fair are grouped initially and what happens to them in the course of the action. If we are to follow the increasingly frenetic goings-on of the fair, it is essential to see the underlying dynamic principles which give them shape and meaning.

Three groups can be identified in the first act as the main parties who will go to the fair in Act II.[8] First there is John Littlewit the proctor, his wife Win-the-fight, her Puritan mother Dame Purecraft, and the zealous Rabbi Busy. Then we have the young men about town, Quarlous and Winwife. The third group centres around Bartholomew Cokes and includes, as we have seen, his sister Mistress Overdo, his fiancée Grace, and the buzzing Wasp. Related to this group, but missing because already at the fair, is Justice Overdo, who is Cokes's brother-in-law and Grace's guardian. These several groups are class-based and are placed in a hierarchy which illustrates their relative social positions. Purecraft and Busy are from the dissident Puritan lower-middle-class: Busy was a baker, until he gave up his profession for full-time preaching, and we hear of a business partner of his, also a Puritan who was a grocer in Newgate-market. A proctor – from Busy's point of view 'a claw of the Beast' – was a clerk of the ecclesiastical court of the Arches. He and his wife are keen that the aristocratic Winwife should marry Purecraft because for them it would mean a step up in the world:

> Littlewit. . . . Win and I both wish you well . . . Win would fain have a
> fine young father i' law with a feather, that her mother might
> hood it and chain it with Mistress Overdo.
>
> I ii 21–5

Mistress Overdo and her symbols of rank are Win Littlewit's envy, and from later references we can tell that the rank is still sufficiently new for Mistress Overdo to be extremely proud of her hood and chain: her husband started life as plain 'Adam the clerk, . . . Adam scrivener'. The Cokes party are in fact in the social stratum immediately above that of the Littlewits – Cokes is an 'esquire of Harrow', minor landed gentry, Overdo is a justice of the peace in the pettiest sessions of the country. The incongruity of Grace Wellborn in this group is made immediately apparent by her name. The very opening lines of the play would have given the audience the clue to her situation: 'Here's Barthol'mew Cokes, of Harrow o' th' Hill, i' th' County of Middlesex, Esquire, takes forth his licence to marry Mistress Grace Wellborn of the said place and county.' (I i 3 − 5). The conjunction of Cokes − a fool − with Grace Wellborn might have made them suspect, what is afterwards confirmed, that this is another case, so common at that time both on and off the stage, of an aristocratic ward of court being forced to marry an imbecile relative of her unscrupulous guardian. Finally, Tom Quarlous, in the *dramatis personae* listed as a 'gamester', and Ned Winwife 'a gentleman', are the traditional impecunious upper-class young men out to restore their fortunes by mercenary marriages or otherwise.

In the first act, therefore, we are presented with a cross-section of the middle to upper classes of society. To this is added in the second act an anatomy of the underworld of the fair people. There are distinctions among the traders themselves, based on the scale of their enterprises. Lantern Leatherhead, whose hobby-horse stall is worth nearly thirty shillings including three shillings for his 'ground' and who has the puppet-show as a second string, is inclined to bully Joan Trash the gingerbread woman, whose whole business sells for less than five shillings 'ground and all'. [9] Of those who frequent the fair some are professional crooks, Edgworth the cut-purse, or Cutting the 'roarer', while some are in the shady region of half and half. Jordan Knockem, for instance, is 'a horse-courser and ranger o' Turnbull', that is both a horse-dealer and a pimp, Turnbull (properly Turnmill) street being associated with prostitutes. Knockem has presumably legitimate business at the Horse Fair as well as his illegitimate activities based on Ursula's booth. It is noticeable that Winwife and Quarlous know some of the fair-people but not others − Knockem but not Edgworth, Whit but not Cutting. Yet whatever the varying shades of disreputability, the natives of the fair all work together. Trash and Leatherhead may squabble between themselves but where either is attacked the other rallies to the defence. Ursula acts as fence for the stolen goods of Edgworth and Nightingale, Knockem and Whit, and will find them whores when the day's work is over. Even the officers of the watch are in league with Whit who directs them to lucrative brawlers to arrest.

The central interest of the play is the effect of the fair and the fair-people on the visitors. In purely formal terms we become aware of an overall pattern of dispersal. After each group has made an initial appearance as a group, we watch it begin to dissolve with couples and individuals breaking away until no two characters from one group are left together. If we imagine each group as a single molecule at the beginning of the action we can show

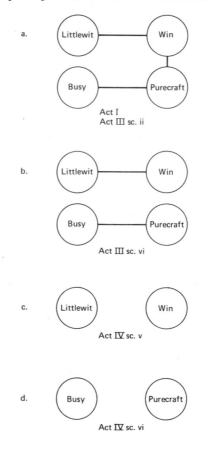

FIG 1 Littlewits

with diagrams the process by which it is split up into its several constituent atoms. The Littlewits, for example, (Fig. 1) appear all together and go to eat pig in Ursula's booth in III ii. When they emerge, however, Littlewit, anxious lest they be marched right home by Busy, contrives a ploy to have him arrested, so that he and his wife manage to escape from the rabbi who is marched off to the stocks with Purecraft in attendance (III vi). The Littlewits are forced back to Ursula's by a call of nature, and when they come out again (IV v) the injudicious Littlewit leaves Win in the tender care of Knockem and Whit. The dispersal of the other half of the group is completed in the next scene (IV vi) when we see Purecraft abandoning Busy to pursue her beloved madman. The pattern with Quarlous and Winwife is necessarily

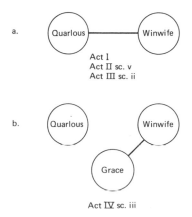

a.

Quarlous —————— Winwife

Act I
Act II sc. v
Act III sc. ii

b.

Quarlous   Winwife

Grace

Act IV sc. iii

FIG 2 Aristocrats

simpler as there are only the two of them (Fig. 2). They stay together for more of the fair than the others, united by their common amusement and contempt for what they see. But with the introduction of Grace as catalyst, their bond is quickly broken and they separate in IV iii, Winwife effectively taking possession of Grace although that possession is not confirmed until the final act. With the third group, the Cokes party, (Fig. 3) we are introduced to four of them in Act I, and the missing member, Justice Overdo, in the first scene of Act II. We first see them all in the fair in II vi, with Cokes madly rushing from stall to stall pursued by the infuriated Wasp and with Mistress Overdo and Grace in tow. As with anything supposedly in the charge of Bartholomew Cokes, his group rapidly get lost or mislaid. Grace drifts away with Quarlous and Winwife (III v); Cokes appears solo without either Wasp or Mistress Overdo in IV ii, and these two in turn are separated in the vapours-scene (IV iv) when Wasp is haled off to the stocks.

The whirling movement of the fair acts as a centrifugal force in which bonds of social relationship vanish until there is a mere mass of human atoms in accidental conjunction. It is worth stressing this pattern because it integrates many other features of the play which might otherwise seem only local or casual ironies. The stripping of Cokes, for example, which we looked at in isolation as a single theatrical sequence, is a part of the general reductive process of the fair. His clothes, his possessions and his attendants are all the outward visible signs of his social position; he must be parted from all of them in order to become the pure Cokes he really is. With other characters,

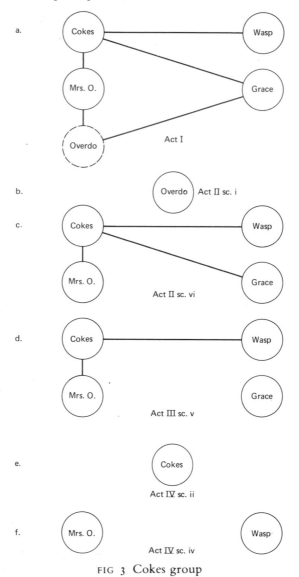

FIG 3 Cokes group

as with Cokes, change of clothing and disguise are not mere slapstick devices. There is the obvious irony of Justice Overdo in the fool's coat, playing the fool indeed, or Quarlous as Trouble-all the madman. These, one might say, are the stock-in-trade of any Elizabethan comedian. But the emphasis on the women's clothes, particularly as they represent their social status, becomes of increasing importance in the final scenes. The last three scenes of Act IV, the culmination in the pattern of dispersal, leave in turn Win, Mistress Overdo, and Purecraft alone and without their male protectors. Both Win and Mistress Overdo are pressed into the service of the pimps. Win now gains the terms of equality she sought for her mother — to 'hood it and chain it with Mistress Overdo' — but it is in the ironic shape of the common uniform of the whore. Alice the professional (Dame Overdo's namesake, one notices) objects vehemently to the competition represented by these amateur ladies. 'The poor common whores can ha' no traffic for the privy rich ones; your caps and hoods of velvet call away our customers and lick the fat from us.' (IV v 64−6). It is typical of the levelling quality of the fair that what began as the token of Mistress Overdo's superior social standing, her 'justice-hood' to borrow Wasp's pun, makes her in the end no more than a higher-grade whore, a twelve-penny 'velvet-woman'. With justice in the stocks, the wards removed from their guardians, the ladies turned into whores, the whole system of society with its complicated network of shibolleths is subverted.

There are signs in the play, moreover, that Jonson deliberately intended it to be seen as the whole system of society. One of the peculiarities of *Bartholomew Fair*, and one which causes most trouble to readers, is the continuous thickening with new characters which we get right through the action. As late as IV iv, we meet three characters we have never heard of before, Northern, Puppy and Cutting, and it does not help matters that we never hear of them again after this one scene. This is the point at which people reading the play who have been finding it hard to follow tend to give up in disgust, understandably in view of the fact that Northern and Puppy as well as Whit are given speeches in dialect, notoriously hard to read. It is not enough to appeal to the stage, where Jonson would have wanted large crowds for his fair and where dialect is always far more intelligible, to defend this feature of the play. There must have been some better reason for this practice, which may have put a strain on the resources of the company, and which has no parallel in other plays of Jonson.[10]

It may be that the very prevalence of dialect in these late-appearing characters gives the clue to their function. Whit, one of the principal figures among the fair-people, speaks what is apparently for the period a very consistently and carefully written stage-Irish.[11] He appears first in III i accompanied by two of the watch, Haggis and Bristle. Now Bristle we know from Wasp's abuse of him much later on is a Welshman — 'Sir, you are a Welsh cuckold, and a prating runt . . . You stink of leeks, metheglin, and cheese, you rogue' (IV vi 42−6). (The Welsh were traditionally supposed to be fond of cheese and metheglin is a form of mead brewed in

Wales.) It is tempting to leap to the assumption that Haggis is Scots and that what we are offered is a representative trio like Fluellen, Captain Jamy and Captain Macmorris in *Henry V*. A number of problems, however, attach to this attractive theory. One is that Haggis is not automatically to be regarded as Scots because of his name, as haggis, at least according to the O.E.D., was not yet in the Elizabethan period exclusively associated with Scotland. Even more puzzling is the fact that neither Bristle nor Haggis are given any indication of dialect in their speech, in striking contrast to Whit. It is possible that Jonson had in his cast a Scot and a Welshman who could be relied on to supply their own accent, and that he therefore found it unnecessary to write in phonetically what they were to say. But however we explain this anomaly, the appearance of Northern, a clothier from the north of England (not from Scotland although Knockem calls him a Galloway nag) and Puppy, a western wrestler, in the vapours-scene, suggests strongly that Jonson wanted to include representatives from the provinces and from the constituent nations of Great Britain.

Clearly Haggis and Bristle, much less Northern and Puppy, are not important parts in themselves; no more indeed than the parts of Captain Jamy and Captain Macmorris are. In *Bartholomew Fair*, as in *Henry V*, it is as representative presences that they are significant. Jonson wants to show an image of the whole realm in holiday disorder, as Shakespeare wanted to show the whole realm assisting in the glorious victory of Agincourt. There are surprisingly few plays in the Elizabethan /Jacobean period in which such representative trios appear, and it may even be that Jonson had *Henry V* at the back of his mind. Justice Overdo incognito at the fair could be seen as a parody version of the king giving his soldiers their 'little touch of Harry in the night'. In any case *Bartholomew Fair* provides a strange instance of the Tudor and Stuart concept of the union of the nations, so strongly emphasised for obvious reasons by James I of England and VI of Scotland. If in the earlier acts of the play we seem to be watching the usual sort of city comedy, with its close but limited view of the world of London, through Acts III and IV the spiralling movement of the action seems to circle out to take in the provinces and the whole of the rest of Great Britain. Or, to change the metaphor, the whole of the country is sucked towards the maelstrom of the national fair at Smithfield. What Jonson is presenting to his London audience and to his monarch, is a view of their society, James's kingdom, in process of reduction to a mass of crooks and fools, pimps and whores, drunkards and madmen. What status of reality had this reduction, and how was an audience to react to it and its comprehensiveness? It would seem an odd dish to set before the king.

There are several ways to go about answering these questions, several sorts of moral attitude which can be seen as the appropriate response to *Bartholomew Fair*. Some critics, for example, have tried to establish one or two of the characters as *raisonneurs*, or audience sponsors on stage; Quarlous and/or Winwife have been the only obvious candidates. They would seem to correspond to the type of gentlemen wits used already by Jonson in *Epicoene* with Truewit and Clerimont, the type later to be developed into the heroes of Restoration comedy. Richard Levin, for example, argues that their attitude to the fair, amused but detached, is the correct one from Jonson's and the audience's point of view: 'these men can be said to be our representatives at the fair, guiding our response, in the manner of a chorus, to the comic behaviour it brings out in the Cokes and Littlewit parties'. [12] It can be claimed that they come out on top, each winning a wife, and Quarlous directing the final dénouement. Other critics prefer to discriminate between the two and suggest that one is morally contrasted with the other; J. A. Bryant Jnr. argues that it is Quarlous whose development in the play is central and representative, [13] whereas for Jackson I. Cope it is Winwife who alone provides a hopeful exemplar. [14]

It is true that the two young gentlemen get off relatively lightly, and indeed profit from the fair; they also appear to be the only characters with whom an audience could identify without damage to their self-respect. But all the same they scarcely fit the part of *raisonneurs* either singly or together. The analogy with the wits of *Epicoene* does not altogether hold. Truewit, Clerimont and Dauphine all have names which mark them quite clearly for the audience's approval, whereas Quarlous and Winwife have satiric-descriptive names which would suggest that they are to be viewed with the other comic characters. And, as we have seen, the fair exerts the same sort of pressure on the two of them as a group, as it does on the other fair-goers. They go as observers in a spirit of disdainful amusement – 'these flies cannot, this hot season, but engender us excellent creeping sport' – but before long they are taken by as nonsensical vapours as any of the rest. Grace's lottery choice of a husband is surely as comically reductive an incident as one could wish for in a Gilbert and Sullivan operetta. As for isolating one as preferable to the other, though they are differentiated in character – Quarlous being more aggressive, Winwife more prudent and fastidious – there is morally little to choose between them. The whole joke of Quarlous's final marriage to Dame Purecraft turns on our recollection of the virtuoso comic diatribe he directed against Winwife when he, Winwife, was courting her. The logic of the play forces us to see them as a Tweedledum/Tweedledee couple, neither of whom are of very compelling individual importance.

If those who see the aristocrats as representative of audience opinion might be characterised as the élitist critics, there are also the democrats who stress the very levelling of all the fair-goers, including Quarlous and Winwife, as the moral of the play. Quarlous's final injunction to the justice has inevitably attracted moral interpretation: 'remember you are but Adam, flesh and blood! You have your frailty; forget your other name of Overdo and invite us all to supper'. (V vi 94–6). All those that pretend to be better, wiser, more holy than the inhabitants of the fair are revealed as the same flesh and blood, the same sinful and foolish men as their despised fellows. This is close to the Christian anarchism of *King Lear*: 'see how yond justice rails upon yond simple thief. Hark in thine ear: change places; and handy-dandy, which is the justice and which the thief?'[15] Thus the spirit of forgiveness characteristic of comedy may be said to be associated at the end of *Bartholomew Fair* with a proper Christian attitude of humility – 'Judge not that ye be not judged'.

There are dangers here, however, dangers particularly of sentimentalising the whole concept of the fair. If the opponents of the fair are Busy, Wasp and Overdo, if its victims are such nincompoops as Cokes, it is inevitable that we should tend to cheer on the fair-people. But it would be a mistake to think that Jonson or his audience looked upon Ursula and Edgworth, Knockem and Whit as lovable rogues in whom we all recognise our common humanity. There are indications throughout the text of a much more tough-minded and astringent attitude towards the fair, which makes it difficult to sustain what we might call the Christian democrat interpretation.

Grace Wellborn objects when the eager Cokes proposes the outing to the fair: 'Truly, I have no such fancy to the Fair, nor ambition to see it; there's none goes thither of any quality or fashion' (I v 121–2). Any modern director, or actress cast for the part of Grace, would presume on the strength of such a line that the character was intended to be played as a snob and a prig. But it is likely that for a seventeenth-century audience Grace's attitude would have had no such taint; indeed it might be considered a sensible point of view. Winwife and Quarlous also regard themselves as accidental onlookers rather than the natural clientèle of the fair: Winwife is indignant at being accosted by Trash and Leatherhead. 'That these people should be so ignorant to think us chapmen for 'em! Do we look as if we would buy gingerbread? Or hobbyhorses?' Quarlous's reply is to the point – 'Why, they know no better ware than they have, nor better customers than come. And our very being here makes us fit to be demanded, as well as others.' (II v 12–16). The force of such tolerance, however, is not to suggest that the aristocrats should accept the levelling spirit of the fair, and admit costermongers as their equals. All Quarlous is saying is that if they go slumming they must expect to be taken for slum-dwellers. The same point is registered in Quarlous's reaction to Edgworth's familiarity with him after the cutpurse has successfully stolen the licence on Quarlous's instructions:

> *Quarlous* . . . go your ways, talk not to me, the hangman is only fit to
> discourse with you; the hand of beadle is too merciful a punishment for
> your trade of life. [*Exit Edgworth.*] I am sorry I employed this fellow; for
> he thinks me such: *Facinus quos inquinat, aequat.* IV vi 23−7

Again a modern response to this might well be that the affronted Quarlous is
standing on his dignity, and the quotation from Lucan would add to the
sense of pomposity. But the tag − 'crime levels those whom it pollutes' − is
probably intended by Jonson to be taken perfectly seriously. The invocation
of the hangman is a reminder that the cutting of purses was not a trivial
crime, and that Edgworth and his companions were people to be avoided.

The fair is not a great hearty entertainment in which all creeds and classes
jostle one another in democratic union, or at least it is not regarded with the
sort of twentieth-century approval which such an image would seem to
imply. People of superior social standing, or of superior sense, do not
normally frequent *Bartholomew Fair*; if they do they must take the
consequences:[16] this seems to be Jonson's attitude, and it is the attitude which
he assumes in his audience. And yet, in some sense, he is allowing them to
have their cake and eat it, because he simultaneously implies that the fair,
with all its foolishness, is familiar to them and that they will enjoy the
familiarity. What Jonson is offering the audience at the Hope seems to be the
opportunity to enjoy the fair without incurring the hazards of being fair-
goers. He is not issuing an open and genial invitation to come to Bartholomew Fair; instead he asks them to sit where they are and watch it. It
is because the audience are not participants that they can laugh securely. But
it is time to look at the way in which this relationship with the audience is
built up in the Induction.

The Induction to *Bartholomew Fair* has drawn a great deal of attention for
its much valued information about current theatrical practice, and for its
characteristic Jonsonian grimaces against Shakespeare. Of course one of its
principal functions is to re-affirm Jonson's principles of art, his disapproval of
obscenity and slapstick, his dislike of fantasy and mixed dramatic form −
Shakespeare's 'Tales and Tempests'. But it is also, formally, a fascinating
example of a comic dramatist establishing a mood for his comedy, setting up
a relationship with his audience. The opening with the Stage-keeper
apologising for the delay in beginning the play is like the start of Jonson's
1612 masque *Love Restored* in which one of the performers is sent out to
announce that the show cannot go on. In each case a preliminary ground of
reality is established with the supposed revelations of behind-the-scenes

confusion. Particularly effective is the device of making the Stage-keeper a man of the theatre of the old school, who whispers his disapproval of Jonson's play, anxious 'lest the poet hear me, or his man, Master Brome, behind the arras'. The views of the Stage-keeper are discredited, and anyone who like him comes to the play expecting the traditional figures of Smithfield or the crude stage business that went with them, is deftly disabused. At the same time we are given an amusing glimpse of the waspish Jonson: 'these master-poets, they will ha' their own absurd courses; they will be informed of nothing! He has, sir-reverence, kicked me three or four times about the tiring-house, I thank him, for but offering to put in, with my experience'. (Induction 23 − 6). The audience, flattered by its position of privilege, given the run of the green-room, is tactfully directed by the irony towards an understanding with the author.

The prompter who comes on and swiftly dispatches the stage-keeper is Jonson's representative, elaborately scornful of the 'grounded judgements' of the pit. And yet in the articles of the contract which the scrivener is ordered to read out, Jonson's pugnacious defiance of popular taste is balanced by a more conciliatory attitude. He offers his wares, proudly asserting their high standard of merit, contemptuously dismissing his rivals, and yet admitting that his audience as the customers have the right to judge for themselves. Balanced too in a similar way is the universal and the particular, the traditional principles which Jonson is restating, and the topical in-jokes by which he cements his league with the present audience. He laughs with them at anyone who will still argue that the first plays of the Elizabethans have never been surpassed:

> He that will swear *Jeronimo* or *Andronicus* are the best plays yet, shall pass unexcepted at here as a man whose judgement shows it is constant, and hath stood still these five and twenty, or thirty years. Though it be an ignorance, it is a virtuous and staid ignorance, and next to truth, a confirmed error does well; such a one the author knows where to find him.   Induction 95− 100

This, with the stage-keeper's nostalgic reference to 'Master Tarleton's time', suggests that there were plenty of people already in 1614 looking back sentimentally to the beginnings of the great period of Elizabethan theatre. There is a wry allusion to the conditions in the newly-opened Hope theatre, where *Bartholomew Fair* was probably the first major production. 'And though the Fair be not kept in the same region that some here, perhaps, would have it, yet think that therein the author hath observed a special decorum, the place being as dirty as Smithfield, and as stinking every whit'.

(Induction 138–142). The joke about Henslowe's bear-baiting, which was the alternative function of the theatre, is turned on an ironic appeal to decorum.

Jonson meets his spectators on their own ground of here and now, and cajoles, bullies, and blackmails them into assuming the role of his ideal audience. He will give them, he says, 'a new sufficient play called *Barthol'mew Fair*, merry, and as full of noise as sport, made to delight all, and to offend none; provided they have either the wit or the honesty to think well of themselves' (Induction 73 – 5). In other words nobody present need think he is satirised in the play unless he is so foolish as to recognise himself among the fools. This attitude, (derived from Martial, Jonson's editors tell us) has always been the satirist's best line of defence, and is always coupled with the claim that he offers only general images of absurdity, species not individuals. It is equally ridiculous to attempt to discover political allegory in the play, and Jonson invites the mockery of the audience on 'any state-decipherer, or politic picklock of the scene, so solemnly ridiculous as to search out who was meant by the gingerbread-woman, who by the hobbyhorse man, who by the costermonger, who by their wares' (Induction 122–5).[17] He takes his spectators to be people of commonsense and good humour, who will understand his play in the spirit in which it is intended. They are, therefore, at once the group of people assembled on a particular day, in a particular place – full details given in the contract – to watch a new play, and a hypothetical audience for this sort of comedy at any time. 'To make the spectators understanders', Jonson describes as the function of the preface to one of his masques, and the same might be said of the Induction to *Bartholomew Fair*: it draws them into the position of an understanding and responsive audience for his play.

For the second performance of the play, the King himself was assigned this role of understanding and responsive audience. For that occasion Jonson wrote a special Prologue 'to the King's Majesty' which presumably served as a substitute for the Induction, and which makes the same points as the Induction did, particularly the insistence that no individual is attacked:

> These for your sport, without particular wrong,
> Or just complaint of any private man
> Who of himself or shall think well or can,
> The maker doth present . . .

But some of those politic pick-locks whom Jonson complained of in the Induction, might well have seen a satiric view of James himself in the play. Many of the opinions well known to be those of the monarch appear in

Bartholomew Fair in the mouths of the least admirable characters. Was it tactful, for example, to have Zeal-of-the-land Busy fulminating against the uncleanness of pig, when James's dislike of pork was a court byword? Several critics have remarked that Justice Overdo's tirade against tobacco might have been drawn from the King's own pamphlet *A Counterblaste to Tobacco*, published in 1604. Overdo's fondness for Latin tags, again, could have been maliciously interpreted as a glance at the king's pride in his classical learning, and one critic has gone so far as to suggest that in Overdo's excessive concern for the 'proper young man' Edgworth, there may be an allusion to the king's attraction to his handsome favourite Robert Carr.[18]

And yet as Ian Donaldson sensibly argues, 'it would seem unlikely that in a play dedicated to the king and designed (partly, at least) for a royal occasion Jonson would have held James up to derision'.[19] Jonson covers himself against the suspicion of any such intention by the terms of his Prologue:

> Your Majesty is welcome to a Fair;
> Such place, such men, such language and such ware,
> You must expect. . . .

This is the same appeal to decorum which we saw in the Induction, and it invokes the monarch's sense of proportion in watching what is to follow. He is to see what he might expect to see in a fair – if he ever went to such a place – knaves, fools, drunkards and charlatans. If there are resemblances between these characters and the king himself, they would serve only to make the characters funnier, not derogate from the dignity of the king. James would hardly be likely to be identified or identity himself with the Puritan elder, in spite of their common dislike of pork; Busy's abhorrence of pig is in any case quite palpably assumed. Some of the arguments in *A Counterblaste to Tobacco* may seem to us almost as ludicrous as Overdo's speech, for example, the conclusion:

> A custome loathsome to the eye, hateful to the Nose, harmfull to the braine, dangerous to the Lungs, and the blacke stinking fume thereof, neerest resembling the horrible Stigian smoke of the pit that is bottomelesse.[20]

Yet one suspects that James was aware of the element of mock-heroic in his rhetoric and he would never have committed the absurdity of trying to preach against ale and tobacco in the middle of *Bartholomew Fair*. Overdo's opinions are funny because of their context and because of Overdo's own foolishness, not because they are inherently ridiculous. The gap between James and Overdo was so enormous that it would hardly have occurred to the king that it could be intended as a satire on himself and if he recognised his own ideas grotesquely distorted in the mouth of the foolish justice he could have laughed contentedly.

As the person of the king was said to represent the whole state, so in the court performance of *Bartholomew Fair*, James takes the place of the whole community embodied in the audience of the Hope theatre. The delight which had been offered them in the Induction is, in the Prologue, tendered as a person 'fairing' for the King. But is there more to this delight than the trivial and ephemeral pleasure of watching ridiculous 'noise and sport'? If the audience, whether the people at the Hope or the King himself, are exempted from seeing themselves as involved in the comedy, surely this drastically limits its seriousness. If it is not the audience or the audience's own society which is exposed to mockery, their laughter is pure escapism. We seem to be left with a view of the play similar to that of L. C. Knights, 'a stage entertainment . . . in which the fun is divorced from any rich significance'.[21]

Bartholomew Fair is, in fact, an excellent test-case for the broader question with which we shall be concerned throughout much of this study: how far and in what way are those who watch a comedy intended to see themselves represented on stage? Are we ever really laughing at ourselves? *Bartholomew Fair* is Jonson's most realistic comedy. With its centre in the national institution of the great London fair, with its carefully pointed hierarchy of social groupings and its comic delegates from the several nations of the united kingdom, it is a systematic and comprehensive anatomy of the range of Jacobean society. In that sense Jonson's audience were undoubtedly watching an image of their own world, delightfully familiar to them in all its detail and all its absurdity. They are asked, however, not to censure or applaud the way of that world but to watch and enjoy it. The play contains comparatively little of the contemporary satire so common in Jonson's earlier works. It is true that there is the continuing vendetta against the Puritans but by comparison with the polemic portraits of *The Alchemist* Busy is a figure of almost pure comic fantasy. If the play may be called an anatomy of Jacobean society it is with none of the sense of satiric diagnosis which that term often implies. Jonson is not out to show his audience what is wrong with them or their community. Instead the realistic, the topical, the specific, are generalised into a fantastic comic pattern which by-passes satire altogether.

From Cicero on, comedy has been traditionally compared to a mirror. It is, however, a distorting mirror.[22] Watching our reflection, we in the audience can comfort ourselves that this is not what we really look like, and yet recognise that it is our image that we see. The delight of the grotesque lines of distortion is based always on a controlling mental image of the normal perspective. It is in this sense that festive comedy's holiday period of allowed misrule implies its opposite – a controlling idea, even an ideal, of order. But in *Bartholomew Fair* we must supply this idea ourselves; it is not represented on the stage by a satisfying return to normality. While the play lasts we accept that the fair is an appropriate metaphor for man's condition as a creature of meaningless appetite and equally meaningless aggression, whose only redeeming feature, if it might be called that, is a mad and undirected vitality. We have agreed with the author in the comic contract to see things in this way, and yet not to take offence at the implication that we too are included in the indictment. If we are able to transcend the play's comprehensive and authentic vision of chaos, which has the force of imaginative truth, it is exactly because we can share together with the author in the laughter which distances us from it. In this understood relationship of comedian and audience *Bartholomew Fair* supplies us with a paradigm for a whole range of differing comic contracts with which the rest of this book will be concerned.

2 The Triumph of Nature

Naturam expellas furca, tamen usque recurret.
You may throw nature out with a pitchfork, she'll return nonetheless.

The Horatian tag might stand as the epigraph to any number of comedies. A variety of pitchforks are used in the attempt to expel nature: the old man defies the natural decorum of like to like when he marries a young wife; the tyrannical father tries to prevent the natural rhythm of the generations when he opposes the marriage of his son or daughter; the fop, the hypocrite or the pedant by their absurd behaviour offend against a social idea of naturalness. But in the final act of the play nature returns to triumph, with the jealous old husband cuckolded, the heavy father outwitted, and the comic butts mocked and humiliated. All of these deviate not merely from a norm of reason, or of socially acceptable behaviour, but from what is taken to be a natural norm. It is easy to move on from the observation of this recurrent pattern to the general concept of comedy as a celebration of the forces of nature. The theme of the triumph of nature may be related to the rhythms of fertility-ritual from which comedy is assumed to have originated. Suzanne Langer's view is representative of that of many modern theorists: 'Comedy is an art-form that arises naturally wherever people are gathered to celebrate life, in spring festivals, triumphs, birthdays, weddings, or initiations.'[1] In these terms, comedy enacts the victory of the new over the old, spring over winter, nature over death.

It is, however, important to distinguish between different valuations, different associations which the concept of the natural may have in comedy. It is not always the same nature that returns to triumph over the forces which oppose it. A low or reductive view of nature is the underlying principle of a whole tradition running from Mediaeval fabliau to English Restoration comedy. It is the natural course of events that Chaucer's Alison or Wycherley's Country Wife should be unfaithful. Men and women, it is implied, must satisfy their appetites like animals, and the attempts to restrain those appetites are inevitably bound to fail. By the 'natural' we understand the basic physicality which the comic characters repress at their peril. In this context, human ideals are seldom much more than hypocritical pretensions used to cover up reality. Honour, love, virtue, fidelity, are meaningless mouthings; society itself is a system which nature is out to beat if it can. Yet there is another tradition of comedy in which nature is seen as an underlying ideal rather than an inescapable reality. There are comedies which conclude 'all's well that ends well' not ironically or cynically, but with a genuinely triumphant triumph of nature. Although these, too, often begin with a conflict of natural impulses with social law, they can find their way to a satisfactory harmony between the two. Moreover the nature that wins out in the end is not very readily identifiable with the primal life-giving force which the rites of ur-comedy are supposed to celebrate. So far from representing a victory of the new over the old, it often suggests a return to an original, a pristine order. At times it seems no more than an optimistic view of the way of the world, an innate tendency for things to turn out for the best. At times it seems that nature is identified as those instincts in man which make for harmonious social life. The natural, so far from being in complete opposition to the social, is very much a concept of man in society. The purpose of this chapter is to analyse two comedies which may illustrate such an idealistic conception of nature – *As You Like It* and *L'Ecole des Femmes*.

AS YOU LIKE IT

As You Like It begins, as so many comedies begin, with an unnatural situation. Already in the opening speech of the play Orlando alerts us to the perversion of natural rights in his position. He is treated less well, he tells Adam and the audience, than his brother's animals for he, a gentleman, is given no better nurture than a beast:

> Besides this nothing which he so plentifully gives me, the something that nature gave me his countenance seems to take from me. He lets me feed with his hinds, bars me the place of a brother, and, as much as in him lies, mines my gentility with my education.   I i 16–21

The natural potential of Orlando's gentle birth is being deformed by an education out of keeping with his blood. Orlando reproaches Oliver and reminds him of their equality of status:

> I know you are my eldest brother, and in the gentle condition of blood you should so know me. The courtesy of nations allows you my better, in that you are the first-born, but the same tradition takes not away my blood, were there twenty brothers betwixt us. I have as much of my father

in me as you, albeit I confess your coming before me is nearer to his reverence. I i 43−50

Orlando is, in fact, the true heir to Sir Rowland de Boys, the figure who throughout the play is used to represent a lost order of aristocratic integrity. An insult to Orlando is an insult to the memory of his father:

> Oliver. Wilt thou lay hands on me villain?
> Orlando. I am no villain. I am the youngest son of Sir Rowland de Boys:
>   he was my father, and he is thrice a villain that says such a father
>   begot villains. I i 55−9

Oliver has betrayed his father's trust in him by cheating Orlando out of his inheritance, both the actual legacy bequeathed to him and the gentleman-like upbringing that is his due. Characteristically for such a villain, when Oliver paints a slanderous picture of Orlando to convince Charles the wrestler to do his worst, he casts him in his own image as an unnatural brother:

> I'll tell thee Charles, it is the stubbornest young fellow of France, full of ambition, an envious emulator of every man's good parts, a secret and villainous contriver against me his natural brother . . . I assure thee − and almost with tears I speak it − there is not one so young and so villainous this day living. I speak but brotherly of him, but should I anatomise him to thee as he is, I must blush and weep, and thou must look pale and wonder. I i 139−56

As Edmund accuses Edgar to Gloucester of just his own crimes, and compounds the slander by pretending to put in a brotherly plea for clemency, so Oliver's false character of Orlando is a true character of himself. He is the 'envious emulator of every man's good parts', as he reveals in the soliloquy which follows Charles's exit:

> Now will I stir this gamester. I hope I shall see an end of him; for my soul − yet I know not why − hates nothing more than he. Yet he's gentle, never schooled and yet learned, full of noble device, of all sorts enchantingly beloved, and indeed so much in the heart of the world, and especially of my own people, who best know him, that I am altogether misprised. I i 161−9

The envious elder brother who grudges his younger sibling the universal love his goodness wins is a standard figure from folk-story or romance. What is interesting here in the light of Orlando's earlier complaints, is that his natural gentility has clearly not been obscured by his lack of a proper education. His gentle blood shows itself not only in an instinctive goodness which is recognised by his inferiors, but even in an almost miraculous knowledge of what he has been deprived of learning. This assertion of innate qualities seems an unequivocal stand for nature as against nurture in the traditional debate. In this early assurance that 'blood will tell', that the spirit of Sir Rowland will live on in his son, we are prepared for an ultimate victory of natural truth, however much it is at present suppressed and distorted.

Shakespeare begins the play with the domestic sub-plot of Oliver and Orlando but when we move to the main plot and the full court setting we find just the same atmosphere. The opening conversation between Rosalind and Celia involves a wit-match on Fortune and Nature and the court-scenes show us indeed an environment governed by the capriciousness of fortune, rather than a natural order.[2] The Duke, who should applaud and reward Orlando's achievement in vanquishing Charles, will do nothing for him when he learns his parentage.

> I would thou hadst been son to some man else.
> The world esteem'd thy father honourable,
> But I did find him still my enemy.   I ii 213−15

The honourable son of an honourable father is slighted, even persecuted for his merit. The 'humorous' duke, like all tyrants, lives by caprice and not by law. He banishes Rosalind, arbitrarily and suddenly, although, as she points out to him, it was at his command that she remained at court when her father was banished. For justification all he will say is 'Thou art thy father's daughter, that's enough' (I iii 54). She is punished for her parentage as Orlando was for his, and she, like Orlando, defiantly defends the honour of her father:

> Treason is not inherited, my lord,
> Or if we did derive it from our friends,
> What's that to me? My father was no traitor.   I iii 57−9

Orlando and Rosalind both stand for a principle of natural succession and inheritance which the Duke has perverted.

Perhaps the most striking token of the corrupt atmosphere of the court, because incidental, is the conversation between Orlando and Le Beau. Le

Beau, who appears first with Rosalind and Celia as an empty-headed courtier, an Osric, is moved to warn Orlando of the Duke's anger. He hesitates at the brink of indiscretion:

> The Duke is humourous; what he is indeed
> More suits you to conceive than I to speak of. I ii 256−7

The modicum of humanity to be found in a professional courtier like Le Beau must not be allowed expression if he values his place or his life. In the context of the court, a friendly hint to Orlando to escape is as much as he can risk.

> Sir fare you well.
> Hereafter, in a better world than this,
> I shall desire more love and knowledge of you. I ii 273−5

It would seem uncharacteristic for Le Beau to be looking forward to a heavenly reunion, and he is probably doing no more here than acknowledging the wickedness of the world he is in where friendship is impossible. But for the audience there is a clear indication that a better world does exist and not only in heaven. We have heard already of the Duke and his companions in the Forest of Arden 'fleeting the time carelessly as they did in the golden world'. The whole rhythm of the first act leads us to expect a shift from the unnatural world of the court to the natural world of the forest.

Arden, however, is no Eden. If we were tempted to lay undue emphasis on Le Beau's 'Hereafter in a better world than this' and look for an image of Paradise, Duke Senior's opening speech of Act II which introduces us to Arden shows us a setting quite definitely within the fallen world:

> Now my co-mates and brothers in exile,
> Hath not old custom made this life more sweet
> Than that of painted pomp? Are not these woods
> More free from peril than the envious court?
> Here feel we not the penalty of Adam,
> The seasons' difference, as the icy fang
> And churlish chiding of the winter's wind,
> Which when it bites and blows upon my body
> Even till I shrink, I smile, and say
> 'This is no flattery.' II i 1−10

Even if we do not accept Theobald's emendation of line 5 to 'Here feel we but the penalty of Adam', it is evident that Arden has the same fallen weather as everywhere else; it is only that in contrast to the cares of court, the discomfort of the woods may be comfortable to a contented mind. Amiens congratulates the Duke on his ability to see good in evil:

> Happy is your Grace,
> That can translate the stubbornness of fortune
> Into so quiet and so sweet a style.   II i 18−20

This is not hypocritical enthusiasm for a pastoral life which has been forced upon the Duke and which he will forsake for a return to the court at the end of the play, as has sometimes been suggested.[3] The speech is not a eulogy of idyllic rural bliss, but a stoical assertion of the power of man to find consolation even in the harshness of exile in the wilds.

The forest is not naturally kind or bountiful to those who seek it as a refuge. When Rosalind and Celia arrive they are worn out and hungry, and Touchstone seems to speak for all three: 'Ay, now am I in Arden, the more fool I; when I was at home I was in a better place'. Orlando and Adam enter the forest in still worse state, with Adam near death. Orlando tries to comfort him:

> Live a little, comfort a little, cheer thyself a little. If this uncouth forest yield anything savage, I will either be food for it, or bring it for food to thee . . . Come I will bear thee to some shelter and thou shalt not die for lack of a dinner, if there live anything in this desert.   II vi 5−17

Arden, for those who approach it, is desert − the two meanings of 'uninhabited' and 'infertile' having full force − a savage place in which nourishment must be hunted savagely. There is no suggestion of a nature like Marvell's in 'The Bermudas', an unspoiled paradise of fruitfulness and fecundity. Instead we have something like an illustration of Blake's aphorism, 'Where man is not, nature is barren'.

The opposition between nature and human nature is brought out most strongly in the confrontation between Orlando and the Duke's company. Orlando enters with drawn sword and demands food, but he is disarmed by the civility he finds.

> Speak you so gently? Pardon me, I pray you.
> I thought that all things had been savage here,
> And therefore put I on the countenance
> Of stern commandment. But whate'er you are

That in this desert inaccessible
Under the shade of melancholy boughs
Lose and neglect the creeping hours of time;
If ever you have look'd on better days;
If ever been where bells have knoll'd to church;
If ever sat at any good man's feast;
If ever from your eyelids wip'd a tear,
And know what 'tis to pity and be pitied,
Let gentleness my strong enforcement be;
In the which hope, I blush, and hide my sword.   II vii 106—19

In this unlikely setting Orlando invokes the attributes and activities of human society which represent the antithesis of the savage desert. The Duke's reply, which repeats the terms of Orlando's appeal line for line, confirms this ideal of mutuality. Orlando finds in the forest just what he least expects, a community of people living in peace and good-will, living, that is, in the natural state of civilised man.

Arden is not then necessarily in any very significant sense a 'green world' — Northrop Frye's term — if what we look for in a green world is a special awareness of external nature.[4] The forest in fact may be little more than a large empty space in which it is plausible for various pastoral or rural figures to appear. It must be large enough and empty enough to dissolve the sense of an organised and centralised society, to make possible sufficient 'other parts of the forest', so that each individual or group of individuals can exist separately. There are a series of different 'pageants' playing in the forest simultaneously, as the Duke realises:

This wide and universal theatre
Presents more woeful pageants than the scene
Wherein we play.

One such detachable 'pageant' is the relationship between Silvius and Phoebe, the conventional lovers of Theocritean pastoral, to which Corin acts as prologue:

If you will see a pageant truly play'd
Between the pale complexion of true love
And the red glow of scorn and proud disdain,
Go hence a little, and I shall conduct you
If you will mark it.   III iv 48—52

Similarly there is the separate side-show of Touchstone and Audrey, Sir Oliver Martext and William. The difference between Duke Frederick's court and Duke Senior's court in exile, is that Duke Senior's is no centre for the world of Arden, controlling it for better or for worse. The band of courtier/outlaws make up no more than one scene in the kaleidoscope of scenes in the forest.

Our awareness of these separate pageants makes possible the series of strange encounters by which the action advances. Individual characters or groups stray away from the play in which they have allotted conventional parts, and meet up with other totally different, totally unexpected *dramatis personae*. Orlando's abrupt entrance into the Duke's banquet is representative of what we find continuously through the scenes in the forest. He bursts in, having prepared himself for the part of desperate young hero turned highwayman, and finds, bewilderingly, that he is in the middle of a gentleman's dinner-party. Similarly Jacques has been startled to discover 'a fool i' the forest', a fool whose sophisticated persona Jacques the malcontent/satirist envies, and yet finds completely astonishing because so absurdly out of context. Phoebe and Silvius are indulging in the highly conventional, highly stylised routine of hopeless lover and heartless mistress, when Rosalind suddenly marches in and kicks over the whole Dresden shepherdess outfit. The inhabitants of the forest are as much *dépaysés* as the visitors in this extraordinary pattern of incongruous confrontations.

The strange encounters do not work towards a one-way levelling of pretensions. In the juxtaposition of court and country the irony is neutral, and it is not a question of showing up the courtiers by their translation into a rural or natural environment. The bout between Touchstone and Corin, for example, the most formal court-country debate of the play, is like a boxing-match between a highly skilled dancing fly-weight and a rock-solid heavy-weight slugger who cannot even see where the punches are coming from, but is more bemused than injured. Touchstone's ingenuity is delightful as he proves that the courtier's civet perfume is as unclean as the sweat and tar of the shepherd's hand. Yet Corin's unflustered statement of his philosophy must surely command respect.

> Sir, I am a true labourer: I earn that I eat, get that I wear; owe no man hate, envy no man's happiness; glad of other men's good, content with my harm; and the greatest of my pride is to see my ewes graze and my lambs suck.   III ii 71−5

This is too dignified to be laughed at as boorish simplicity. Yet if Corin scores a moral victory here, the dialectical triumph is Touchstone's, and the points come out even in the end. Similarly in the scene between Touchstone and Audrey, observed by Jacques, the emphasis is on incongruity rather than satiric mockery of one or the other party. Audrey and Sir Oliver are much more obviously country bumpkins than Corin, yet they too have a sort of unshakeable stolidity which survives both the elaborate mockery of Touchstone and the gentlemanly contempt of Jacques. Sir Oliver has the last word — ' 'Tis no matter. Ne'er a fantastical knave of them all shall flout me out of my calling'.

Touchstone moralises on his memories of his youthful love for Jane Smile: 'as all is mortal in nature, so is all nature in love mortal in folly'. If Arden exposes the variable shapes of nature, it sets together also a wide variety of types of 'nature in love'. Phoebe, in Silvius' eyes, is the unobtainable cruel mistress to be adored but never possessed. Rosalind reminds her forcefully that she is of the same stock as her lover:

> Who might be your mother
> That you insult, exult, and all at once,
> Over the wretched . . .
> Why what means this? Why do you look on me?
> I see no more in you than in the ordinary
> Of Nature's sale-work.   II v 35–42

She deliberately reduces love to the commercial exchange of marriage:

> Down on your knees
> And thank heaven, fasting, for a good man's love;
> For I must tell you friendly in your ear,
> Sell when you can, you are not for all markets.   III v 57–60

Similarly reductive is Touchstone's reaction to Orlando's tree-verses. For Orlando, as for so many Renaissance love-poets, the beloved is the soul of the world, the distilled elixir of nature:

> Her worth being mounted on the wind
> Through all the world bears Rosalind.   III ii 88–9

> But upon the fairest boughs
> Or at every sentence end,
> Will I Rosalinda write
> Teaching all that read to know
> The quintessence of every sprite
> Heaven would in little show.

> Therefore Heaven Nature charg'd
> That one body should be fill'd
> With all graces wide-enlarg'd.   III ii 132–40

Touchstone's response is a crudely sexual parody:

> If a hart do lack a hind,
> Let him seek out Rosalind
> If the cat will after kind,
> So be sure will Rosalind.   III ii 99–102

Where Orlando speaks of a goddess-like Nature, Touchstone insists on 'kind', the basic mating instinct.

Rosalind's function in the play is to provide a centre which can assimilate both Touchstone and Orlando's view of 'nature in love' as well as that of Silvius and Phoebe. Her therapeutic education of Orlando involves the assumption of the knowing and cynical role of the comic mistress. She gives him a taste of the stereotyped fickle and shrewish wife, not because it is likely that she will be such a wife to him, but in order to control and exorcise that possibility by playing the role. A full and genuine romantic love can only be achieved when its sexual counterpart has been recognised. Modesty and virtue in Shakespeare's heroines does not depend on blank ignorance of the facts of life: Beatrice in *Much Ado*, Helena in *All's Well*, Desdemona in *Othello*, all like Rosalind can hold their own in *double-entendre* and sexual repartee. As Ganymede, Rosalind plays her witty page-boy part to the full, a 'worm's eye view' of love, to borrow a phrase which G. K. Hunter has used in connection with Lyly.[5] And yet by incorporating this worm's eye view into her persona, she can in the long run endorse all the more strongly Orlando's concept of love, and isolate and place Touchstone's. There is more to the concluding union of lovers than the collection of 'country copulatives' Touchstone would have us believe; and the reason why we can be assured that this is so, is that Rosalind has taken Touchstone's view of the conclusion into account.

As You Like It seems to drift rather than hurry towards a dénouement. Without the dynamics of plot complication, there scarcely seems a compelling reason for the end to come when it does. Shakespeare does make use of Rosalind's double disguise – playing Ganymede to Phoebe, and Ganymede as Rosalind to Orlando – to bring a climax of bewilderment in Act V scene iii, where the apparently inextricable knot of cross-loving is given stylised expression in a formal quartet. The formality of confusion prepares us for the aesthetic satisfaction of the formal ending. Generally, however, no pressure seems to prevent the leisurely life of sport and conversation from going on in Arden indefinitely. Yet the direction of the action, if it can be called action, has its own logic, and crucial to that logic is the appearance of the transformed Oliver.

An awareness of the court is kept alive after we have moved to Arden by two scenes (II ii, III i) in which the villains Duke Frederick and Oliver are shown frustrated and angry, deprived of the objects of their hatred. We are prepared for the process by which they too will be attracted or drawn from the emptying court to the increasingly crowded forest. It may, therefore, not be a complete surprise to find Oliver in Arden. But it is certainly a surprise to find him changed as he is and Shakespeare makes the most of that surprise by having him reveal his own story in an impersonal narrative, seen through the eyes of Orlando. Rosalind and Celia are shown Orlando coming upon 'a wretched ragged man, o'ergrown with hair', menaced by the snake and lioness, and register his sense of shock when he discovers who it was:

> This seen, Orlando did approach the man,
> And found it was his brother, his elder brother.
> *Celia.* O I have heard him speak of that same brother,
> And he did render him the most unnatural
> That liv'd amongst men.
> *Oliver.* And well he might so do,
> For well I know he was unnatural.
> *Rosalind.* But to Orlando. Did he leave him there,
> Food to the suck'd and hungry lioness?
> *Oliver.* Twice did he turn his back, and purposed so,
> But kindness, nobler ever than revenge,
> And nature, stronger than his just occasion,
> Made him give battle to the lioness,
> Who quickly fell before him; in which hurtling
> From miserable slumber I awak'd. IV iii 119–32

The contrast between the two brothers is here worked out in exactly the same terms in which it was established in the first scene. Oliver the 'unnatural' is saved and consequently converted by the nature of Orlando. Nature is that spirit of love and forgiveness which will triumph over the base instinct of vindictiveness. 'Kindness' here — as in 'the milk of human kindness' — has its semantic force of 'kindred'. This instance of natural kindness has translated Oliver into what he has never been before, a natural brother.

The conversion of Oliver is crucial to the movement towards dénouement. The love at first sight match between Oliver and Celia which follows will be the first marriage to be arranged, the nucleus of the final multiple wedding party. But more importantly it suggests that the unnatural situation of the first act is beginning to work itself out and that we are about to return to a more natural state of harmony. All that is needed is the conversion of Duke Frederick, which the conversion of Oliver anticipates. It is easy to see the news of the Duke's sudden change of heart brought by the anomalous Jacques de Boys as no more than a convenient device for returning the exiles to power. But that return to power is significant and it is also significant that Duke Frederick is linked with Jacques as the figures excluded from the pattern of reconciliation. Frederick cannot be reintegrated into the natural pattern, as Oliver just barely can. For him there must be a special, even a mysterious, change, which leaves him finally isolated from the normal bonds of kindred and love in his hermitage, as he was in his usurped dukedom.

How is nature involved in the happy ending of *As You Like It*? How far do we feel that the changes brought about have been due to a natural process, or to a return to nature? At first sight the range of concepts of nature with which the play has been concerned seem to make it impossible to see more here than a playful kaleidoscope of contrasting images. All is well in the end not by virtue of the healing powers of nature but as a result of the light and good-humoured attitude of the dramatist towards his subject. There is certainly little or no feeling that the characters have been purified by their return to a simple country life. Their encounters with one another are quite as important as their encounters with the forest's aborigines and few of the characters actually engage in any rural pursuits beyond the odd day's hunting. Does the play illustrate anything other than the pastimes of a court-world on holiday?

Perhaps not. All the same, it is not meaningless to say that in the ending of *As You Like It* we experience the triumph of nature. The principle of natural right and the inheritance of tradition are vindicated. The natural heirs, Rosalind and Orlando, who were banished, are now repossessed and united and the Duke, who represented an older order of justice and goodness, is reinstated. This has been brought about, not by a positive victory of the forces of natural goodness over unnatural evil, but instead by a complete withdrawal from conflict and confrontation. Basic to the 'retreat to the green world', here as so often in Shakespearean comedy, is not so much its greenness as its emptiness. The social mechanism which has become overheated and is running awry needs room in which it can be disengaged, in which its constituent parts can run idle for a time. Given that space for disengagement, the underlying comic understanding seems to be that the society will naturally right itself.

Our sense of what is natural in *As You Like It* ranges from Orlando's forgiveness of Oliver to Touchstone's desire for Audrey. But in the final pattern of the play there is room for both of these and more, in what Fielding's Mr. Square would call the 'eternal fitness of things'. Jacques puts everyone in their place:

(*To Duke Senior.*)	You to your former honour I bequeath,
	Your patience and your virtue well deserve it.
(*To Orlando.*)	You to a love that your true faith doth merit:
(*To Oliver.*)	You to your land and love and great allies:
(*To Silvius.*)	You to a long and well-deserved bed:
(*To Touchstone.*)	And you to wrangling, for thy loving voyage
	Is but for two months victuall'd. V iv 185–91

This has a special authority coming from the man who is opting out, who has presented the cankered view of the satirist throughout. From outside he observes and acknowledges the formal harmony of natural justice – from each according to his capacity, to each according to his deserts – while he himself is temperamentally incapable of participating in it. By the comprehensiveness of its vision of nature, by the sense it gives us of the necessary pluralism of the concept, *As You Like It* wins our assent for its underlying concept of natural order as an ideal to which social man inevitably returns.

L'ECOLE DES FEMMES

It might seem difficult, on the face of it, to find any points of similarity at all between *As You Like It* and Molière's *L'Ecole des Femmes*. The two, indeed, might almost stand as representative examples of the extraordinarily different genres of Shakespearean and Molièrean comedy. *As You Like It* is pastoral romance, incorporating all the improbabilities of an avowedly imaginary story. *L'Ecole des Femmes* has the solidity of realistically observed bourgeois life. Where *As You Like It* moves through space with complete fluidity, to the forest and back to the court, from place to unnamed place within Arden, Molière not only preserves unity of location, but emphasises the very fixity of his action: Horace is always congratulating himself on the happy accident of meeting Arnolphe at just that place on the street outside the house of M. de la Souche. Molière exploits for all it is worth a single plot mechanism, one ironic situation, *As You Like It* moves almost entirely by its lack of plot. Almost any general antithesis to be drawn between the comic approaches of Shakespeare and Molière could be illustrated from these two plays. With all of these differences, partly because of all of these differences, it is worth looking for a common underlying pattern. What Molière means by nature may be something quite unlike what we have seen in *As You Like It*. All the same, *L'Ecole des Femmes* like Shakespeare's play ends with a triumph of nature, and it may be interesting in the light of the preceding discussion to, consider by what process we are brought to that conclusion.

We begin in *L'Ecole des Femmes*, as so often in Molière's comedy, with a debate between the comic protagonist and the *raisonneur*. This establishes the terms of reference of the play, defining by the contrasting attitudes of the *raisonneur* the specific absurdity of the comic butt. In this case, Arnolphe the man determined at all costs to avoid cuckoldry by taking an innocent wife is opposed by Chrysalde who warns him of the dangers of this method. Ignorance does not ensure virtue, Chrysalde argues, for,

> Une femme d'esprit peut trahir son devoir;
> Mais il faut pour le moins qu'elle ose le vouloir;
> Et la stupide au sien peut manquer d'ordinaire,
> Sans en avoir l'envie et sans penser le faire.   I i 113–16

In any case, Arnolphe, who has always been so offensive in his jokes about other men's domestic misfortunes, runs exceptional risks of disgrace if he too is cuckolded. But to such reasoning Arnolphe will not listen, and he speaks for all of Molière's comic egoists in his determined idiosyncrasy—'en femme, comme en tout, je veux suivre ma mode' 'In a wife, as in everything else, I want to follow my own fashion'.

The status of the *raisonneur's* views has been one of the most argued issues of Molière criticism. It is no longer widely considered, as it was up until the last thirty years, that the *raisonneur* is the unquestionable moral spokesman of the author. We hear less now from critics about Molière's philosophy of the 'juste milieu', and it is no longer generally supposed that Molière's ideology can be inferred from the views expressed by his *raisonneurs*. And yet within the context of the individual comedy, the *raisonneur* must by definition represent the point of view which the author asks the audience to adopt as true. Chrysalde stands here for good sense and good will, and it is understood that the audience will agree with him. This is the more remarkable because it is by no means clear that an ordinary seventeenth century Parisian audience would have taken Chrysalde's view rather than Arnolphe's outside the theatre. How many of Molière's contemporaries would have been prepared to accept that cuckoldry is no more than an accident of fate which should be accepted with resignation?[6] The viewpoint of the *raisonneur*, though it is expected that the audience will agree with it, is by no means the standard view of the 'silent majority'.

The *raisonneur* is like the winning speaker of a debate; his arguments are convincing against those of his opponents, but need not be absolutely true. He defines his opposite in the comic butt, as the ordinary reasoning of the tragic confidant defines the extraordinary situation of the Racinian hero by contrast. In this instance in which Molière is assigning to Chrysalde a point of view not self-evidently acceptable, he aligns it with attitudes of his great predecessors – the stoicism of Montaigne, the comic humanism of Rabelais.[7] Chrysalde preaches tolerance, and a humane acceptance of life, including if necessary the misfortune of cuckoldom. This brings out all the more emphatically Arnolphe's contrary determination to be the master of his fate, to control and direct life rather than accept it. The theme of the play is thus introduced: what we are to be shown is the conflict between control and spontaneity, the willed and the involuntary, the natural against the artificial.

Arnolphe is a convinced educationalist. He believes in the concept of the *tabula rasa*, that Agnès will take whatever impression or lack of impression he determines:

> Ainsi que je voudrai, je tournerai cette âme;
> Comme un morceau de cire entre mes mains elle est,
> Et je lui puis donner la forme qui me plaît.   III iii 809–11

He speaks of secluding her from outside influences to avoid 'spoiling her natural goodness', but that natural goodness is for Arnolphe no more than the inability to sin. Human nature in itself, from his point of view, is morally neutral though prone to corruption. By a resolute exercise of authority Arnolphe believes that it is possible to create for himself a wife unsullied by knowledge and therefore wholly innocent, wholly to be possessed by her husband. Sophistication is synonymous with promiscuity, and Arnolphe comprehends in his denunciation all the refinements of civilisation from dancing to preciosity. Agnès is isolated to prevent contamination. But as with the old experiments which supposedly illustrated the theory of spontaneous generation, we will see in the play Agnès grow in her isolation to disprove Arnolphe's concepts and vindicate the principle of a living autonomous human nature.

Arnolphe speaks in the name of ideals – honour and morality – in justification of his method, but Molière steadily undermines these pretensions and by a series of comic sidelights shows us how deeply vitiated and self-deceived Arnolphe's motives are. Most splendidly in the scene between

Alain and Georgette, following Arnolphe's first violent attack of jealousy, the basic character of his possessiveness is exposed. Alain and Georgette, classically moronic country yokels, puzzle over why Arnolphe should be so upset at Horace's visits to Agnès. 'Why all this fuss?' asks Georgette.

> *Alain.* C'est que cette action le met en jalousie.
> *Georgette.* Mais d'où vient qu'il est pris de cette fantaisie?
> *Alain.* Cela vient . . . : cela vient de ce qu'il est jaloux.
> *Georgette.* Oui; mais pourquoi l'est-il? et pourquoi ce courroux?
> *Alain.* C'est que la jalousie . . . entends-tu bien, Georgette,
> Est une chose . . . là . . . qui fait qu'on s'inquiète . . .
> Et qui chasse les gens d'autour d'une maison.
> Je m'en vais te bailler une comparaison,
> Afin de conçevoir la chose davantage.
> Dis-moi, n'est-il pas vrai, quand tu tiens ton potage,
> Que si quelque affamé venoit pour en manger,
> Tu serois en colère, et voudrois le charger?
> *Georgette.* Oui, je comprends cela.
> *Alain.*   C'est justement tout comme:
> La femme est en effet le potage de l'homme.   II iii 423 — 36

This childishly reductive account of sexual jealousy beautifully underlines the truth which Arnolphe wraps up in pomposities of honour and dignity. The hypothetical ignorance of Georgette serves to expose in an especially ridiculous light Arnolphe's motives, just as later the innocence of Agnès will have a similar but even more devastating effect.

In his relations with Horace, Arnolphe's self-deception is painfully brought home to him. The quiproquo on which the whole plot turns is more than a convenient device. It is another mark against Arnolphe that he should want absurdly to elevate himself to the nobility with the title Monsieur de la Souche. But even more importantly it makes possible the double identity which is crucial to the satiric attack on him. Arnolphe, we know from Chrysalde, has always taken a malicious delight in learning and broadcasting stories of marital infidelity. When Horace appears on the scene, he is almost indecently eager to see in him a potential cuckold-maker:

> Les gens faits comme vous font plus que les écus
> Et vous êtes de taille à faire des cocus.   I iv 301 — 2

He casts himself directly in the role of delighted onlooker and assistant to the young man's love affairs. He is preparing the appropriate sniggers when it suddenly emerges that he has also been cast for the role of ludicrous cuckold.

> Pour l'homme
> C'est, je crois, de la Zousse ou Souche qu'on le nomme:
> Je ne me suis pas fort arrêté sur le nom;
> Riche, à ce qu'on m'a dit, mais des plus sensés, non;
> Et l'on m'en a parlé comme d'un ridicule.   I iv 327—31

Arnolphe's role of lover's confidant involves a voyeuristic sexuality and a vicarious pleasure in the thought of the cheated husband. A cruel comic justice forces him to play through that part when it is he himself who is being cheated and scorned. The culminating humiliation in the series of confrontations with his double is the vivid picture Horace gives him of his actions overheard from inside the cupboard in Agnès' room:

> Il est entré d'abord; je ne le voyois pas,
> Mais je l'oyois marcher, sans rien dire, à grands pas
> Poussant de temps en temps des soupirs pitoyables,
> Et donnant quelquefois de grands coups sur les tables,
> Frappant un petit chien qui pour lui s'émouvoit,
> Et jetant brusquement les hardes qu'il trouvoit.   IV vi 1154—9

Arnolphe must listen and accept this version of himself, 'ce becque cornu', reduced to speechless violence by his desperate anxiety.

When we first see him with Agnès (I iii), however, he seems very much in control, and she seems very much what he takes her to be. She complains of the fleas biting her at night; Arnolphe replies with a meaning look, which she completely fails to register, that she will shortly have someone to get rid of them for her. But in the second interview between them (II v), after Arnolphe has learned of the visits of Horace, we begin to see qualities in Agnès unsuspected by Arnolphe. He is at first dismayed by her small talk, the weather, the domestic news — 'Le petit chat est mort' — and so on. How could this girl have been receiving a lover and show so little signs of it? The answer is, of course, that she does not recognise that she has been 'receiving a lover', an action of which she should be highly conscious, highly ashamed. Agnès' account of Horace's courtship is splendidly funny in that she accepts literally all the tired euphemisms of poetic metaphor. She can only imagine that Horace has been actually wounded by her eyes, and is delighted when he makes such a quick recovery. She relates her own emotions with a completely unselfconscious hedonism:

Il juroit qu'il m'aimoit d'une amour sans seconde,
Et me disoit des mots les plus gentils du monde,
Des choses que jamais rien ne peut égaler,
Et dont, toutes les fois que je l'entends parler,
La douceur me chatouille et là dedans remue
Certain je ne sais quoi dont je suis toute émue.   II v 559—64

Chrysalde's point is being illustrated: Agnès has no idea that there is anything wrong with love-making, though perfectly willing to accept the preliminary of marriage with Horace if that will stop it being a sin.

It is this unselfconsciousness of Agnès which misleads Arnolphe. Someone so naive as to confess all of her relations with her lover to her guardian, is surely still unspoiled enough so that a few sharp stern words will put her right. The next time we see Agnès she is being drilled through the Maxims of Marriage, in preparation for her elevation to the exalted and honourable rank of *bourgeoise*. Once again Agnès seems entirely submissive to the will of her master, having done her duty by forcibly repulsing Horace. It is therefore a surprise to us as well as to Arnolphe when, in the following scene, Horace reveals that appearances have been deceptive. Agnès behind her mask of silence, has been thinking, and the results of her thought can be seen in the letter which accompanied the stone she was forced to throw at Horace.

Agnès' letter is central to the play. It is interesting to compare it both with a sketch for it in Molière's earlier play *L'Ecole des Maris*, and the imitation of it in Wycherley's *The Country Wife*. In *L'Ecole des Maris* Sganarelle is the unwitting go-between who carries a letter from his ward Isabelle to the young man whom he wants to prevent her from marrying, Valère. Isabelle, although like Agnès she has been kept away from society by her guardian, writes a letter which shows her well aware of social conventions. She explains that it is the threat of immediate marriage with Sganarelle that forces her to this breach of propriety: 'Ce n'est pas la contrainte où je me treuve qui a fait nâitre les sentiments que j'ai pour vous; mais c'est elle qui en précipite le témoignage, et qui me fait passer sur des formalités où la bienséance du sexe oblige', 'It is not the constraint I am under which has given rise to the feelings I have for you; but it is that which has forced me to confess them, and which has made me pass over the formalities which the conventions of our sex demand'. (*L'Ecole des Maris* II v). Isabelle is perfectly conscious of the requirements of 'la bienséance' — she knows entirely what she is doing.

Agnès, by contrast, is touchingly, movingly, confused.

Je veux vous écrire, et je suis bien en peine par où je m'y prendrai. J'ai des pensées que je désirerois que vous sussiez; mais je ne sais comment faire pour vous les dire, et je me défie de mes paroles.

She is only beginning to discover herself and to discover the world of which she has been kept in ignorance, and she is anxious lest what she is doing may be considered wrong.

En verité, je ne sais ce que vous m'avez fait; mais je sens que je suis fâchée à mourir de ce qu'on me fait faire contre vous, que j'aurai toutes les peines du monde à me passer de vous, et que je serois bien aise d'être à vous. Peut-être qu'il y a du mal à dire cela; mais enfin je ne puis m'empêcher de le dire, et je voudrois que cela se pût faire sans qu'il y en eût.

She has listened to Arnolphe's preaching but she remains unconvinced.

On me dit fort que tous les jeunes hommes sont des trompeurs, qu'il ne les faut point écouter, et que tout ce que vous me dites n'est que pour m'abuser; mais je vous assure que je n'ai pu encore me figurer cela de vous, et je suis si touchée de vos paroles, que je ne saurois croire qu'elles soient menteuses.

She appeals to Horace's generosity to prove her right.

Dites-moi franchement ce qui en est; car enfin, comme je suis sans malice, vous auriez le plus grand tort du monde, si vous me trompiez; et je pense que j'en mourrois de déplaisir.   III iv [947]

The natural delicacy of Agnès is all the more striking when contrasted with the kittenish naiveté of Margery Pinchwife. Wycherley uses the letter she writes to Horner to bring home his point that a country wife may be as promiscuous as a London one. As she reads aloud her composition, we are given a glimpse of country flirtation which is more awkward than a city amour, no doubt, but scarcely more innocent:

Dear, sweet Mr. Horner . . . my husband would have me send you a base, rude, unmannerly letter – but I won't . . . and would have me forbid you loving me – but I won't . . . and would have me say to you I hate you, poor Mr. Horner – but I won't tell a lie for him . . . for I'm sure if you and I were in the country at cards together . . . I could not help treading on your toe under the table . . . or rubbing knees with you, and staring in your face till you saw me . . . and then looking down, and blushing for an hour together.[8]

Country or city, human nature is all one, and in *The Country Wife* this means all are equally lustful, potentially all equally hypocritical. But this is not Molière's nature in *L'Ecole des Femmes*, for where Wycherley shows natural lubriciousness, Molière pains in Agnès a picture of natural innocence. Horace sums it up, when he describes Agnès' letter:

> Tout ce que son coeur sent, sa main a su l'y mettre,
> Mais en termes touchants et tout pleins de bonté,
> De tendresse innocente et d'ingénuité,
> De la manière enfin que la pure nature
> Exprime de l'amour la première blessure.   III iv 941−5

For Wycherley, as indeed for Arnolphe, there is no such thing as 'la pure nature', an instinctive feeling which is good and beautiful.

The clear difference between Horace and Arnolphe is that Horace can understand Agnès and appreciate her, whereas Arnolphe cannot. Horace sees the awakening of love working naturally to bring Agnès to a new awareness, and sees the wickedness of the attempt to suppress this development:

> Malgré les soins maudits d'un injuste pouvoir,
> Un plus beau naturel peut-il se faire voir?
> Et n'est-ce pas sans doute un crime punissable
> De gâter méchamment ce fonds d'âme admirable,
> D'avoir dans l'ignorance et la stupidité
> Voulu de cet esprit étouffer la clarté?   III iv 950−5

Arnolphe can only reproach himself for having had her taught to write at all, since this is the use she makes of it. He cannot imagine where she could have learned such presence of mind, such ingenuity, which he associates only with the sophisticated and the wordly. This is the force of the play's ambiguous title. Arnolphe thinks that he has set up a school for wives, in which by 'maxims of marriage' and other means Agnès will be perfectly trained for her position as his wife. But the real school for wives is the natural power of love which helps Agnès to grow into a wife for Horace. Arnolphe is in a position of authority, knowledge and control throughout, and at each turn of events he is defeated by thoughtless innocence and chance. He comments frequently on the silliness of Horace unwittingly confiding all of his secrets to his rival. Yet each time he plans definitively to out-manœuvre 'ce jeune évente', 'this young fool', his apparently assured victory is turned into disaster. Arnolphe is driven to wonder what fate can be against him.

> Quoi? l'astre qui s'obstine à me désespérer
> Ne me donnerá pas le temps de respirer?
> Coup sur coup je verrai, par leur intelligence
> De mes soins vigilants confondre la prudence?
> Et je serai la dupe, en ma maturité,
> D'une jeune innocente et d'un jeune évente?   IV vii 1182−7

How could a 'sage philosophe' like himself, who has formed his theories over years of close observation of cheated husbands, be overcome by a couple so naive? The comedy is here that of the theorist defeated by the facts of life. All of his calculations are mistaken because he has reckoned without the autonomous life of the person who is the subject of his experiment.

The cruellest irony of all, however, is the fact that Arnolphe is moved beyond possessiveness towards love by the transformation brought about in Agnès, the transformation he cannot understand. The more he rages against her ability to deceive him, the more he is attracted to her:

> Plus en la regardant je la voyois tranquille,
> Plus je sentois en moi s'échauffer une bile;
> Et ces bouillants transports dont s'enflammoit mon coeur
> Y sembloient redoubler son amoureuse ardeur;
> J'étois aigri, fâché, désespéré contre elle:
> Et cependant jamais je ne la vis si belle.   IV i 1016−21

In the final brilliant interview between Arnolphe and Agnès, he demands why she loves Horace and not him:

> *Arnolphe.* Vous ne m'aimez donc pas, à ce compte?
> *Agnès.* Vous?
> *Arnolphe.* Oui.
> *Agnès.* Helas! non.
> *Arnolphe.* Comment, non!
> *Agnès.* Voulez-vouz que je mente?
> *Arnolphe.* Pourquoi ne m'aimer pas, Madame l'impudente?
> *Agnès.* Mon Dieu, ce n'est pas moi que vous devez blâmer:
> Que ne vous êtes-vous, comme lui, fait aimer?
> Je ne vous en ai pas empêché, que je pense.   V iv 1531−6

This is, of course, unanswerable. Reason, argument, impassioned pleas or commands, all of which Arnolphe uses by the end of the scene, are worthless in the vain attempt to awaken love.

The beauty and innocence of Agnès not only overcomes Arnolphe, it converts Horace. When he is first asked about his affair with Agnès, it is clear that Horace is planning the sort of intrigue that Arnolphe expects, if not a seduction at least a casual amour. Even as he admires the natural sweetness of her letter, there is still a touch of the complacent aesthete about him, relishing the refinement of being the object of a first love. Arnolphe is of course convinced that Horace has no notion but to seduce Agnès.

> Je sais que, pour punir son amour libertin,
> Je n'ai qu'à laisser faire à son mauvais destin,
> Que je serai vengé d'elle par elle-même.   III v 990−2

But here, as throughout, Arnolphe's low view of human nature is proved incorrect. When she finally manages to escape with Horace, the appeal of Agnès' trusting innocence and helplessness is enough to make him change his 'dishonourable' intentions, as he explains to Arnolphe:

> Considérez un peu, par ce trait d'innocence,
> Où l'expose d'un fou la haute impertinence,
> Et quels fâcheux périls elle pourroit courir,
> Si j'étois maintenant homme à la moins chérir.
> Mais d'un trop pur amour mon âme est embrasée;
> J'aimerois mieux mourir que l'avoir abusée;
> Je lui vois des appas dignes d'um autre sort,
> Et rien ne m'en sauroit séparer que la mort.   V ii 1412−19

Horace is not a romantic lover at the beginning of the play; he is more or less the libertine that Arnolphe imagines. The effect of Agnès is all the more impressive, therefore, in that she can change what was started as a light-hearted affair into a serious love. There is such a thing as a better nature in man, and the natural in Agnès calls it forth.

Horace by the end of the play has reached the position which is the starting-point of so many comedies − he wants to marry for love against the wishes of his father. It is here that Arnolphe has his last card to play. Horace begs him to help persuade his father to defer the arranged marraige prepared for him, to pave the way for a marriage with Agnès. Arnolphe of course promises his asssitance and then double-crosses him. He throws all his weight on to the other side and strongly advises Oronte to press on with the marriage in spite of his son's objections:

> Quoi? se laissera-t-il gouverner par son fils?
> Est-ce que vous voulez qu'un père ait la mollesse
> De ne savoir pas faire obéir la jeunesse?   V vii 1687–9

Obviously Arnolphe has his reasons for taking this line but it is entirely consistent with his character in any case. He has stood all through the play for the rights of authority, the rights of property. He believes in a rigid application of the letter of social law, children and wives must be completely submissive, vassals of their legitimate masters, be they fathers or husbands.

As always, however, what looks like a winning trick for Arnolphe is turned into its opposite. He finds that he has been pressing forward the marriage he so much wanted to prevent, the marriage of Horace and Agnès. The dénouement of the play has often been considered very implausible and arbitrary, and some critics have suspected Molière of parodying the plot-mechanics of romantic comedy.[9] But the ending has its own sort of logic, admittedly not realistic logic, and it is typical of a very basic pattern in comedy. It is, of course, highly improbable that Agnès should turn out to be the long-lost daughter of Enrique, the niece of Chrysalde, and the proposed daughter-in-law of Oronte. But an audience accepts that it should be so, as audiences accepted the convention by which the slave-girl of Roman comedy whom the young hero wanted to marry is revealed as the daughter of some respectable citizen. The love-match is initially opposed to the arranged *mariage de convenance* but in the end the love-match turns out to be as *convenable* as the other.

In *L'Ecole des Femmes* this dénouement is satisfying as it contributes to the comprehensive defeat of Arnolphe. For Arnolphe possession is nine-tenths of the law, yet he is made to discover that it is not all of the law. His insistence on absolute rights of authority over others denies not only the independent life of another human being, but also the sociality of man. He is defeated ultimately both by nature itself working through the love of Horace and Agnès, and also by the unseen webs of relationship which make up society. For society will corroborate what nature achieves — this is the essential tenet of the comic contract which underlies a play like *L'Ecole des Femmes*. Arnolphe may assume that he has the force of social authority behind him but as he attempts to abrogate and suppress the full scope of human nature he will not have the final support of society. His flight from the stage, his exclusion from the harmony of the conclusion, is representative of the self-defending, self-righting mechanism of society which will not permit absolute control or absolute authority to any individual within it.

Molière and Shakespeare both expect their audiences to agree that nature will out, not as the basic animal drives, but as the natural goodness of man. Both *As You Like It* and *L'Ecole des Femmes* admit that human beings are animals, driven by physical needs. 'As the ox hath his bow, sir, the horse his curb, and the falcon her bells, so man hath his desires, and as pigeons bill, so wedlock would be nibbling'. 'La femme est, en effet, le potage de l'homme'. The low view of human desires as expressed by Touchstone or Alain is included, but included in order to be transcended. The innocent sexuality of Agnès, or the sophisticated awareness of sex shown by Rosalind, convince us that physicality is a perfectly consonant part of the best human natures. People are animals indeed, but they are higher animals. To Agnès and Horace, to Rosalind and Orlando, feelings of self-consciousness, delicacy, loyalty or love are as natural and instinctive as the simpler instincts are to the simpler animals.

Such a view of nature, so far from the familiar Renaissance preoccupations with the divisions of soul and body, is curiously secular. Many critics have interpreted *As You Like It* in religious terms, arguing that 'during the play's final moments, a divine presence is more than laughingly asserted'.[10] But it is surely perverse to place much theological emphasis on Duke Frederick's miraculous conversion, or the masque-like appearance of Hymen to celebrate the marriages. The grace by which the happy ending is brought about is a natural rather than a supernatural grace. *L'Ecole des Femmes* has been read as distinctly anti-Christian, evidence of Molière's humanist and libertine 'philosophy of nature'. It scarcely seems necessary, however, to place it so specifically as the individual and possibly polemic ideology of Molière himself. For with both plays the secular, non-Christian concept of human nature is due to the comic context itself rather than the personal views of the dramatists. The triumph of nature is brought about often by indirect even mysterious means, but from within not from above. The sequence of events which brings the action to a happy conclusion in each play is beyond the control of any character or characters involved; confusions and mistaken purposes are essential to the comic causality. But the movement towards harmony is not directed from outside of the action. Where in tragedy the accidents of chance are attributed to an unseen power which 'shapes our ends, rough-hew them how we will', in comedies such as *L'Ecole des Femmes* and *As You Like It* that power is felt to be nature itself. In the next chapter we shall be looking at plays in which this comic providence is achieved by one particular character. Here, however, it is immanent force rather than transcendent authority which is the dynamic principle of the comic structure.

3 Comic Controllers

The switchback action of comedy repeatedly throws off those characters who try to ride it towards a fixed goal of their own choosing. The dogmatist Arnolphe who believes in the possibility of total control is defeated at every turn by the sequence of circumstances which moves always to the benefit of spontaneity and unwilled impulse. The crusade of Justice Overdo to enforce his literal-minded and pedantic code must necessarily end in mockery. Almost any character in a comedy who begins by asserting with assurance his capacity to shape his own and others' lives is marked out for the punishment which this comic version of *hubris* demands. Yet only in pure farce does the series of events appear a totally meaningless and absurd concatenation of chances beyond the control of anyone involved. Much more frequently in comedy there are characters who can exploit the absurd logic of the plot, who do contrive to master the perverse movement of the action. Why should some be allowed to dominate, when the officious attempt at domination is one of the most signal comic sins? Who are the controllers of comedy and by virtue of what circumstances do they control?

One class of characters, most strikingly, are not directors of the action — the *raisonneurs*. The *raisonneur*, the person from whose point of view the comedy is seen, whose views can be accepted as sound, is seldom given a decisive role in the plot. In Molière, indeed, the *raisonneur* is a curiously impotent figure. Chrysalde puts his argument against that of Arnolphe, sets up the terms of the debate, but then disappears for the greater part of the play. Even at the end when he returns to the scene he is only a party to the dénouement, not its organiser. Philinte follows Alceste around, trying to make him moderate his anti-social manners, advising him sensibly on his lawsuit or his love-affair, but by definition he can achieve nothing. The reasoning of Cléante in *Tartuffe*, the reasoning of the whole family indeed, does not stop Orgon from plunging them all into the near disaster from which the miraculous intervention of the king must rescue them. It seems that it is one of the rules of the game that the Molièrean *raisonneur*, like the Greek tragic chorus, is not permitted an active role.

Some counterexamples from Jonson suggest the rationale for Molière's

43

practice. It is hard to stop the *raisonneur* – the man who is always right – from sounding priggish and self-righteous. As long as he is only an observer, and his observations are tactfully managed, he is tolerable. But when he is given the ultimate control of the action, as Jonson's presenters are in the 'comical satyres', then no audience or reader is prepared to put up with him. Even though he is split into different personae, the properly indignant Asper as against the perniciously envious Macilente, we still feel that the game is rigged and fair play impossible. It is not only that the self-congratulatory self-portraits of Jonson as Asper or Horace are dramatically tactless. But once the reasonable man, or in Jonson's case the moral dogmatist, has become openly identified with the comedian who pulls the strings, then the comedy is a dead duck. The essentially accidental quality of the comic action is lost, and we are railroaded towards a 'happy ending' with every man purged of his humours by the authoritarian Doctor Jonson.

The men of reason who are spokesmen for the principle of commonsense and humanity may advise from the sidelines but may not join in. However, they have allies, in Molière particularly, who are right in the middle of the action. The high *raisonneurs*, if we may call them that, the Cléantes, Philintes and Chrysaldes are spectators only, but the pert servants, the Toinettes and Dorines, may intrigue on behalf of their young masters and mistresses against the tyrannic parents and guardians. If the *raisonneur* appeals to an ideal of reason, the servant speaks as a pragmatic realist, and as such is often more practically effective. In fact, Molière's servants have rarely anything like the powers of achievement granted to their ancestors, the Roman tricky slaves of Plautus and Terence. The emphasis is put on their verbal facility and daring in defying the comic enemies rather than their skill in outmanoeuvring them. But they do have some active influence where the *raisonneurs* have none.

Perhaps this is because in comedy we prefer to see power in the hands of those who would normally be powerless, the servants rather than the masters, the women rather than the men. The generalisation suggests one other group of characters who are given a hand in organising the comic action – the disguised heroines of Shakespearean comedy. Rosalind, Portia, Viola might be said to be in some sort descendents of the tricky slave, via the page-boys of early Elizabethan comedy. In their male disguises, one of their functions is to supply an impertinent, cynical and knowing stance like that of the intelligent slaves regarding the follies of their betters. As women, also, in the society of their time assumed to be normally passive and incapable of action, they are shown in the comic context taking control and engineering a happy outcome, where the men are baffled or despairing. There are always moments at which their deficiencies in masculine qualities such as physical courage are comically apparent. But as executives and organisers they run rings round their ineffective husbands-to-be.

In many comedies, therefore, we enjoy the transfer of dominance to the less dominant figures of the audience's community – children, servants, women. Equally we resent the attempts at dominance on the part of those who normally speak with authority in real life, magistrates, teachers, or even surrogate comedian-preachers. This is no doubt related to the spirit of iconoclastic inversion which is so pervasive in comedy. We might almost argue for a rule of inverse proportion between the degree of influence normally associated with a social persona and the degree of influence he or she is accorded in the comic action. But there are outstanding exceptions, and it is with such exceptions that this chapter will be concerned. There are comedies watched over and controlled by a figure of high authority, in which the pattern of comic providence is ultimately executed by a masterful agent of that providence. Two instances will serve as the focus for the present discussion – Theseus in *A Midsummer Night's Dream*, and Prospero in *The Tempest*. What is the effect of the comic action when ordered by these figures of exceptional authority? How does the anti-authoritarian stance which we may think of as characteristically comic accord with the magisterial presence of the Dukes of Athens or Milan?

A MIDSUMMER NIGHT'S DREAM

> Whilom, as olde stories tellen us
> There was a duc that highte Theseus
> Of Atthenes he was lord and governour . . .

Shakespeare's most immediate source for the Theseus of *A Midsummer Night's Dream* was probably Chaucer's *Knight's Tale*, but behind that figure lay the numerous different versions of the 'olde stories', the *Teseide* of Boccaccio, the *Thebaid* of Statius, Plutarch's *Life of Theseus*, the Greek tragedies, receding back into legend and myth. Although Theseus had his full share of hero's adventures, monster-killing and lady-rescuing, he is often portrayed at a later stage of his life, as king rather than hero. He is a survivor who emerges from the world of Herculean demi-gods to become the founding-father of Athens. In tragedy, whether he is played as the wise king of Sophocles' *Oedipus at Colonus*, or the rash king of Euripides' *Hippolytus*, he is rarely if ever the tragic protagonist. His womanising is disapproved of by Plutarch, yet he never seems to suffer for it. Indeed by the Renaissance Theseus had become a glorious example of heroic success in both love and war, a conqueror who could turn his military force into civil authority.[1]

It is as 'lord and governour' of Athens that Shakespeare introduces us to his Theseus and, like Chaucer, he introduces him on the eve of his marriage to Hippolyta. The transformation from warrior to lover is stressed:

> Hippolyta, I wooed thee with my sword,
> And won thy love doing thee injuries;
> But I will wed thee in another key:
> With pomp, with triumph, and with revelling.   I i 16–19[2]

This is the mature Theseus, whose marriage may be taken as confirming him in his settled role as Duke and magistrate. And it is as arbitrating magistrate that he is approached by Egeus who complains that Lysander has misled his daughter Hermia's affections away from Demetrius, the man he has chosen to be his son-in-law. Egeus demands the full rigour of the law – one of those capricious laws which tend to turn up in the first acts of comedies – by which he has the right to prescribe a husband for her or, if she refuses, condemn her to death. Theseus appears to endorse the father's absolute authority, and gives the conventional justification of that authority:

> What say you Hermia? Be advised, fair maid:
> To you your father should be as a god;
> One that composed your beauties – yea, and one
> To whom you are but as a form in wax
> By him imprinted, and within his power
> To leave the figure or disfigure it.   I i 46–50

Yet Theseus's language and bearing in this scene distinguish his position clearly from the peremptory and tyrannic will of the father Egeus. He puts to Hermia the choices before her, introducing a third option which Egeus did not mention – she may choose a nunnery rather than death – and advises her kindly on how she should make up her mind:

> Therefore, fair Hermia, question your desires,
> Know of your youth, examine well your blood,
> Whether, if you yield not to your father's choice,
> You can endure the livery of a nun,
> For aye to be in shady cloister mewed,
> To live a barren sister all your life,
> Chanting faint hymns to the cold fruitless moon.
> Thrice blessed they that master so their blood

To undergo such maiden pilgrimage;
But earthlier happy is the rose distilled
Than that which, withering on the virgin thorn
Grows, lives, and dies in single blessedness. I i 67–78

Theseus is *l'homme moyen sensuel*, wise and humane, arguing against the emotional absolutism of the nunnery with the pragmatic logic of 'better any husband that no husband at all'. Where Egeus is the father-ogre of Oedipal fears, thwarting and menacing, Theseus is a paternalistic father-figure, persuading and cajoling.

The impression of paternalism is extended in his later speech in which he recalls hearing of Demetrius's prior commitment to Helena:

I must confess that I have heard so much,
And with Demetrius thought to have spoke thereof;
But, being overfull of self affairs,
My mind did lose it. But Demetrius, come;
And come Egeus. You shall go with me.
I have some private schooling for you both. I i 111–16

This is a Duke in whom we may have some confidence, familiar and concerned as he evidently is with the doings of his subjects. He proclaims that he is unable to 'extenuate' the threatening law, yet there remains a residual assurance that with him in charge things will not go badly wrong. As a lover himself, he is likely to look kindly upon the needs of the lovers, though as a mature man he will see those needs in perspective. He is understandably preoccupied at present with 'self affairs', but he will not long neglect his public responsibilities, and we may hope for the best from his conference with Demetrius and Egeus.

However, for the greater part of the action of *A Midsummer Night's Dream* this reassuring presence is withdrawn. Theseus does not appear at all between Act I and Act IV, the period of the night wanderings of the lovers, a period presided over by a very different figure of authority, Oberon. Or is he so very different? Peter Brook, who doubled the parts of Theseus and Oberon in his celebrated production of 1970, would presumably argue not. But what sort of significance would this equivalence of the two roles have in our understanding of the play? It is worth discussing this issue because it bears directly on the question with which we started, the question of what authority controls the comedy.

Oberon rules the night as Theseus rules the day; to each in his own sphere is given the same sort of commanding presence. This is the basic feature of congruence. In favour of the doubling of the parts, Brook argues, also, that the relationship between Theseus and Hippolyta is echoed in the relationship between Oberon and Titania, that the quarrel between the king and queen of the fairies is used as an exploration of the meaning of the mortal union celebrated in the final marriage.[3] Paul Olson, in an influential scholarly article, likewise sees Oberon as the counterpart of Theseus, though for very different reasons. Oberon, he claims, represents the same principle of reasoned masculine authority as Theseus, and the refusal of Titania to submit to his will shows that improper spirit of female assertiveness which Theseus in conquering the Amazonian Hippolyta had successfully subdued.[4] Concord is restored when the source of the dispute, the changeling boy, is ceded by Titania, and the way is prepared for the final marriage blessing.

   This sort of equation of Theseus/Hippolyta − Oberon/Titania is no doubt attractive, whether it is posed in theatrical or thematic terms. But it may distort or neglect fundamental distinctions between the various types of experience in the play. (It is worth remarking, by the way, that there is no precedent in what we know of the original staging of *A Midsummer Night's Dream* for Brook's doubling; 'significant' doubling does not seem to have been common in the Elizabethan theatre.)[5] The most basic distinction between the rulers of the night and the rulers of the day derives from the simple fact that Oberon and Titania are non-human. Where Theseus and Hippolyta, whatever their legendary antecedents, are flesh and blood, mature lovers at a recognisable stage of a human life, Oberon and Titania are ageless deities unlimited by time or space. Their dispute over the Indian boy has that lack of moral implications which we associate with the conflicts of the pagan gods. To suggest, as Olson does, that we are intended to see in Titania a reprehensible failure of respect for hierarchical principle, is surely to belie dramatic effect in the interests of ingenious emblematic interpretation. In so far as we take sides between the two, indeed, it is rather with Titania, who has moving personal reasons for keeping the child of her dead friend, than with 'jealous Oberon' who merely wants a toy which is denied him. But the impact of the confrontation is not to make us take sides. Instead the whole ambiance of the fairy world inclines us to regard the conflict as a morally neutral clash of natural forces which we watch with wonder, delight, and perhaps a suspicion of fear.

   The danger of too close an identification of Oberon with Theseus, Titania with Hippolyta, is that the sense of the separateness of the night-realm will be lost. The influence of the fairies on the human action as we see it in the play is accidental, casual, arbitrary. Oberon and Titania, like the Greek gods, have their human favourites whom they jealously protect and their patronage of, respectively, Hippolyta and Theseus is used as a plot-device to explain their appearance for the wedding, as well as for an amusing piece of tit-for-tat mudslinging. Such an interest in mortals is, however, necessarily exceptional. Titania gives a disturbing view of the effect of her quarrel with Oberon on the human environment:

> The fold stands empty in the drowned field,
> And crows are fatted with the murrion flock.
> The nine men's morris is filled up with mud,
> And the quaint mazes in the wanton green
> For lack of tread are undistinguishable. II i 96—100

But this is a side-effect of their dissension, not an intentional curse upon the natural world.

Oberon's control of the various visitors to the wood is of this accidental kind. He does not specify to Puck that Bottom, much less Bottom-plus-ass's-head, should be used for his revenge upon Titania. By chance he happens to overhear Helena wooing the reluctant Demetrius but he gives no inkling of why he decides to intervene. He merely comments,

> Fare thee well nymph. Ere he do leave this grove
> Thou shalt fly him, and he shall seek thy love. II i 245—6

There is in Oberon a cool love of power for power's sake. Titania by refusing him the boy he wants affronts his absolute will and his revenge is to make her feel the full force of his power over her. He sorts out the mismatchings of the lovers without any marked benevolent intention; more, perhaps, with the amusement of a grown-up effortlessly reversing the drift of play in a children's game. Yet Oberon is too remote from the game even to feel malicious pleasure at the children's dismay. This is left entirely to Puck, to whom Oberon delegates executive responsibility.

With Puck we find a comic controller who does match one of our earlier categories of those whom we expect to control the comic action. Puck as the cunning and mischievous servant is like a Roman tricky slave with wings. He is loyal and industrious in the service of his master but he has also a pure love of absurdity and confusion and, as Robin Goodfellow, is the author of all sorts of minor human mischances. His is the idea of the ass's head for Bottom. He genuinely makes a mistake in anointing the wrong Athenian with the love-juice, yet the resulting confusion he finds delightful:

> so far am I glad it so did sort,
> As this their jangling I esteem a sport. III ii 352—3

His attitude to the lovers is one of good-humoured contempt – 'Lord what fools these mortals be'. His final assurance to us that the tangle will be sorted out, with its parody of country proverbs, has a similar knowing cynicism,

> Jack shall have Jill
> Naught shall go ill
> The man shall have his mare again, and all shall be well.
>
> III ii 461–3

The combination of Oberon's lofty indifference and Puck's amused mockery provides a detached view of the pattern of human loves being worked out in the wood.

Thus we have what might be called a separation of powers in *A Midsummer Night's Dream*. The authority of Oberon is different in kind from that of Theseus, not the authority of paternal human concern but a presence of grace and power quite divorced from human commitments. In so far as he does engage with the doings of the mortals who wander into his realm, it is through the agency of Puck, a jester who uses the bewildered night-travellers as the butts of his jokes. It is wrong to identify the figures of the Athenian court with those of the fairy kingdom because the play depends on the sense of the lovers (and of Bottom) that in the course of the night they have been somewhere else, somewhere totally alien. As so often in Shakespeare's comedy this alienation or disorienting experience is a crucial part of the progress towards the final resolution. The otherness of the other world which they encounter should not be diminished; the wood near Athens must be a bewildering, an enchanted, a frightening place in which the humans become conscious that powers prevail beyond their comprehension in whose hand they are casual toys.

Act IV scene i brings a gradual lighting-change as Titania and Oberon make their exit and we shift to the hunting-scene which again Shakespeare borrows from Chaucer. Nothing better illustrates the distinctness of the two worlds than this. For Oberon and Titania the lark is the signal for the ending of the night's sport:

> Then my queen in silence sad
> Trip we after night's shade.
> We the globe can compass soon,
> Swifter than the wandering moon.   IV i 94–7

With Theseus and Hippolyta there is the energy of a day beginning – the dawn of a May morning when they have done their 'observation' and will make use of their early start for a full hunting session. Their discussion of the cry of the hounds takes us straight into the reality of their lives. Hippolyta's recollection reminds us of her heroic past yet the casualness of her reference to her hunting-companions, the mythical Hercules and Cadmus, scales them down to human size:

> I was with Hercules and Cadmus once,
> When in a wood of Crete they bayed the bear
> With hounds of Sparta. Never did I hear
> Such gallant chiding, for besides the groves,
> The skies, the fountains, every region near
> Seemed all one mutual cry. I never heard
> So musical a discord, such sweet thunder. IV i 111–17

This is Theseus's cue to describe the breeding of his dogs and insist that they are no less 'tuneable' than those of Hercules. But the image of musical discord provides a metaphor for the pattern of the play and we are now reaching the vantage-point from which the cacophonous confusions of the lovers are heard to be an orchestrated harmony.

The lovers are awakened formally, deliberately, by the call of the huntsmen's horns. With this flourish the tribunal of the first act is re-assembled, the rivals Demetrius and Lysander standing once again before the accuser Egeus and the judge Theseus. Lysander confesses to his intention of eloping with Hermia, and this is enough for Egeus:

> *Lysander.* . . . Our intent
> Was to be gone from Athens where we might
> Without the peril of the Athenian law . . .
> *Egeus.* Enough, enough – my lord you have enough!
> I beg the law, the law upon his head. IV i 150–4

But the attempt to escape from Theseus's jurisdiction is not treated as the flagrant contempt of court which Egeus would have it to be. In the light of Demetrius's avowal that his love for Hermia has mysteriously vanished and his loyalty returned to Helena, Theseus gives the case against Egeus and for the lovers:

> Fair lovers, you are fortunately met.
> Of this discourse we more will hear anon.
> Egeus, I will overbear your will;

> For in the temple by and by with us
> These couples shall eternally be knit.   IV i 176—80

So what has become of the law which in Act I Theseus could 'by no means . . . extenuate'? Here it is set aside by a bland ducal decree which may make us suspicious of the original legal reasoning. Clifford Leech, placing Theseus in the context of other comic dukes in Shakespeare, comments on this 'moment of arbitrary forgetfulness'. He compares it with similar actions of the Duke of Ephesus in *A Comedy of Errors*, or the Duke in *The Merchant of Venice*, where justice is done but is manifestly not seen to be done.[6] Leech's conclusion, however, that we are intended to view with irony such contradictory actions of authority, is arguable. On the most literal-minded and rationalistic level, Theseus's decision can be defended. We saw him in Act I retiring for a private hearing with Egeus and Demetrius and it may well be that what he heard there, particularly of Demetrius's former engagement to Helena, has quite properly influenced his judgement. But this sort of logical defense is not really necessary. The change in Theseus's attitude reflects a change in the lovers' relations to one another brought about by the night in the wood and a change in our, the audience's, reaction to the comedy. We are now ready for Theseus to shift from the compassionate but just magistrate of the first act to the benign and merciful duke of the dénouement. It may not be a defensible turn-about for a judge on the bench but it is quite the development we expect from the father-figure to whom we have entrusted the happiness of the people concerned.

This pattern of reversal is analogous to that which we considered in the previous chapter in *As You Like It* and *L'Ecole des Femmes*. There we began with an apparent opposition between nature and the tyranny of social law and convention. But ultimately society vindicated what nature demanded. In the same way the law of Athens is initially the law of Egeus, endorsed, however regretfully, with the authority of Theseus. The interval in the moonlit wood, however, makes it possible for that law to be overruled or replaced. Once the irregular pattern of cross-wooing has been resolved into the symmetry of the properly paired lovers, then the frustrating will of Egeus becomes impotent and Theseus can fulfil his function as civil magistrate sanctioning the socially fruitful marriage union. If there is irony in this scene it is directed not against Theseus and the authority he represents, but at the naive confession of Demetrius:

> But, my good lord — I wot not by what power,
> But by some power it is — my love to Hermia,
> Melted as the snow, seems to me now

As the remembrance of an idle gaud
Which in my childhood I did dote upon;
And all the faith, the virtue of my heart,
The object and the pleasure of mine eye,
Is only Helena. To her, my lord,
Was I betrothed ere I saw Hermia;
But like a sickness did I loathe this food;
But as in health come to my natural taste,
Now I do wish it, love it, long for it,
And will for evermore be true to it.   IV i 163 – 75

We know by what power his love for Hermia melted and we may well smile at the images of the change of affections as a progress from childhood to maturity, sickness to health. Demetrius's present (permanent) enchantment is no more natural or adult than Lysander's temporary love for Helena during the night, which he justified with a similar type of argument (II ii 141 ff.) The impersonality and arbitrariness of the powers that played with the lovers like puppets, leave us in no doubt about the relativism and irrationality of young love. All the same, by whatever good mismanagement, those irrational impulses do find their correct direction and by Act IV scene i they are ready to be drawn into the dance of social harmony.

The final act of the play gives us a full picture of the court of Theseus in nuptial celebration. Additional details body out the figure of Theseus as a recognisable duke in Elizabethan terms. He receives the list of proposed entertainments from his Master of Revels, Philostrate, as one well used to such matters; he only needs the title to alert him to 'an old device' revived or a satirical piece unsuitable to the occasion. His vivid account of the 'great clerks' of a civic reception breaking down in their 'premeditated welcomes' suggests an English monarch on a royal progress rather than a mythical Athenian hero. His behaviour throughout, his noble courtesy and magnanimity, would seem intended to be admirable, even ideal. But we are left with the much debated issue of how we are to interpret his great speech – 'The lunatic, the lover, and the poet' – and whether the authority of his presence commands our assent for the point of view it expresses. It has been suggested that in this controversy opinion is divided into Theseus-critics and Hippolyta-critics, those who feel that Theseus's attitude is to be regarded as normative, and those who argue that the final word is Hippolyta's? In spite of their familiarity, it is worth quoting the lines at length, in order to look at the argument in detail:

Hippolyta. 'Tis strange, my Theseus, that these lovers speak of.

Theseus. More strange than true. I never may believe
These antique fables, nor these fairy toys.
Lovers and madmen have such seething brains,
Such shaping fantasies, that apprehend
More than cool reason ever comprehends.
The lunatic, the lover, and the poet
Are of imagination all compact.
One sees more devils than vast hell can hold.
That is the madman. The lover, all as frantic,
Sees Helen's beauty in a brow of Egypt.
The poet's eye, in a fine frenzy rolling,
Doth glance from heaven to earth, from earth to heaven.
And as imagination bodies forth
The form of things unknown, the poet's pen
Turns them to shapes, and gives to airy nothing
A local habitation and a name.
Such tricks hath strong imagination
That if it would but apprehend some joy,
It comprehends some bringer of that joy.
Or in the night, imagining some fear,
How easy is a bush supposed a bear?
Hippolyta. But all the story of the night told over,
And all their minds transfigured so together,
More witnesseth than fancy's images,
And grows to something of great constancy;
But howsoever, strange and admirable.   V i 1 – 28

Theseus's statement is undoubtedly one of the most eloquent expressions ever written of the 'all poets are liars' point of view. But in spite of the eloquence, critics have been understandably reluctant to see Shakespeare offering for our approval such a reductive theory of the poetic imagination. Paul Olson, arguing that a great poet is unlikely to be disparaging poetry, suggests that Theseus's description is perfectly consonant with the Renaissance humanist tradition by which the poet, divinely inspired, figures in earthly terms the unknowable mysteries of heaven — 'imagination bodies forth The form of things unknown'.[8] This, however, seems to disregard the pragmatist, anti-idealist tone of the whole speech. It is surely impossible to turn Theseus into a neo-Platonist. Other critics have seen ironies which undermine Theseus's position from within: for example, his scoffing dismissal of 'antique fables' is belied by his own fictional nature as a character in just such a fable.[9] Much more commonly, however, it has been felt that Hippolyta's wondering and tentative belief is to be preferred to Theseus's brusque rationalism. In other words, if we are to place Shakespeare between the two points of view, he is closer to Hippolyta than to Theseus.

In one respect, no doubt, Hippolyta is right and Theseus is wrong. There was more to the 'story of the night' than mere 'fairy toys', 'fancy's images'; the lovers we actually saw being 'transfigured so together' by the power of Oberon. Theseus will allow no level of experience beyond that of daytime reality and therefore he dismisses the whole night-world of the fairies as fantasy. Yet there are features of his description which also tally with what we have seen. The traditional allusion to the distorted vision of the lover who sees 'Helen's beauty in a brow of Egypt' is warranted by the enchanted changes of perception in Demetrius and Lysander. Having watched Puck at work we can testify to how easy it was for him to make the lovers suppose a bush was a bear. However we might regard Theseus's view of poetic creation in itself, as a theory of the imagination, at this stage in the comedy he is a steadying voice, reassuring in his commonsensical solidity. We must live, after all, in Theseus's world, not Oberon's and we are grateful for the sanity of his daylight vision. Hippolyta's words may well act, in Stanley Wells's phrase, as a 'corrective' to Theseus's statement, but it is a corrective, not a rebuttal.[10] The frenzied fantasies of young love are left firmly behind and the dominant mood of the final act, for which Theseus sets the key, is of down-to-earth joviality.

What then of the re-entry of Oberon and Titania and their train with which the play ends? What of the admission implicit in Theseus's retiring remark — 'Lovers, to bed; 'tis almost fairy time'? Does the play not conclude with the reassertion of the dimension of experience which Theseus had tried to deny and therefore expose the hollowness and complacency of his point of view? It might well be argued that this coda reduces to a sham the authority and control that Theseus has assumed by showing us the superior power of the supernatural world. However, this is not necessarily its effect. Puck's ominous speech, 'Now the hungry lion roars . . .', is no doubt disturbing, with all its associations of the 'witching-time' of night, but Oberon earlier reassured us that he and his followers were 'spirits of another sort' from the damned who may walk only between midnight and cock-crow. We know, also, in advance the reason for this appearance — Titania and Oberon, in their renewed concord, come to bless the beds of the lovers. The effect is like that of the final stanzas of Spenser's *Epithalamion*. The public and private celebration of human happiness in marriage must include finally a propitiation of those forces beyond human control whose assistance is necessary to full and fruitful union. The social and personal harmony of the lovers is extended in the fairies' dance into the non-human world of the natural and supernatural. But this is not to deny the substance of Theseus's anthropocentric vision. For Oberon and Titania become in the final scene tutelary spirits who protect and bless rather than deities who dominate and control the human lives.

Theseus throughout *A Midsummer Night's Dream* is a figure whose qualities are not intended to be slighted or despised. If his perspective seems limited by his lack of imagination, that limitation is necessary if he is to fulfil his proper function. The comforting security of his presence depends upon his authoritative defiance of the irrational. We can have confidence in him as ruler and judge — in the best and fullest sense, the father of his country. But his actual control of events within the action is also limited. He can and will confirm with the seal of his authority the pattern which we expect as the happy ending, but only when that pattern has been shaken out by the kaleidoscope of the night misadventures. In the night world of Oberon he has no part and indeed no belief. Theseus is the representative of just social authority; he is not against life, as the Oedipal father Egeus is, but he must wait on the forces of life itself before he can employ his moral strength on the right side.

THE TEMPEST

Shakespeare may not have intended the parts of Theseus and Oberon to be doubled, but in *The Tempest* he compressed them into a single role — Prospero, Duke of Milan. What is more, he included the part of Egeus for good measure. Prospero's triple persona as father, duke and magician is represented emblematically in the theatre by his costume-changes. When we see him first in Act I scene ii, he is wearing his 'magic garment' — presumably he has just been conjuring up the tempest — and he takes it off to talk to Miranda.

> Lend thy hand,
> And pluck my magic garment from me. — So:
> Lie there, my Art.   I ii 23 — 5

We have no clue as to just what he wears throughout most of the play but it must be sufficiently humble and drab to suit his description of himself to Miranda — 'Prospero, master of a full poor cell, And thy no greater father'. (I ii 20 — 21). The transformation, at least, when he presents himself in the last act as he 'was sometime Milan', must be startling enough to impress Caliban by the contrast — 'How fine my master is'. (V.i 262). (He sends Ariel to fetch 'hat and rapier', and one guesses from the use of the word 'discase' and from the fact that he changes on stage, that he merely removes some form of outer gown to reveal a splendid ducal costume underneath.)[11] These three aspects of Prospero alternate throughout, and together make up the complex sense we have of his control over the action.

The long Act I scene ii shows Prospero in all his varying characters. The exposition takes the form of a conversation between father and daughter — or rather a recital of the past by Prospero broken by dutiful noises from Miranda. This exposition is so protracted that it has lent weight to the theory that The Tempest, as we know it, is an abridgement of an earlier text in which the events which Prospero here relates were actually represented. Whether this is so or not — and most modern editors seem to think not — it is clear that Shakespeare felt the need to add life to his slabs of expository monologue. This he did by giving Prospero a series of irritable injunctions to Miranda to listen — 'Dost thou attend me?', 'I pray thee, mark me', 'Dost thou hear?' These might be used theatrically to suggest the disparity between his absorbed re-living of the past and her relative lack of interest in the story, or his obsessive desire to make her share his own passionate indignation at his wrongs. But its general effect is to make us think of Prospero as a peremptory, if not a tyrannic, father. Although he assures Miranda that he has 'done nothing but in care of thee, of thee, my dear one, thee, my daughter', we may suspect that he belongs to that tribe of comic fathers, of whom Egeus in A Midsummer Night's Dream is one, who are devoted parents while their children are obedient but who become violent the instant they are opposed.

The exposition, of course, not only relates the past but prepares us to meet some of the principal characters of the play — notably 'the noble Neapolitan Gonzalo' whose help to Prospero and Miranda is stressed. The story of the usurpation sets up as the play's ultimate goal the restoration to Prospero of the dukedom of Milan. There is in Prospero a desire for vengeance and a concern for regaining power which makes him a very different banished Duke from such as Duke Senior in As You Like It. Where Duke Senior never once mentions his usurping brother, Prospero still after twelve years nearly bursts with rage at the thought of Antonio's action. Mingled with the sense of personal injury there is the feeling of the disgrace brought upon the dukedom itself. Milan was 'at that time, Through all the signiories . . . the first And Prospero the prime Duke'. The most infamous part of Antonio's conspiracy was his pact with the King of Naples,

> To give him annual tribute, do him homage,
> Subject his coronet to his crown, and bend
> The dukedom, yet unbow'd . . .
> To most ignoble stooping.   I ii 113 – 16

The irony is that Antonio's need to be 'absolute Milan', rather than merely Prospero's regent, leads him to destroy the absolute sovereignty of Milan. Though there are elements of self-pity and self-righteousness in Prospero's portrait – 'Me, poor man, my library was dukedom large enough' – yet we may be expected to sympathise with his desire not merely to regain his position as Duke but to restore that position itself to its former dignity. The relationship between the dukedom of Milan and the kingship of Naples will recur several times through the play and is to be crucial in the dénouement.

Prospero ends his conversation with Miranda by putting her to sleep. Although she is familiar with his magical powers and now knows that he has caused the tempest and why, yet it appears that she is not allowed to meet the spirit who 'performed' the tempest, Ariel, who now enters. It was Coleridge who remarked that 'Miranda is never brought into comparison with Ariel, lest the natural and human of the one and the supernatural of the other should tend to neutralise each other'.[12] There is besides an intimacy in the relationship between Ariel and Prospero which would not admit of a third presence. Like Oberon and Puck they alone share the highest possible plateau of irony. Ariel's description of the effect of the tempest on the ship's passengers has the delight in the observation of human folly which was Puck's key-note too. Ferdinand, who is to be the play's juvenile lead, is introduced to us in very undignified posture by the mocking Ariel:

> the King's son, Ferdinand,
> With hair up-staring, – then like reeds, not hair –
> Was the first man that leap'd; cried, 'Hell is empty,
> And all the devils are here'.   I ii 212 – 15

Contrasting this with the very real panic which we experienced with the characters in the opening scene, we can see that we have been transferred to the distant pinnacle of power from which such antics are laughable because we know that they are over-reactions.

Prospero and Ariel share, as Oberon and Puck did, this pure pleasure in power for its own sake though, again as in *A Midsummer Night's Dream*, the servant shows a delight in mischief which is beneath the dignity of the master. There are other parallels as well. Just as Oberon reassures us of the difference between his sort of night-wanderers who may linger until after dawn and the black spirits of the damned, so Prospero's art of white magic is deliberately contrasted with the damnable power of the witch Sycorax, Ariel's former mistress. But the relationship between Prospero and Ariel is more complicated, or at least more fully drawn, than that between Oberon and Puck. Puck serves his master happily, without any suggestion that he might do otherwise; it is quite simply the function of Robin Goodfellow to be page and jester to King Oberon. With Ariel, however, there is an ultimate desire for liberty and willing service is only a means to that end. Prospero's anger at Ariel's demand for freedom is disconcerting. In the aggressive and self-assertive tones with which he reminds his servant of all that he has done for him, we may hear again the voice of the father threatened by rebellion. (Prospero's attitude to Ariel has, at times, a paternal tenderness and warmth which he scarcely shows to Miranda.) But more generally the scene makes us aware of a question which the play repeatedly asks: by what right does one being have power over another?

It is a question which is certainly asked most strikingly in the next encounter, that between Prospero and Caliban. It is no wonder that twentieth-century directors have seen in *The Tempest* an analysis of the evils of imperialism, for the argument between Prospero and Caliban does seem astonishingly to prefigure the whole vicious circle of colonial conflict. What starts as practical help from the native to the colonialist – 'I lov'd thee, And show'd thee all the qualities o' th' isle,' – in exchange for education – 'I endow'd thy purposes with Words that made them known'[13] – rapidly sours into exploitation and enslavement. We must, of course, beware of reading back too much of a post-colonial interpretation into this scene. Yet once again the harsh anger of Prospero, fitting with what we have seen of his behaviour with Miranda and Ariel, bears out the gathering impression of arbitrary and tyrannic authority associated with him. His absolute power is not so absolute but that he feels an almost obsessive need to defend it.

We pass directly from the slave Caliban back to his opposite, the servant Ariel, who now enters leading on Ferdinand, the first of the castaways. Here, as elsewhere in the play, Ariel, the elusive spirit who beguiles people into following with light or music, is like Robin Goodfellow, the will o' the wisp. With the appearance of Ariel Prospero's attitude to Miranda changes, and it is as a conjuror rather than a father that he stage-manages the meeting between her and Ferdinand. Miranda herself is sure that this is another of her father's magical displays:

> What is't? a spirit?
> Lord, how it looks about! Believe me, sir,
> It carries a brave form. But 'tis a spirit. I ii 411–13

Throughout the scene Prospero continues to address asides partly to himself, partly to Ariel, rejoicing in his ironic control over the whole situation.

> It goes on, I see,
> As my soul prompts it. Spirit, fine spirit! I'll free thee
> Within two days for this.   I ii 422−4

To put it in *Midsummer Night's Dream* terms, Prospero is primarily Oberon in this scene.

But he can make use of his other personae also. To Ferdinand, for example, he is the jealous and authoritarian ruler. He questions him closely on his claim to the Kingdom of Naples: Ferdinand is convinced his father is drowned − and then produces the sort of preposterous charge we expect from tyrannic dukes in renaissance drama:

> One word more; I charge thee
> That thou attend me: thou dost here usurp
> The name thou ow'st not; and hast put thyself
> Upon this island as a spy, to win it
> From me, the lord on't.   I ii 455−9

To Miranda he plays an equally stock angry father, when she pleads on Ferdinand's behalf:

> Silence! one word more
> Shall make me chide thee; if not hate thee. What!
> An advocate for an imposter! hush!   I ii 478−80

But in this instance we know that his assumption of these parts is merely a means towards a benign end − 'this swift business I must uneasy make, lest too light winning Make the prize light' and that the opposition to Ferdinand and Miranda's love is explicitly the ritual trial of the fairy-tale. We are assured that from the beginning his will is for them and that the blocking father-ogre is a pure fiction manipulated by a figure of benevolent control. Such control gives its own ironic flavour to the love affair but it suggests that Prospero's final role will be that of comic controller rather than punitive authority.

The theme of power and domination is thus threaded through the expository Act I scene ii. In Acts II and III it is extended and amplified by a study of all the different visitors to the island. We have already seen

Ferdinand trying on uneasily the title of king which he imagines that he has inherited from his drowned father:

> myself am Naples
> Who with mine eyes, never since at ebb, beheld
> The King my father wrack'd. I ii 437–9

His attitude is the correct one for a respectful but responsible heir, like that of Hal in *Henry IV Part II* trying on the crown. In Act II scene i, however, when we meet the court party who are nearly as convinced that Ferdinand is lost, we see much less admirable views on the succession to the throne of Naples. To Ferdinand the shipwreck is the unhappy occasion of his accession; to Sebastian, prompted by Antonio, it is an unexpected opportunity for a quick *coup d'état*. The situation is perfect: the heir-apparent Ferdinand is drowned, the next heir Claribel is married in Tunis 'ten leagues beyond man's life', and here they are on a desert island where there is no-one to witness an assassination but a few easily bribed courtiers. With straightforward villains like Antonio and Sebastian the natural surroundings of the island turn covert ambition into a naked flame of aggression.

However it is not only in the evil politicians that the conditions of the shipwreck encourage the aspiration for power to blossom. The innocent and honest lord Gonzalo is prompted to a colonialist vision by the island:

> Had I plantation of this isle, my lord . . .
> And were the King on't, what would I do? II i 139–41

What follows is the famous adaptation of the lines from Montaigne outlining a perfect natural republic. But, as Antonio and Sebastian are quick to point out, 'the latter end of his commonwealth forgets the beginning'. Gonzalo would have no 'sovereignty' in his state and yet his initial premise is that he would be King. This can be interpreted as Shakespeare's refutation of Montaigne's naturalism by showing that power and organisation are necessary in any society, even in order to free men from the threat of power and organisation, but in terms of the structure of the play it gives one more instance of the effect of the island's alienating atmosphere. As the wood near Athens liberates in the characters the irrational impulses of love, so the 'uninhabited Island' of *The Tempest* frees from inhibition the fantasies of domination that lurk in every man, even if they are as beneficent fantasies as Gonzalo's.

The range of forms which such fantasies may take is completed by the introduction of the low comics Stephano and Trinculo. In the first scene in

which they appear we see Caliban changing allegiance from the tyrant
Prospero to the god who 'bears celestial liquor', alias Stephano the drunken
butler. A change in masters is, tragically, the farthest Caliban can aspire
towards freedom. 'Ban ban Cacaliban, Got a new master get a new man'. In
the earlier scene Caliban had complained of his enslavement to Prospero
with the telling words:

> For I am all the subjects that you have,
> Which first was mine own King.   I ii 343 – 4

But he can never regain that state of independence; he is imprisoned in the
slave mentality which can only conceive of liberation in terms of his master
being defeated by a new and stronger master. Shakespeare understood the
various different sides to the colonial process. Along with the high-minded
Prosperos, the educators and developers, come the totally irresponsible
Stephanos who contemputuously hoodwink the natives with a few cheap
tricks. But within the play perhaps the effect of the Stephano-Trinculo sub-
plot is partially to vindicate Prospero. At least his idea of dominion is not as
short-sighted or banal as Stephano's — endless drink and a good-looking
wench for his queen. The low comedy scenes in the play are very funny, but
there is a bitter edge of satire to the perception of how much more degraded
the 'civilized' butler and jester are than the 'salvage and deformed slave'.

   All these characters, whose desire for power is exposed, are all the time in
the power of Prospero. His plan is to make each aspiration a punishment to
itself. For those capable of remorse like Alonso, the supposed loss of his son is
presented as retribution for the crime of ambition which led him to sentence
Prospero and Miranda to death. To Sebastian and Antonio, who confidently
planned to carve out their own destiny on the island, comes distraction and
complete loss of control. Stephano and Trinculo are diverted from their
attempt on Prospero's life and sovereignty by cheap trumpery such as they
themselves, or other colonialists like them, might have used to dazzle the
natives. Prospero gives to each man his dream of power, and then turns it
into a nightmare. The process ends when all of them are thoroughly
distracted, throughly unnerved, as the bewilderments of *A Midsummer
Night's Dream* end with the exhausted collapse of all four lovers on the
ground.

> At this hour
> Lies at my mercy all mine enemies.   IV i 262 – 3

Prospero's moment of gloating triumph is a real climax, a real point of suspense in the play. What will he now do with his absolute control over his enemies? Which of the several aspects of his character that we isolated in Act I will emerge now? In Act IV we have seen him taking off his harsh father disguise and giving his paternal blessing to Ferdinand and Miranda, although his repeated injunctions on the need for chastity still have the ring of the authoritarian father of the earlier scenes. His magical display in honour of the lovers is broken off by the news of the Caliban plot, to which he seems to over-react in the same way that he did to previous challenges to the absolutism of his power. We may well wonder in what mood this multiple personality will direct the dénouement.

The cue for Prospero's final change of attitude comes from Ariel, who is reporting the state of the courtiers, spell-bound by Prospero:

> *Ariel.* . . .   Your charm so strongly works 'em,
> That if you now beheld them, your affections
> Would become tender.
> *Prospero.*   Dost thou think so, spirit?
> *Ariel.* Mine would, sir, were I human.
> *Prospero.*   And mine shall.   V i 16—20

The irony is that the non-human spirit should prompt Prospero to the act of forgiveness which is the defining characteristic of Christian humanity. The inner need for vengeance is now at an end:

> Though with their high wrongs I am struck to th' quick
> Yet with my nobler reason 'gainst my fury
> Do I take part: the rarer action is in virtue
> Than in vengeance: they being penitent,
> The sole drift of my purpose does extend
> Not a frown further.   V i 25—30

Now that he has satisfied the impulse to punish his enemies, to salve his pride injured by the usurpation, the wrathful over-assertiveness which we saw in earlier scenes may wither away. He exorcises it finally by an address to the still bewitched members of the court, in which he spends his remaining emotion upon friend and enemies, Gonzalo, Alonso, Sebastian and Antonio. He thus prepares for his ultimate apparition as the rightful Duke of Milan, stern but magnanimous, the Duke whose authority is no longer questioned.

But with the decision to end his project of revenge comes the larger decision to renounce his magic altogether. His renunciation is prefaced by a triumphant celebration of all that he has achieved by his art and it is not surprising that those who saw autobiographical allegory in *The Tempest* should have read this speech as Shakespeare's nostalgic pride at the moment of retirement in the achievements of his stage magic. Within the structure of the play, however, it is representative of that return to the real world which we except from this phase of the comic pattern. It is like the change from night to day in *A Midsummer Night's Dream* and, though it is here actually evening, Prospero's metaphor for the thawing back to normality of the courtiers recalls the dawn awakening of the lovers:

> The charm dissolves apace;
> And as the morning steals upon the night,
> Melting the darkness, so their rising senses
> Begin to chase the ignorant fumes that mantle
> Their clearer reason.   V i 64−8

As Oberon disappears to make way for Theseus, so Prospero the magician vanishes and we are left with the Duke of Milan who can convince King Alonso of his solid reality by a warm bodily embrace. It is as Duke, with no more power than a Duke has, that he must preside over the final happy ending. For it is a happy ending in the real world of Dukes and Kings, with Alonso renouncing his claim to homage from Milan − 'thy dukedom I resign' − and an entirely satisfactory dynastic solution achieved in the marriage of Ferdinand and Miranda.

If Prospero is to be identified with Shakespeare, then it should perhaps be with Shakespeare the comedian. In *The Tempest* Shakespeare was notoriously careful about keeping to the unity of time, as he had been nowhere else in his dramatic work. Prospero in Act I and again Act V is at pains to remind the audience that the stage-action parallels the time of its representation, from two to six in the afternoon.[14] We remember Jonson's injunction to the audience of *Bartholomew Fair* to be patient for two hours and a half or somewhat more. The comedian is conscious that he has at his disposal a limited time to amuse and divert the spectators with a fantastic sequence of confusion and inversion. For that duration he may use as his surrogate the fairy King Oberon or the wizard Prospero. But then control must pass from this extraordinary authority to a ruler of the here and now. The Lord of Misrule must break his staff and resign his office to a real lord of order, a stage director who can take authoritative charge.

In one sense, therefore, it would seem from the analysis of this chapter that our initial hypothesis was right: no single figure of authority is allowed to dominate the comic action. Theseus reigns only in the day-time, and the crucial events of *A Midsummer Night's Dream* are played out at night under the auspices of Oberon. Prospero does control throughout, but by his capricious and arbitrary behaviour he is at least partly identified with that form of authority which comedy conspires to defeat. He succeeds, it is true, but it is an empty success and makes him realise that such total control is of limited value. Yet we can perhaps go beyond such a negative conclusion. What comedy most often resists is not so much power or authority as the individual will which claims for itself the force of law. The heavy father Egeus demands as a right due to his paternity an obedience which is really just the consummation of his will, and he arouses accordingly just as arbitrary opposition. Of such arbitrariness the comic community must be purged. A period beyond the control of human law altogether is the common path to such purgation. Oberon's power is disinterested because non-human and therefore, although his control of events is also completely capricious, we have faith that its effects will be ultimately beneficial. Theseus can then take over as the representative of responsible authority whose task it is to control and direct the individual wills into social harmony. What Shakespeare has done in *The Tempest* is to internalise and in part to psychologise this comic pattern. The figures representing arbitrary human will, capricious power and responsible authority are all compounded into one strange and complicated personality. Prospero must purge himself of his tyrannic tendencies as well as chastening the wills of the castaways; he must limit his own power down to the legitimate sway of the Duke of Milan, before he can inherit the role of Theseus. That role, however, is not an insignificant one. For the comic audience the figure of just and benevolent authority is the ultimate guarantor of the security of the social union which the play has achieved by such unexpected and mysterious means.

Yet, for all the parallels between Theseus and Prospero, there are profound differences of tone and atmosphere between the two plays, that edge *The Tempest* away from the comic pattern represented by *A Midsummer Night's Dream*, perhaps away from comedy altogether. Even before Prospero actually renounces his magic there is a disengagement from the world of the imagination in the celebrated valedictory speech:

> Our revels now are ended. These our actors
> As I foretold you, were all spirits, and
> Are melted into air, into thin air:
> And, like the baseless fabric of this vision,
> The cloud-capp'd towers, the gorgeous palaces,
> The solemn temples, the great globe itself,
> Yea, all which it inherit, shall dissolve,
> And, like this insubstantial pageant faded,

> Leave not a wrack behind. We are such stuff
> As dreams are made on; and our little life
> Is rounded with a sleep.   IV i 148–58

This is similar to Theseus's 'the lunatic, the lover, and the poet' speech, in so far as it represents a withdrawal for the audience from the realm of fantasy in which much of the action is played. But, of course, the effect is utterly different. Whereas Theseus scoffs at the poet's vision by stamping his foot very hard on *terra firma*, Prospero makes of reality itself a solipsist dream like the poet's. This metaphysical dimension seems non-comic at least, if not anti-comic. A precedent for it may be found in other Shakespearean comedies – Jacques' 'All the world's a stage', for instance, but Jacques has not the authority of Prospero, and his eloquence is placed by the irony of his persona. Comedy on the whole remains loyal to the life of the senses, however much it may divert us with the vagaries of that life. Prospero's transcendental vision seems to take us outside that area in which the comic action is worked out.

The atmospheres of the plays' endings are different. Prospero's re-established authority does not have the solid assurance and confidence of Theseus, nor does the play end with the sense of joy and security which we experience with *A Midsummer Night's Dream*. This is not only because some of the characters remain unredeemed – Antonio is given no sign of re-pentance, Caliban's conversion is problematic, to say the least. It is partly the very fact that the issues are those of redemption: guilt and retribution, penitence and forgiveness. Prospero's final resignation of control involves a Christian realisation of the vanity of power. He has achieved what can be achieved, his enemies are at his mercy and their attempts at domination have been rendered laughable, but beyond that, within the individual souls where true change must come if at all, there he can have no power. He returns to his dukedom, therefore, not confidently resuming his sovereignty, but begin-ning the preparation for death:

> And thence retire me to my Milan, where
> Every third thought shall be my grave.   V i 310–11

It is the quietude of the close of a tragedy, rather than the buoyant ending of a comedy.

The final contrast between the plays' epilogues confirms the sense of the differences between *The Tempest* and *A Midsummer Night's Dream*. Both are based on the tradition, deriving ultimately from Roman comedy, by which a chief character asks the audience for their approval and demands their applause. It is a confirmation of the comic contract and Puck's Epilogue to *A Midsummer Night's Dream* is a very good specimen:

> If we shadows have offended
> Think but this, and all is mended;
> That you have but slumbered here
> While these visions did appear.
> And this weak and idle theme,
> No more yielding but a dream
> Gentles do not reprehend.

Puck extends the dream metaphor of the play's title into his mock-modest apology. The sympathy and goodwill which Puck has earned through the audience's appreciation of him in the play is here to be turned into a general approval of the whole design. In Prospero's epilogue there is an exactly similar variation upon the images of the play:

> Now my charms are all o'erthrown
> And what strength I have's my own,
> Which is most faint: now 'tis true,
> I must be here confin'd by you,
> Or sent to Naples. Let me not,
> Since I have my dukedom got,
> And pardon'd the deceiver, dwell
> In this bare island by your spell;
> But release me from my bands
> With the help of your good hands:
> Gentle breath of yours my sails
> Must fill, or else my project fails,
> Which was to please. Now I want
> Spirits to enforce, Art to enchant;
> And my ending is despair,
> Unless I be reliev'd by prayer,
> Which pierces so, that it assaults
> Mercy itself, and frees all faults.
> As you from crimes would pardon'd be,
> Let your indulgence set me free.

The renunciation of magic here explicitly becomes the actor-manager removing his make-up. But this further stripping of Prospero of his several mantles of authority, combined with the repeated imagery of prayer and forgiveness, gives to the epilogue a moving and solemn effect quite unlike the normal knowing comic appeal to the audience. Prospero, from being duke and magician, all-powerful within the confines of the play's action, has become a man like any other, as dependent on mercy as any single member of the audience. It is as individuals that we face this appeal, not as the corporate community of the comic audience, as at the end of *A Midsummer Night's Dream*.

4 Quacks and Conmen

'*The Tempest* is concerned with illusion . . . Jonsonian comedy is concerned with the theory and practice of delusion', as Harry Levin points out in his essay on *The Tempest* and *The Alchemist*.[1] The distinction is a useful one. Though Prospero finally steps back from the images of his conjuring and acknowledges them to be illusion, yet throughout the play the audience is prepared to believe in his magic as magic. We share with him the knowledge of how and why the visitors to the island are hallucinated, but we accept that his powers to enchant are real. To Prospero's art itself we lend willing suspension of disbelief, and we may remind ourselves that disbelief would have been less hard to suspend in 1611, when benevolent white magic was considered to be distinctly possible. Subtle, the alchemist, a year before Prospero, also claimed power over winds and waves:

> No, you scarab,
> I'll thunder you in pieces. I will teach you
> How to beware to tempt a Fury again
> That carries tempest in his hand and voice.   I i 59—62

But even though Subtle has the excellent alchemical authority of Paracelsus for such a claim,[2] no audience would ever have dreamed of taking it literally. It is no more than a grotesque comic metaphor in his slanging-match with Face, appropriate to his thundering aggression but a ludicrous boast coming from the conman we see before us. For Jonson deliberately starts his play with his tricksters *en deshabillé*, exposed for what they are, so that we are never likely to grant the least shred of credit to their subsequent pretensions. The scurrilous word pictures which each of the two paints of the other provide a deft exposition in which the reality of their characters as frauds is definitely established. From then on the business of the play will be, indeed, deception not illusion. Instead of focusing, as *The Tempest* does, on the strange bewildering effects of magic on the enchanted, we will watch a series of dupes being hoodwinked, cheated, deceived, and we will remain conscious throughout of the fraudulent intentions of the deceivers.

The basic confidence-trick of the play centres around Subtle's profession as alchemist; he blinds with 'science' the gulls who are already blinded with greed. But it is not only pseudo-sciences like alchemy which are regarded in this light in comedy. Very often the more respectable learned professions are seen as an equally dishonest means of exploiting human weaknesses. M. Filerin, the leading spokesman of Molière's doctors in *L'Amour Médecin* puts his own calling on a par with those of alchemists and astrologers:

> Nous ne sommes pas les seuls, comme vous savez, qui tâchons à nous prévaloir de la foiblesse humaine. C'est là qui va l'étude de la plupart du monde, et chacun s'efforce de prendre les hommes par leur foible, pour en tirer quelque profit . . . Les alchimistes tâchent à profiter de la passion qu'on a pour les richesses, en promettant des montagnes d'or a ceux qui les écoutent; et les diseurs d'horoscope, par leurs prédictions trompeuses, profitent de la vanité et de l'ambition des crédules esprits. Mais le plus grand foible des hommes, c'est l'amour qu'ils ont pour la vie; et nous en profitons, nous autres, par notre pompeux galimatias et savons prendre nos avantages de cette vénération que la peur de mourir leur donne pour notre métier. III i

Molière's medical satires, like *The Alchemist*, are directed towards audiences who are not 'crédules esprits', 'credulous minds'. We are expected to watch the comedies in a spirit of knowing specticism, laughing alike at the credulity of those who believe in the hocus-pocus of medicine or alchemy and at the pretensions of the practitioners. The universal comic impulse to mock the language of learning is sharpened by the knowledge that it is being manipulated for profit. The comedy of the quack and the charlatan is built upon the comedy of the pedant.

Reading or seeing such plays as *The Alchemist* or *Le Malade Imaginaire* in the twentieth century, we may well assume that the attitude Jonson and Molière invite us to adopt is no more than that of commonsense. The alchemical jargon of Subtle is to us pure abracadabra nonsense and the ministrations of Messieurs Purgon and Diafoirus we may regard from the security of modern medicine as equally absurd. It is perhaps necessary to remind ourselves that the seventeenth century audience would not have had the same presuppositions. Alchemy was not by any means universally discredited in Jonson's time: Bacon, for example, though sceptical of the general theory, thought the actual process of making gold possible.[3] Still later, and even more spectacularly, Newton was so absorbed in alchemical experiments that he apparently spent a greater proportion of his time on them than on physics.[4] As for Molière and medicine, however grotesque the double-barrel torture of bleeding and purging may seem to us, it continued to flourish throughout the reign of Louis XIV, whose medical treatment is detailed meticulously in the *Journal de la Santé du Roi*. One of the most apparently fantastic scenes in Molière, the induction of the newly qualified doctor at the end of *Le Malade Imaginaire*, in fact quite closely approximated to the real ceremonial at Montpellier.[5]

We have limited evidence of Molière's personal views on medicine or Jonson's on alchemy outside the context of the plays, though the question with regard to Molière has often been discussed. We are not in a position to take a public opinion poll of an average seventeenth century audience (whatever that may have been) in order to establish what their normal ideas on such professions were. No doubt there were many people who were at times sceptical of the doctors' healing powers: Mme. de Sévigné, although she was not generally a disbeliever in medicine, could applaud heartily the view expressed in *Le Malade Imaginaire*. 'Ah! que j'en veux aux médecins! quelle forfanterie que leur art!'[6] – 'Oh! how I hate doctors! what quackery their art is!' Swindling alchemists were notorious in England from the time of Chaucer's Canon down to that Simon Forman. What the comedians appeal to, however, is not the particular opinions of the 'man in the street' of their time, but a strain of comic scepticism which is universal and traditional. After all, medical satires are quite as common in the twentieth century, when we have some grounds for supposing that doctors can cure diseases, as they were in any earlier age when medical success rates must have been far lower. What we have in *The Alchemist* or in Molière's doctor plays is one more type of comic contract in which, instead of disbelief, it is belief which is willingly suspended. To analyse the nature of this response and to illustrate the way in which it is built up we must look to the plays themselves rather than attempting to identify their viewpoint primarily in terms of the background of contemporary ideas.

MOLIÈRE AND MEDICINE

Molière's attacks on doctors, ranging from one end of his writing career to the other through five pieces in which medicine is a central subject beside numerous side-swipes in other plays, may well look like a personal vendetta. Various critics have supplied conjectural biographical motives for this animus against the medical profession. John Palmer, noticing that the first all-out denunciation of doctors comes in 1665 in *Dom Juan*, followed closely by *L'Amour Médecin*, reminds us that it was at this period that Molière's serious illness first began.[7] John Cairncross argues that the hostility to doctors may have originated a year earlier with the deaths of Molière's close friend

La Mothe Le Vayer and his own first son.[8] A row with D'Aquin, the Court doctor who was Moliere's landlord in 1665, has been suggested as another personal grievance against the profession at this period.[9] On the other hand, the little we know of Molière's relations with his own doctor, M. de Mauvillain, suggests that they were cordial. In the third 'placet' to the king on behalf of *Tartuffe* we find Molière soliciting a royal favour for him, although he couches the petition in the form of a typically Molièrean anti-doctor joke. What is more important, from our point of view, than Molière's possible motivation for writing medical satires is that the plays accord an opportunity for studying the way in which the subject was adapted for different audiences. The jokes remain much the same from *Le Médecin Volant* down to *Le Malade Imaginaire*, but the character of the comic contract varies depending to some extent on whom Molière was writing for, the provincial audience of his early farces, the Parisians who regularly attended his theatre at the Palais-Royal, or the King and Court at Versailles or elsewhere.

Le *Médecin Volant* is no more than a brief sketch written for performance in the provinces, and not everyone is agreed that it is Molière's.[10] But whether the actual text is authentic or not, there can be little doubt that Molière did write such farces and that it was from farces like this, close to the Italian tradition, that his doctor satires evolved. Considering how often Molière cannibalised his own earlier work, the fact that the plot of *Le Médecin Volant* reappears in later plays might well be used to strengthen the attribution. What is most striking about the play, in the context of the pieces that were to succeed it, is that it is scarcely an attack on doctors or medicine at all. Sganarelle, who pretends to be a doctor to further his master's love-intrigue, is too gross an imposter to be taken as a parody of the real thing. The humour of the piece derives from the confidence with which he covers up his ignorance:

> *Sganarelle.* . . . . Il faut que je vous fasse une ordonnance.
> *Gorgibus.* Vite une table, du papier, de l'encre.
> *Sganarelle.* Y a-t-il quelqu'un qui sache écrire?
> *Gorgibus.* Est-ce que vous ne le savez point?
> *Sganarelle.* Ah! je ne m'en souvenois point; j'ai tant d'affaires dans la tête, que j'oublie la moitié. *Le Médecin Volant* v

The audience laughs at the simple absurdity of the familiar Sganarelle, the ignorant/cunning valet, in a doctor's gown. In fact, *Le Médecin Volant* contains what may be the only serious appreciation of medical skill in Molière's work. An 'avocat', quite unnecessary to the plot, is brought in to give a eulogy of doctors, addressed to the uncomprehending Sganarelle:

> Il faut avouer que tous ceux qui excellent en quelque science sont dignes de grande louange, et particulièrement ceux qui font profession de la médecine, tant à cause du son utilité, que parce qu'elle contient en elle plusieurs autres sciences, ce qui rend sa parfaite connoissance fort difficile . . . Vous n'êtes pas de ces médecins qui ne vous appliquez qu'à là médecine qu'on appelle rationale ou dogmatique, et je crois que vous l'exercez tous les jours avec beaucoup de succès: *experientia magistra rerum*. *Le Médecin Volant* viii

It is of course impossible to say that this represents Molière's own point of view, particularly as there are doubts over the authorship of the farce. But it is consistent with his later attacks on doctors in which it is their tendency to divorce theory from practice, their neglect of empirical observations which is ridiculed. There was certainly little to upset any self-respecting doctor in *Le Médecin Volant*.

Nor yet is there much in *Le Médecin Malgré Lui*, a later more elaborate farce, hastily written, it is often supposed, as a booster to support the dubious success of *Le Misanthrope* in 1666. Again Sganarelle, this time a woodcutter, is a pretend doctor though the pretence is forced upon him. He is given some colour for the success of his disguise in the opening scene in which he is shown as 'un faiseur des fagots qui sache . . . raisonner des choses, qui ait servi six ans un fameux médecin, et qui ait su, dans son jeune âge, son rudiment par coeur', 'a woodcutter who knows how to argue about things, who worked for a famous doctor for six years, and who learned his grammar by heart at an early age'. (*Le Médecin Malgré Lui* I i). He has one or two anti-doctor jokes of the traditional variety – no-one ever blames the doctor, he claims, as one of the principal advantages of the profession is that the deceased is always at fault – 'c'est toujours la faute de celui qui meurt'. But once again it is the imposture which is funny rather the doctor's rôle itself, as in his famous line defending his misplacing of the heart and liver:

> Oui, cela étoit autrefois ainsi; mais nous avons changé tout cela, et nous faisons maitenant la médecine d'une méthode toute nouvelle. II iv

This does perhaps catch the absurd complacency of the doctor's belief in progress, but we laugh at it mainly for its delightful implausibility. We take pleasure in the audacity and outrageousness with which Sganarelle carries off his part, and if some of this pleasure derives from the debunking of the learned rigmarole which he mimics, *Le Médecin Malgré Lui* yet remains farcical comedy, not satire.

Turning from the popular farces to the court *comédie-ballets*, we might well expect to find a greater degree of refinement or sophistication, but, if so, we would be disappointed. Molière, like Jonson, catered for the personal tastes of the monarch and both Louis XIV and James I enjoyed simple, not to say crude, forms of humour. The *comèdie-ballet* and the Jonsonian masque with anti-masque were both developed to meet royal preferences for a roughly similar combination of dancing, display and dirty jokes. This accounts for why pieces such as *The Gypsies Metamorphosed* or *M. de Pourceaugnac*, neither of which are their authors' most artistic creations, nevertheless met with great success. Molière in putting together *L'Amour Médecin*, for instance, ('putting together' seems the right phrase, as he assures us in the preface that he composed, rehearsed and produced it in five days) did little more than take one of his stock farce situations and contrive more or less plausible occasions for *entrées de ballet* in between the acts. The plot is virtually the same as that of *Le Médecin Volant* and *Le Médecin Malgré Lui*.

There is, however, an important difference in that *L'Amour Médecin* does attack real doctors rather than making comedy out of pretend doctors, and in fact it caricatures the most eminent practioners of the time. There is no question here of satire of the species rather than the individual — to the court the identifications would have been unmistakable either by the resemblance of names or physical mannerisms: Tomès is D'Aquin, one of the King's own doctors, Filerin is Yvelin, Des Fonandrès, (the name is taken from Greek roots meaning 'man-killer') is Des Fougerais, Bahis is marked as Esprit by his stammer, Macroton as Guenault by his slow speech. All of these were either attached to the royal household or well-known in Paris. The farcical scenes in which the doctors dispute might have been founded on the real arguments which took place around the death-bed of Cardinal Mazarin as to what he was dying of, or on the controversial crisis over the King's fever in 1658 when D'Aquin, Esprit, Guenault and Yvelin were all involved. The play, in which the doctors are ridiculed as total incompetents, if not frankly conscious hypocrites, does seem remarkable evidence of Molière's hostility towards the medical profession. It may be, however, that the apparent directness of the attack is due to the circumstances of the production. Whether or not Louis actually suggested the subject, Molière would certainly not have ventured on a public mockery of the royal physicians without knowing that the king would approve. It may be, in fact, that he returned to the subject of medicine so often after 1665, not because of any personal animus, but simply because he discovered that it was a favourite comic butt of the king's. 'Les médecins font assez souvent pleurer pour faire

rire quelquefois', was Louis' attitude, 'Doctors make us weep often enough
for us to laugh at them sometimes.'

If we look at it in the light of a court entertainment, what does the medical
satire of *L'Amour Médecin* amount to? Many of the ideas are derived from
Montaigne, as so often with Molière, and parts of the speech of M. Filerin,
already quoted, are borrowed almost word for word from the long essay
which Montaigne devotes to the demolition of the doctor's art.[11] But there
can be little of Montaigne's serious purpose in as slight a piece as *L'Amour
Médecin* and the whole play gives an impression of spoof rather than satire in
earnest. Within the court context, in fact, the personal caricatures of the
royal doctors should not necessarily be taken as the measure of Molière's
'impiety in medicine'; they may instead have had something of the character
of an enjoyable if slightly malicious in-joke. Personalities in comedy are only
funny within a restricted circle — one thinks of undergraduate revues — and
it is unlikely that Molière would ever have written *L'Amour Médecin* in the
first instance for a public performance. It was no doubt a pleasure for the
courtiers who normally had to submit to the authority of Messieurs
D'Aquin, Yvelin etc., to see them guyed by the King's actors. It is in this
spirit that Mme. de Sévigné much later relished the jealous rage of D'Aquin
at the success of an English rival and wished Molière were alive to write a
comedy about it.[12] Yet the authority of the doctors need not have been
seriously undermined. *L'Amour Médecin* belongs to that very simplest form
of comedy which is pure escapism. The audience can laugh with impunity at
the antics of the doctors because no real illness is in question. The play ends
with the neatly turned claims of La Comédie, Le Ballet, and La Musique to
be the only true doctors:

> Sans nous tous les hommes
> Deviendroient mal sains,
> Et c'est nous qui sommes
> Leurs grands médecins.

It is the appropriate finale for this divertissement, light-heartedly setting
aside the reality of doctors or disease in its celebration of its own gaiety.

Monsieur de Pourceaugnac seems very much the mixture as before, a cruder,
more heavy-handed *comédie-ballet* than *L'Amour Médecin*, in which Molière
added to the jargon of the doctors a whole range of different provincial
dialects and patois to make up a complete patchwork of barbaric sounding
language. *Le Malade Imaginaire*, although it too was planned as a court
comédie-ballet, is obviously a major work of a quite different kind from the
earlier medical satires. It took a long time to produce: projected as an

offering for the King's return from the wars in the winter of 1672, it was denied presentation at court, probably by the influence of Molière's rival Lulli, and Molière had to write a new Prologue adapting it for the public theatre where it finally appeared in February 1673. It is the nearest Molière came to a *grande comédie* on the subject of medicine. It has many of the features of his other major comedies, a fully drawn central comic character, a *raisonneur* presenting the logical alternative point of view. If for no other reason, the dreadful ironies of the circumstances of its performance would demand for it a more serious consideration than the other medical satires.

LE MALADE IMAGINAIRE

Argan stands as the last in line of Molière's comic monomaniacs; he is infatuated with medicine, as Harpagon was with money, or Orgon with religion. This infatuation, however, although it dominates his life, does not deprive him of what might pass for practical common sense. When we meet him first he is reading aloud and reckoning up his apothecary's bills for the month, scrutinising each item and making the traditional deductions — seventeenth century apothecaries apparently always charged twice what they expected to be paid. Argan is, in his own eyes, nobody's fool, and is determined to get value for money:

'Plus, du vingt-quatrième, un petit clystère insinuatif, préparatif, et rémollient, pour amollir, humecter, et rafraîchir les entrailles de Monsieur'. Ce qui me plaît de Monsieur Fleurant, mon apothicaire, c'est que ses parties sont toujours fort civiles: 'les entrailles de Monsier, trente sols.' Oui, mais, Monsier Fleurant, ce n'est pas tout que d 'être civil, il faut être aussi raisonnable, et ne pas écorcher les malades. Trente sols un lavement; Je suis votre serviteur, je vous l'ai déjà dit. Vous ne me les avez mis dans les autres parties qu'à vingt sols, et vingt sols en langage d'apothicaire, c'est-à-dire dix sols; les voilà, dix sols.   I i

Argan is not so deranged by his hypochondria that he will let his apothecary cheat him, and in everything that relates to money he can be shrewd enough. Later, when he plans to marry his daughter to the imbecile Thomas Diafoirus, he has calculated on the property Thomas will inherit as well as the advantage of having a qualified doctor as a son-in-law. In one sense this solid pragmatism is the measure of Argan's robust good health, for a man who was really as ill as he imagines himself to be would be too weak or too desperate to haggle over medical expenses. His illness and his doctors are

Argan's luxuries, for which he does not grudge payment when he has had satisfaction. This leads to the final lunatic logic of the conclusion of his monologue:

> Si bien donc que ce mois j'ai pris . . huit médecines, et . . . douze lavements; et l'autre mois il y avoit douze médecines, et vingt lavements. Je ne m'étonne pas si je ne me porte pas si bien ce mois-ci que l'autre.   I i

The whole speech has something of the comic impact of the story of the emperor's new clothes; the more literally Argan asseses the benefits of medicine, the more clearly the audience realises that its effects are purely imaginary.

Argan's matter-of-fact calculations serve also to highlight the preposterous number of laxatives and enemas he has taken in the past month. The lavatorial humour of purgation is a basic part of most of Molière's medical satires, and is used as a continuing piece of comic business throughout *Le Malade Imaginaire*. For Anglo-Saxons, with less strong stomachs in such matters than the French, the spectacle of a man who can talk lovingly of a 'bon petit clystère', may be almost too disgusting to be funny. But it is not just for the sake of the scatalogical jokes that Molière harps upon the mechanics of purgation. It was, after, an essential part of the medicine of his time. For seventeenth-century doctors, committed to the concept of the humours, the primary purpose of any medical treatment was likely to be the evacuation of the malignant substances from the body, and this could only be done by emetics, laxatives or bleeding. In the burlesque dog-Latin catechism of the postulant doctor at the end of the play the automatic treatment for every disease is 'clysterium donare, postea seignare, ensuitta purgare'. This may have been no more than a slight exaggeration of the truth for Molière's contemporaries.

It is likely to be a matter of wonder to many of us in the twentieth century how indeed anyone ever survived this system of medicine. When we consider that the orthodox view of the medical Faculty in Molière's time was that a patient could lose 20 out of his estimated 24 litres of blood without doing him permanent harm, and that babies and pregnant women were not exempt from this calculation, the jokes about doctors as killers seem to have considerable point.[13] With bleeding also used as a regular prophylactic measure on perfectly healthy patients, the result must have been chronic anaemia for those who had nothing worse. Would averagely intelligent laymen in the seventeenth century have been in a position to know that such treatment was anything but helpful? How far could Molière expect to carry his audience with him in mocking these standard practices of evacuation? As we have said, it is impossible to know definitely. But we might apply the analogy of the attitude of many modern people towards the use of antibiotics. Although there can be no doubt that the discovery of antibiotics in this century was a step forward in medicine unlike anything before it, many ordinary patients, besides several medical authorities, have remarked on the tendency of general practitioners to prescribe them promiscuously. Even though the lay patient does not understand the nature of the treatment, he can observe from the mechanical way in which his G. P. reaches for the prescription pad that the antibiotics are being used as placebos of panaceas rather than considered remedies. Surely we can infer from the character of Molière's satire that the situation was similar with the doctors of his time and that, even though his audience believed in the efficacy of laxatives and bleeding, they would have seen enough of normal practice to recognise that they were often used unnecessarily, as in the case of Argan.[14]

In *Le Malade Imaginaire*, however, as in no other medical satire of Molière, there is some evidence that he expected on the part of his audience, not just the attitude of thoughtful common sense, but a fairly informed position on medicine. Monsieur Diafoirus' eulogy of his son Thomas has the following significant conclusion:

> Mais sur toute chose ce qui me plaît en lui, et en quoi il suit mon exemple, c'est qu'il s'attache aveuglement aux opinions de nos anciens, et que jamais il n'a voulu comprendre ni écouter les raisons et les expériences des prétendues découvertes de notre siècle, touchant la circulation du sang, et autres opinions de même farine.   II v

The speech is heavily ironic throughout, and the Diafoirus, *père et fils*, are intended quite clearly as satiric models of what doctors ought not to be. In the ancients versus moderns controversy there is no doubt where Molière's audience are asked to stand. As Angélique puts it to Thomas − 'Les anciens, Monsieur, sont les anciens, et nous sommes les gens de maintenant' − 'the ancients, Monsieur, are the ancients, and we are the people of today.' M. Diafoirus' praise for blind devotion to ancient theory as against modern empiricism compares interestingly with the speech of the Avocat in *Le Médecin Volant*, quoted earlier. Molière's irony here suggests that his audience will take for granted the discoveries of their age, including the circulation of the blood. Although Harvey's work on the circulation had been published as long before as 1628, it was still fiercely controversial in France and especially in Paris at the time of *Le Malade Imaginaire*. For in 1671 Louis XIV had decided to institute a chair attached to the Jardin du Roi to teach the new anatomy of the circulation and in 1672 personally intervened in Parliement against the reactionary Faculty of Medicine who were opposing the new chair as an infringement of their privilege. In 1673 the surgeon Pierre Dionys was installed as professor and ordered by the King to give public lectures on anatomy.[15] With this background of public controversy, Molière could no doubt rely on a majority of his audience to follow the King's lead and laugh at the old-fashioned conservatism of the medical establishment.

It may seem, therefore, that Molière in *Le Malade Imaginaire* harnessed the traditional comic scepticism of all medicine to the more specific and topical discredit of one school of medicine. In so far as he seems to be asserting the truth and importance of the anatomical discoveries and empirical methods which form the basis of modern medicine, we may well be tempted to consider Molière as a mind before his time, an avant-garde believer in scientific rationalism. If so, we will be disappointed by the doctrine put forward by Béralde, the play's *raisonneur*, apparently for our approval. Béralde's reasons for disbelieving in the medicine of his time are closer to those of a Christian Scientist than to a twentieth century doctor's. He argues that a disease should be allowed to take its course without interference:

> La nature, d'elle-même, quand nous la laissons faire, se tire doucement du désordre òu elle est tombée. C'est notre inquiétude, c'est notre impatience qui gâte tout, et presque tous les hommes meurent de leurs remèdes, et non pas de leurs maladies.   III iii

Such passive trust in nature is made necessary by our inability to understand her mysteries:

> Les ressorts de notre machine sont des mystères, jusques ici, où les hommes ne voient goutte, et . . la nature nous a mis au-devant des yeux des voiles trop épais pour y connoître quelque chose.   III iii

Although the qualifying 'jusques ici' might be taken to imply the possibility of future understanding, the attitude of Béralde seems to have the quietism of the traditional 'if God had intended us to fly he would have given us wings'.

Béralde's attitude has been related to the philosophy of Gassendi, popularised by Bernier, who is known to have worked with Molière, or to the 'naturism' which originated with Hippocrates but was generally out of fashion in the seventeenth century.[16] But it is surely unnecessary to make *Le Malade Imaginaire* one more debating-ground for the controversy over Molière's philosophical allegiances. The primitivist idealisation of things natural, and its corresponding rejection of everything artificial, is a recurrent phenomenon through the ages, a popular attitude which need not be ascribed to the influence of one current ideology or another. The antipathy for what is felt to be 'meddling with nature' is as strong in the modern environmental and ecological movement as it is in Montaigne – who is as likely a source for Molière as Gassendi. Once again, it is not particularly helpful to place precisely the ideological affiliations of the comic attitudes, or to nail them down as the personal views of Molière. Béralde's position on medicine is available for approval by the comic audience by reason of its strong but vague emotional attractiveness rather than its congruence with the ideas of the seventeenth century. The wishful optimism of assuming that men are naturally inclined to recover from illness is combined with the underlying atavism of accepting nature's decree without question. The result is an attitude which is felt to be humanly valid, however little it may correspond to the religious and scientific beliefs of a given age.

To think of Molière performing *Le Malade Imaginaire* on the point of death, however, is to stop this argument or any other in its tracks. How could Molière, who must have known that he was critically ill if not dying, have jested about illness? Surely here if nowhere else we are entitled to believe that he was speaking from the heart, on an analogous principle to that which gives death-bed confession an especial authority in a court of law? The play can be read as a final laughing defiance of the doctors and their art, attacking their pretensions even while apparently in greatest need of their services. Béralde's explanation to Argan of why Molière will have nothing to do with doctor's remedies has, certainly, the air of a bitter personal joke:

> Il a ses raisons pour n'en point vouloir, et il soutient que cela n'est permis qu'aux gens vigoureux et robustes, et qui ont des forces de reste pour porter les remèdes avec la maladie; mais que, pour lui, il n'a justement de la force que pour porter son mal.   III iii

But Molière's explanation of the ironies of his own situation is more outrageous and less straightforwardly polemic than this. To begin with, there is the sheer audaciousness of impersonating Argan, the man who pretends to be ill, but whose robust good health is apparent in the raging energy he shows whenever he is thwarted. Argan asks nervously when it is suggested he should sham dead – 'N'y a-til point quelque danger à contrefaire le mort?' But even an unsuperstitious person might feel that for an actor who was desperately sick to play a hypochondriac was tempting fate. The joke of Toinette in her disguise as doctor, mechanically ascribing all Argan's symptoms to a single ailment is no doubt a standard one   we meet another version of it in Shaw's *Doctor's Dilemma*. But is there not a frightening audacity in Molière, in the last stages of tuberculosis, having his pretend doctor diagnose his imaginary illness as originating in the lungs? It is Molière, rather than Sartre's Saint Genet, who deserves the title 'comédien et martyr'. For in *Le Malade Imaginaire* he did martyr himself to his profession of actor. All through his career, Molière had been prepared to exploit caricatures of himself for their comic potential. In *L'Impromptu de Versailles* he painted a delightful, but hardly flattering portrait of M. Molière, the bossy, irritable, harassed theatre director desperately trying to discipline his troupe through a rush rehearsal. From the point when his tubercular cough became so habitual that it could not be suppressed, he wrote it into his parts and turned it to comic advantage, above all in *L'Avare*. Presumably, as with all repertory companies, the pleasure of the audience derived in part from the very familiarity of the actor and the skill with which he could manipulate those familiar features in the interests of a given role. Many critics have suggested that Molière actually took his cue for *Le Malade Imaginaire* from Boulanger du Chalussay's *Elomire Hypocondre*, the malicious portrait in which Elomire/Molière is represented as a querulous hypochondriac. Molière, in taking up the challenge, one might say, was arguing that no-one could satirise him better than he could satirise himself. It was he, playing Argan, who spat with fury when Béralde suggested that a comedy of Molière might do him good:

> Par la mort non de diable! si j'étois que des médecins, je me vengerois de son impertinence; et quand il sera malade, je le laisserois mourir sans secours. Il auroit beau faire et beau dire, je ne lui ordonnerois pas la moindre petite saignée, le moindre petit lavement, et je lui dirois: 'Crève, crève! cela t'apprendra une autre fois à te jouer à la Faculté'.   III iii

This is so vivid that it even seems to have originated a tradition with apparently little other foundation that Molière did actually die with the doctors refusing him aid. But we should not let the aftermath mislead us as to what Molière was doing with such a speech. It was a means of transferring his private illness into the public arena of comedy, making even of this extremity a subject at which his audience could comfortably laugh.

The speculative autobiographical interpretation of Molière which imagined a disturbed personal life feeding the life of the plays is no longer in fashion, if only because the increased caution of twentieth-century scholarship has driven us back to a realisation of how little we know of the facts. What we are left with is the sense of his role as a clown whose art so often includes an element of self-caricature. Molière may really have shared the scepticism about doctors which had been expressed by Montaigne and others before him. He may well have had the impatience of so many chronic invalids with the absurdities of their examinations and prescriptions. What he put upon the stage, however, was not these opinions as opinions, but a version of such views corresponding to a pre-established comic paradigm. In the early farces this amounted to the simple reductivism of the ignorant impersonating the learned. In the *comédie-ballets*, prepared for the King, the farcical jokes of popular tradition were spiked with a personal satire which the exclusive audience of the court could be expected to relish. For the Palais-Royal, where *La Malade Imaginaire* was finally played, the comedy of the doctors was once again generalised beyond personalities – and could incorporate a more serious and informed attitude to the subject. But even here, the realities of pain and death, which must have been so very real to Molière by then, are tacitly ignored, while the audience can observe with uninfatuated amusement the infatuation of Argan and the 'gallimatias' of his doctors.

THE ALCHEMIST

To turn back from Molière's medical satires to Jonson's *Alchemist* is to turn from respectable to disreputable imposture. Although the early links forged between medicine and alchemy – Paracelsus styled himself 'Prince of Philosophy and medicine' – had not been broken by the seventeenth century, there was already an orthodox medical establishment, whereas alchemy, however it may have fascinated individual scientists, belonged in the public mind in the half-light at the edge of the underworld. To anyone less dazzled by the chimeras of their own greed than Dapper, Drugger, or Mammon, the very fact of Subtle's obscure residence in the Blackfriars and his lack of antecedents would have seemed fishy. Messieurs Filerin, Des Fonandrès, Diafoirus etc. were, by contrast, the counterparts of real life doctors of eminent reputation in court and city. Yet for the purposes of comedy the process remains that of imposture, however different the normal credibility of doctors and alchemists. *The Alchemist*, like Molière's medical plays, is a study of deceivers and deceived.

In *The Alchemist*, also, as in *Le Malade Imaginaire*, we laugh as much at the deceived as at the deceivers. One of the play's great pieces of character-drawing is Sir Epicure Mammon, as obsessed with alchemy as Argan is with medicine. By contrast with Argan, however, Mammon is an extravagant and fantastic personality who impresses us not by his simple foolishness but by the extraordinary and abnormal scale of his delusions, his 'elephantiasis of the imagination', as Harry Levin calls it.[17] When we meet him first the disease is already far advanced and the imagination is swollen to monstrous proportions:

> My meat shall all come in in Indian shells,
> Dishes of agate, set in gold, and studded,
> With emeralds, sapphires, hyacinths, and rubies.
> The tongues of carps, dormice, and camels' heels,
> Boil'd i' the spirit of Sol, and dissolved pearl,
> (Apicius' diet, 'gainst the epilepsy)
> And I will eat these broths with spoons of amber,
> Headed with diamond and carbuncle.
> My foot-boy shall eat pheasants, calvered salmons,
> Knots, godwits, lampreys. I myself will have
> The beards of barbels, serv'd instead of salads;
> Oil'd mushrooms; and the swelling unctuous paps
> Of a fat pregnant sow, newly cut off,
> Dress'd with an exquisite and poignant sauce. II ii 72–85

But though the monomanias of Mammon and Argan take such different forms and are so differently expressed, they have a similar underlying tendency. Mammon and Argan are both taken in by a vision of bettering nature. Béralde argues, 'lorsqu' un médecin vous parle d'aider, de secourir, de soulager la nature, de lui ôter ce qui lui nuit et lui donner ce qui lui manque . . il vous dit justement le roman de la médecine'. 'When a doctor talks to you about aiding, assisting, relieving nature, taking away from it what is harmful or giving it what it needs . . . he is giving you the old fairy-tale of medicine'. The 'roman' of alchemy is closely related – to 'teach dull nature what her own forces are', as Mammon puts it to Doll Common. Both have their origins in a theological concept of fallen nature which might conceivably be restored to its prelapsarian capacities. Medicine and alchemy, therefore, offer hope to those who are too impatient, too restless, or too greedy to put up with the natural limitations of the real world.

Molière gives us Béralde to point the moral of Argan's failure to accept nature's way. In *The Alchemist* there is no such clear-cut spokesman for the audience. Surly, Mammon's friend, reasons with him but is not the *raisonneur* of the play in the technical sense. Surly can see through Subtle and Face, as can the audience, and yet the audience is not encouraged to identify with Surly. It is interesting to try to analyse why this should be so. Mammon brings Surly along as a 'heretic' to be converted to the true faith of alchemy. As Mammon's rhetoric soars at the prospect of the new world of riches in view, Surly sticks fast to his attitude of incredulity — 'Faith, I have a humour, I would not willingly be gull'd'. The very word 'humour', and the way in which this fear of gulling quickly becomes established as Surly's mechanical catch-word — 'Sir Epicure, your friend to use: yet, still, loth to be gull'd — might enough to place him for us as one of Jonson's 'humourists', with a single comic over-developed character-trait. But the tone of Surly's deflations of Mammon, also, is important in removing him from the possibility of audience identification. Virtually Surly's first lines in the play are his response to Mammon's assurance that proofs of the alchemical process will convince him:

> Mammon. . . . You will believe me.
> Surly.   Yes, when I see't, I will.
> But if my eyes do cozen me so and I
> Giving 'em no occasion, sure I'll have
> A whore, shall piss 'em out next day.   II i 42 – 5

There is a gratuitous violence and crudity, here, which marks this as an over-reaction, Surly's agressiveness turned against himself for want of any other object. We hardly need the courteous and good-humoured tones of Béralde arguing with his brother for contrast to convince us that Surly is not a character to be trusted.

Surly's ancestor in Jonsonian comedy is Downright of *Every Man in His Humour* who also makes a profession out of being gruff and grum. With Surly as with Downright, Jonson can undercut and expose the pretensions of the affected and fantastic characters, without implying any approval of offensive frankness in itself. Surly, listed in the *dramatis personae* as a 'gamester', is partly discredited as one who can see through the alchemist's cheating only because he is so familiar with cheating at cards himself. He constantly equates the two:

> alchemy is a pretty kind of game,
> Somewhat like tricks o' the cards, to cheat a man
> With charming.   II iii 180 – 2

His scoffing asides or interruptions are mostly knowing allusions to London underworld life — thieving, swindling, the bawdy-houses of Pict-hatch — and in placing alchemy in this context we feel he is bringing it down to his own level. While Face and Subtle are putting on their display for the benefit of Mammon, Surly's reductive gibes point the irony, and no doubt even the crudest of his puns and *double-entendres* raised a laugh among some of the

Jacobean audience. But it is striking that he does not win the argument with Subtle when it comes to a formal debate, and the virtuoso rhetoric of Subtle's exposition of alchemy, though it cannot convince him (or us), leaves Surly looking rather stupid. His disbelief seems the result of temperamental cussedness and Philistine ignorance, rather than an intelligent and reasonable scepticism.

Surly's attitude is that of the proudly uneducated mocking the alchemist's 'worlds of strange ingredients would burst a man to name'. But *The Alchemist* was not written for the Surlys of Jonson's audience. To us the language of alchemy is nothing more than a nonsensical hocus-pocus intended to deceive, and so it probably was for many Jacobeans. But there would have been those, also, who, like Jonson, knew the literature of alchemy and could appreciate the accuracy with which he reproduced the alchemical arguments. We may well laugh at the absurd if unanswerable logic of Subtle's defence of his profession against Surly:

> *Subtle.* Why, what have you observed, sir, in our art,
>   Seems so impossible?
> *Surly.*   But your whole work, no more.
>   That you should hatch gold in a furnace, sir,
>   As they do eggs in Egypt!
> *Subtle.*   Sir, do you
>   Believe that eggs are hatched so?
> *Surly.*   If I should?
> *Subtle.* Why, I think that the greater miracle.
>   No egg but differs from a chicken more
>   Than metals in themselves.
> *Surly.*   That cannot be.
>   The egg's ordained by nature to that end,
>   And is a chicken *in potentia*.
> *Subtle.* The same we say of lead and other metals,
>   Which would be gold if they had time.   II iii 125–36

But once Surly mentioned the Egyptian practice of artificial incubation of chickens, the more alert members of Jonson's audience might have realised that he had played into Subtle's hands, for this was one of the analogies used to support alchemical theory, and Subtle's argument is taken virtually word for word from the Latin of Martin Delrio's *Disquisitiones Magicae*.[18] Sir Epicure's authorities for the truth of alchemy — 'a book where Moses and his sister, and Solomon have written of the art . . . a treatise penn'd by Adam . . . in high Dutch' — may seem too much even for such a glutton for belief as Mammon to swallow. But again such supposed authentic manuscripts were taken seriously by alchemists and Jonson even owned one such work himself.[19] When Mammon goes on to make of the golden fleece an alchemist's book, to see in 'Pythagoras' thigh', 'Pandora's tub', and many more, metaphors for the alchemist's art, he is following a well-established tradition of reinterpreting the classical myths as alchemical allegory.[20]

Those who had used alchemy as the subject of comedy before Jonson had been content to mock its grotesque and fantastic jargon. Lyly, for example, in *Gallathea*, does little more than copy out the barbaric technical terms from Chaucer's *Canon's Yeoman's Tale*, and gives us the simple humour of the prentice sending up his master's learning. But Jonson, in *The Alchemist* as in his court masques, was meticulous in his research, and it is a work of bizarre scholarship as well as a theatrical *tour de force*. Why should Jonson have taken the trouble to read Paracelsus, Arnold de Villa Nova, Geber, or Martin Delrio, in order to get right what he was convinced was nonsense anyhow? If there were people in the audience who were also familiar with these authors, what sort of pleasure did they get from recognising the learned reasoning of such authorities reproduced in the mouth of a conman? It almost seems a breach of decorum to accord so much knowledge to the down-at-heel Subtle.

Jonson allows to Subtle the best answer an alchemist could supply, 'less out of generosity than out of the thorough-going candour of the scholar', as Herford and Simpson put it.[21] It is indeed Jonson's scholarly temperament which enables him to display in *The Alchemist* alchemical learning far beyond anything on medicine we find in Molière. We are sometimes inclined to think of his scholarship as a handicap rather than an asset to Jonson, sitting rather heavily upon his writing, but here it is the very source of comic achievement. The play yields a special delight for those capable of recognising that these fantastic arabesques of argument are not the products of imagination but of genuine authorities, that truth, if one could call alchemical theory truth, is indeed wilder than fiction. Most comic writers who mock learning are not sufficiently interested in learning to go beyond superficial caricature. But there is a tradition of perverse scholarship turned to the benefit of a sort of fantastic dead-pan comedy which runs (at least) from Rabelais to Joyce, and it is in this tradition that Jonson belongs. A part of Joyce or of Jonson enjoys the mock scientific language of 'Ithaca' or Subtle's alchemy for its own sake. It is a parody which is half in love with what it parodies, to the point where the reader or audience may feel puzzled as to whether it is parody at all.

If we return them to Surly and consider why we are not asked to identify with his scepticism, it may be that his attitude of coarse disbelief is felt to be inappropriate to the sheer intricacy of Subtle's deceptions. He sees through alchemy as a swindle, but he fails to see what an accomplished swindle it is. In a similar way, when Stephen Dedalus propounds theories of aesthetics or literary criticism founded upon the scholastic principles of Aquinas, although Joyce invites an ironic reaction, he disassociates us from the trivial sneers of Lynch or Mulligan. Those who have no real respect for the creations of the mind cannot truly appreciate the grotesqueness of its abortions. Jonson wants us to feel the sheer beauty of the alchemical system, meaningless as it is. As Subtle expounds the nature of 'remote matter' (II iii 143 – 76), each step in his exposition follows on logically from the previous one and the whole argument is a model of clarity which might have an audience nodding understanding assent. The language of alchemy is a hypnotic Sirens' song, whose enchanting attraction we can feel, while ourselves ensured against its spell.

Whatever its attractions, there is certainly no possibility of anyone in the audience actually believing in alchemy, any more than anyone in the audience of *Le Malade Imaginaire* could believe in medicine. We start, in both cases, with a basic assumption of scepticism. What is more in *The Alchemist*, we laugh at people in direct proportion to the degree they become involved in belief. The simpletons, Dapper or Drugger, are mocked mercilessly, though their pretensions are harmless, relatively speaking, because of the ridiculousness of the charades they are willing to credit. Sir Epicure's imagination has become so saturated in alchemy that he speaks almost entirely in alchemical metaphors, whether appropriate or not. In a different context, Ananias is the more absurd of the two Puritans because he believes literally in the hypocritical attitudes his sect adopts. A flexible capacity for disengaging from any role is the greatest possible asset in *The Alchemist*. This is where Surly finally falls down. He is cynical about everything except his own role as cynic, and while he is self-righteously glorying in his exposure of the tricksters, Face can set going a whole batch of further deceptions which defeat him. It is this same flexibility which may explain why it is ultimately Face rather than Subtle who wins out. Subtle can play his alchemist part in all sorts of different moods and styles — as a religious anchorite for Mammon, as a temperamental artist for Ananias, as a man of the world, expert in rules of honour to Kastril; he can adjust his act to suit the special weaknesses of the individual gulls. Yet it is always basically the same role and from the fact that he, like Mammon, uses his alchemical jargon out of context we sense that he has half begun to believe in his own powers, or at least to take for granted the awing effects of his persona. He is like an actor who has played star parts too long. Face, the perfect character actor by contrast, can double and treble, now as the blustering Captain, now as the technician Lungs, and finally as 'smooth Jeremy' the butler. Face is ironically faceless because each successive mask is equally plausible. If we feel that there is comic justice in his triumph it is because he matches virtuosity in deception, which all the rogues share, with the mental agility to see when each deception must be replaced by a new one. In a comedy where we are asked to see through and admire every form of cheating trick, the man who can participate in all of them, yet believe in none, may end up as something like the hero.

Disbelief in medicine or alchemy in *The Alchemist* or *Le Malade Imaginaire* has been related by several critics to religious belief or disbelief. Molière's 'impiety in medicine' has been linked with the naturalism of Gassendi, as we have seen, and more generally to Molière's alleged 'libertinage'.[22] It has been claimed that *Le Malade Imaginaire* is a disguised attack upon religion and that 'the play actually gains in coherence whenever a metaphor, an attitude, a gesture suggests an analogy between medical doctors and theologians.'[23] To challenge the authority of the Faculty of Medicine could be construed as a step towards challenging the authority of Theology, and of course the two were closely linked. Under cover of mocking the credulity of Argan, who imagines himself in need of doctoring, Molière is perhaps satirising the orthodox Christian who allowed his priests to convince him that he was in constant need of spiritual attention.

For those who interpret *The Alchemist* as a play with religious significance, Jonson's position is the very opposite of Molière's. Through the religious echoes of the alchemist's patter can be detected not a satire on Christianity, but on the age which has debased Christian language into a swindler's stock-in-trade. Edward B. Partridge, who is the outstanding spokesman of this view in Jonson criticism, sums up:

> the alchemist (Subtle or gold) becomes a parody of the Creator. To sincere alchemists who were mystical idealists, alchemy was a religion or quasi-religion. To Jonson, a moral idealist and a dogmatic Christian who approached alchemy with no sympathy for the religious impulse at its heart, it seemed only an obscure fraud, and alchemic terms only a parody of the Word.[24]

As his attacks on medicine are used to support the image of Molière the progressive freethinker, so *The Alchemist* provides further evidence for Jonson the conservative moralist. Subtle and Face are not only confidence tricksters, they are in some sort blasphemers, and it is this undercurrent of blasphemy which, for such critics as Partridge, deepens and darkens the meaning of the play.

At issue here is the relation of the life of the comedy to the life of ideas of the playwright's time. How far did the audience of *Le Malade Imaginaire* or of *The Alchemist* bring to the theatre with them all their normal ethical, social and spiritual commitments within the real world? How open were they to ideological suggestions in comedy? As a first example let us look at the scene in which Monsieur Purgon anathematises Argan for having refused to take his 'clystère' on time. An effect of ritual is built up with the interjections of Argan and Toinette serving to heighten the rhythm of the denunciation:

> *M. Purgon.* Mais puisque vous n'avez pas voulu guérir par mes mains
> *Argan.* Ce n'est pas ma faute
> *M. Purgon.* Puisque vous vous êtes soustrait de l'obéissance que l'on doit
> à son médecin,
> *Toinette.* Cela crie vengeance.
> *M. Purgon.* Puisque vous vous êtes déclaré rebelle aux remèdes que je
> vous ordonnois . . .
> *Argan.* Hé! point du tout.
> *M. Purgon.* J'ai à vous dire que je vous abandonne â votre mauvaise
> constitution, à l'intempérie de vos entrailles, à la corruption
> de votre sang, à l'âcreté de votre bile et à la féculence de vos
> humeurs.   III v

M. Purgon then proceeds to project the course of Argan's degeneration – 'De la bradypepsie dans la dyspepsie', 'De la dyspepsie dans l'apepsie' – so convincingly that Argan cries out at last 'Ah, mon Dieu! je suis mort'.

This might quite plausibly be compared to an excommunication ceremony, the procedure by which a disobedient heretic is solemnly cut off as a diseased limb of the Church. But the laugh here is against the doctors who take upon themselves an authority as absolute as that of the Church, rather than a disguised satire on the Church itself. It is the disproportion of the sentence to the offence, the absurdity of the doctor's tyrannical pretensions, which is the basis of the parody. Its effect upon the unfortunate Argan, ironically the last person who could justly be accused of medical heresy, is that of an annihilating barrage because it comes from the authority he holds in awe. The sceptical audience, however, can relish the attack as a purely nonsensical rite. The tactics are the same in *The Alchemist*, when Subtle routs Ananias. Ananias has objected to Subtle's 'heathen Greek' alchemical terms, and in indignant demonstration Subtle puts Face through a mock catechism:

> *Subtle* Sirrah, my varlet, stand you forth, and speak to him
> Like a philosopher. Answer i' the language,
> Name the vexations, and the martyrizations
> Of metals in the work.

Face.	Sir, putrefaction,

Solution, ablution, sublimation,
Cohobation, calcination, ceration, and
Fixation.
Subtle. This is heathen Greek to you now?
And when comes vivification?
Face.   After mortification.
Subtle. What's cohobation?
Face.   'Tis the pouring on
Your aqua regis, and then drawing him off,
To the trine circle of the seven spheres.
Subtle. What's the proper passion of metals?
Face.   Malleation.
Subtle. What's your *ultimum supplicium auri?*
Face.   Antimonium.
Subtle. This's heathen Greek to you?   II v 18—31

Of course, the comedy here is that the terms become more and more 'Greek'
to Ananias who is nevertheless driven back on his heels by this onslaught of
quick-fire learning. Once again, as with Purgon, the combination of
wrathful authority and a command of mysterious language gives the
imposter success, and Subtle ends by denouncing 'wicked Ananias', 'the
varlet that cozen'd the Apostles', in the style of one of Ananias's own Puritan
preachers.

The language of alchemy is closely related to the language of mystical
religion as Partridge points out, and as we can see from the excerpt
from Subtle's catechism. 'Martyrization', 'sublimation', 'mortification',
'passion' — all of these terms have spiritual significance, and the association is
not accidental. The alchemist was part scientist, part philosopher, but also
part mystic, as Surly reminds Mammon:

he must be *homo frugi,*
A pious, holy, and religious man,
One free from mortal sin, a very virgin.

But just because there is a normal and accepted relation between alchemical
concepts and those of theology, the parody detected by Jonson's critics may
not have been so striking as they would have us think. Jonson here is unlike
Joyce, who does deliberately use liturgical or sacred images in a profane
context with a fully self-conscious sense of parody. The inverted use of
Christian symbols does not force itself upon the reader or audience of *The*

Alchemist with the shock of Buck Mulligan's shaving Mass. Instead it is part of a much more general inflation and abuse of language. To see Subtle and Face as blasphemers would be to take the claims of alchemy far more seriously than Jonson ever encourages his audience to do. The comic catechism works less by its undercurrent of religious parody, than by the sheer grotesqueness of its literal concepts, the anthropomorphic character of the metaphors applied to the alchemical process. It is the pure absurdity of imagining inanimate metals being 'mortified', 'tortured', 'sublimed', which Jonson mocks here, and which he dramatises so amusingly in his masque *Mercury Vindicated from the Alchemists at Court*.

What Molière and Jonson invite is a general rather than a specific scepticism. Molière's medical satires are not slyly directed against the orthodoxies of the Church, nor is *The Alchemist* intended to satirise those who debased such orthodoxies. In both cases the language of religion is included as it is cognate to all professional language, which, for the purposes of this sort of comedy, can be defined as language which works by means of its obscurity rather than its clarity, its systematic dogmatism rather than its real significance, its emotional charge rather than its logical force. At its simplest we see this in Molière's early medical farces, where the imposter crudely apes the airs of the learned doctor. It is rather different in plays such as *Le Malade Imaginaire* or *The Alchemist*, when the audience is presumed to have a fairly detailed knowledge of what is being parodied. There the pleasure is rather that of seeing the familiar and real, by a process of perhaps only slight exaggeration, turned into the fantastically monstrous. (To read or to watch *Le Malade Imaginaire* is to realise that the techniques of absurdist farce are not innovations of the twentieth century). While the seamy richness of detail in Jonson makes for a very different texture from the tight mad logic of Molière, in both cases it is the mechanics of deception which we are observing, the psychology both of the gulls or fools and of the professionals who cheat them.

Jonson and Molière are not here finally dependent on the private opinions of their audience on medicine or alchemy. As always the comedian will make capital out of the local or the topical, and so Molière caricatured the court doctors, D'Aquin and the rest, and Jonson no doubt relied on the notoriety of men like Kelly, Forman, and Dee to give immediacy to his play. But if we try to characterise the audience attitudes that Molière or Jonson seem to expect towards *Le Malade Imaginaire* or *The Alchemist*, they are not those of any definite sect or faction of the time. They are assumed to be people of common sense, as always, but common sense, in this instance, takes the form of a sceptical disbelief in what as individuals they might have credited or half credited. They are encouraged to watch with no trace of illusion the comedy of human weakness and credulity which plays in tandem with the comedy of mystification; with no trace of illusion, but without indignation either, for indignation is itself a form of self-righteous pretension which may be left to the Surlys. They are above all understood to be pragmatic plain-speakers, those for whom the only true function of language is communication, and who suspect the alchemists or the doctors most of all for their opacity. In the next chapter we shall turn to a different sort of language, but this underlying norm of a plain-speaking audience will remain the same.

5 The Language of Courtship

The topicality of comedy must always present a problem to those who try to study the theatre of the past. Two alternatives seem available: either to hunt down remorselessly every allusion, re-building from fragments the lost design of local satire, or to ignore altogether the in-jokes of the period and concentrate on the general thematic structure of the play. Neither method is ideal; for the archaeological approach by focussing on the deadest part of the comedy makes it difficult to believe in its life, whereas the universalising and generalising tendency must sacrifice the particularity which is so often crucial to the comedy's texture. *Love's Labour's Lost* and *Les Précieuses Ridicules* are interesting cases in point, for they have both been interpreted as satires of specific literary and intellectual coteries. Molière's attack upon preciosity has been a traditional arguing-point. Who were Molière's targets, would-be literary ladies or the distinguished leaders of the salons themselves – *les precieuses vraies où fausses?*[1] What sort of animus made Molière, recently arrived from the provinces, guy the most fashionable literary movement of the time? By comparison with speculations about Molière and the *précieuses*, the theories about topical satire in *Love's Labour's Lost* are not nearly so wide-ranging. The idea that *Love's Labour's Lost* satirised the so-called 'school of night' was an early twentieth-century discovery (or invention) and really only flourished as a critical *point d'appui* in the 1930's, since when it has gone out of fashion. But if it is no longer thought necessary to see the play as a contribution to a literary and political feud, and Shakespeare as the spokesman of the Essex party against that of Ralegh, puzzling allusions which can only be contemporary and satirical remain to annoy and baffle critics and editors. Are *les précieuses* and 'the school of night' just red herrings, or can we relate the satiric occasions of *Les Précieuses Ridicules* and *Love's Labour's Lost* to a more general and universal pattern of comic meaning?

Comedy's objects of riducule are nearly always imitators, never the real thing – or so comedians tell us. Molière was explicitly attacking the pretenders to preciosity, just as later in *Tartuffe* he would protest that it was the 'faux dévots' who were exposed, not the genuinely pious, for whom he had the greatest respect etc. etc. There must always be an element of professional disingenuousness here. Of course, if a satiric comedy is going to be more than a personal polemic, it will centre on ridiculous representatives of a general fashion, rather than the fashion's initiators or best exponents. And yet without the Marquise de Rambouillet or Mlle. de Scudéry there would have been no *précieuses ridicules* to ridicule. When Molière makes an allusion to the Carte du Tendre, he is not necessarily satirising *Clélie* directly, but he is relying on an audience to whom Mlle. de Scudéry's allegorical map of the progress of friendship is familiar and who can be relied upon to laugh when it is mentioned. No doubt it is commonly the case that the general public does not become aware of a cultural movement until it has moved past its creative into its derivative stage and by 1659 the best years of the *précieux* salons may have been over. All the same, it is surely fair to say that the Parisian audiences who made the play a popular success must have come to see a celebrated literary school satirised.

To say what that satire meant in terms of Molière's social, political, or ideological commitments, however, is much more speculative. The *précieux* movement was in origin associated with the aristocracy; does this mean that *Les Précieuses Ridicules* is anti-aristocratic? Not necessarily, for its milieu is bourgeois, and therefore it can be argued that what is derided is the mimicking by the grotesque bourgeois misses of the *grandes dames* of the salons[2]. The argument linking Molière with an anti-*précieuse* faction led by the Abbé d'Aubignac has the strained tones of conspiracy theory.[3] It is more probable, indeed, that the choice of satiric topic for Molière's troupe of actors was a shrewd and lucky guess. *Les Précieuses Ridicules* is closer to farce than to satire, and if once critics tried to identify Magdelon and Cathos with Madeleine de Scudéry and Catherine de Vivonne, Marquise de Rambouillet, it now seems much more likely that Madeleine Béjart and Catherine de Brie, the two actresses who played the roles, were following the traditional conventions of farce in using versions of their own names on stage.

The 'school of night' is still more shadowy and obscure. Even the identification by that name of the group of intellectuals of the Ralegh circle must remain in question. It turns mainly on the fact that Chapman wrote a long poem called 'The Shadow of Night' at about the time when it is conjectured that *Love's Labour's Lost* was first produced and that Ralegh and various of his associates had a reputation as a dangerous band of free-thinkers. This band becomes a 'school of night' and is named in the King's line mocking Berowne's devotion to the dark-haired Rosaline:

O paradox! Black is the badge of hell,
The hue of dungeons and the school of night[4]

It is, to say the least, a glancing reference if this is intended to be a major satiric target in the play. In fact, it is doubtful if the theory would have gained any currency were it not for a whole series of puzzles and loose ends scattered through the text of the play which critics have been eager to tie together into one nèat all-explaining set of topical allusions. Unfortunately the concept of the 'school of night' does not provide this sort of consistent key at all. It is not clear which of the characters are to be identified with which real-life counterparts. One assumes that the 'school' is being mocked in the very notion of the King's 'academe', especially as the early 1590's was the period of Ralegh's disgrace when he lived retired from the court, though not of course by deliberate choice. And yet M. C. Bradbrook, who supported the theory of the 'school of night' to the extent of giving that name to her book on the Ralegh circle, sees Ralegh as Armado and argues that, from quite early on in the play, the King and his party stand for Essex and his followers, Ralegh's rivals at court.[5] And so it is with other identifications — Moth as Nashe, Holofernes as Gabriel Harvey — they obscure as much as they explain. As Bradbrook herself admits, 'The play is on the whole more concerned with theories of living than with personalities; the satire is not sustained and consistent.'[6] The details, if there were details, may be irrevocably lost, and we can let them go.

If we move just a little away from the particular, however, it can be seen that both *Les Précieuses Ridicules* and *Love's Labour's Lost* are concerned with satirising contemporary modes of literary language. A. N. Kaul has remarked on how frequently comedians begin as literary parodists,[7] and these two plays, early on in the writing careers of Molière and Shakespeare, bear out his thesis. Whether Molière was satirising individual *précieuses* or not, there can be no doubt that he hit off the baroque fastidiousness of *précieux* jargon. Indeed phrases like Magdelon's marvellous, 'Vite, voituriez-nous ici les commodités de la conversation' when she wants an armchair are all many readers know of *précieux* diction. The business of purifying the language of the tribe must often throw up tortuous forms of literary distillation ideal for comic satire. Whère Molière had preciosity, the absurder aspect of the language of the 'grand siècle', Shakespeare could revel in the innumerable freaks of Elizabethan poetry and prose. Maybe it is not specifically Lyly's Euphuism which is being parodied in Armado's 'fire-new words', as so many critics have claimed.[8] It scarcely matters, for when Berowne makes his famous farewell to,

Taffeta phrases, silken terms precise,
Three-pil'd hyperboles, spruce affection,
Figures pedantical   V. ii 406–8

he could be describing the work of any number of the writers of the 1580's and 90's, including of course, that of Shakespeare himself.

Both the plays, however, are not only about language, but also about love and marriage. From the point of view of Gorgibus, Cathos and Magdelon have gone off the rails of the established track to respectable bourgeois settlement with their fussing over *précieuse* airs and manners. La Grange and Du Croisy plan their humiliating practical joke in revenge for the scornful way in which their honourable suit has been treated. As Antonie Adam points out, 'The neologisms, the mannered peripharases, the hyperbolic expressions are only secondary features completing the picture of the "Précieuse". She is primarily a woman who condemns love, despises marriage, and claims to set herself above the ordinary emotions.'[9] Similarly in *Love's Labour's Lost* the 'academe' is intended as a defiance of the tradition of courtship which is the normal preoccupation of a court. This defiance is, of course, rapidly abandoned and the King and his courtiers are soon using language as part of their highly elaborate and artificial love-games. Love's labour is finally lost in part because they are as yet incapable of expressing feeling in any more substantial or direct way. The combination of literary satire and love-comedy is not accidental in either play. It implies an audience attitude towards the relationship between language and love which it will be the concern of the rest of the chapter to examine.

LES PRÉCIEUSES RIDICULES

The *précieux* concept of love is recognisably related to mediaeval tradition. A close analogue to the *Carte du Tendre*, with its symbolic journey towards the ultimate goal of 'Tendre' and the hazards to be encountered on the way, is the first part of the *Roman de la Rose*. In both, the lover's long and troublesome struggle to win his lady's grace is dramatised allegorically with the emphasis equally on the difficulty and the desirability of the desired object. The *précieuses* sought to revive the mediaeval concept of unremitting and totally humble service to the mistress as an end in itself, or almost. From their feminist point of view this had the advantage of putting off indefinitely the final surrender to masculine authority, the marriage which they detested. Molière turns the interminable quests of Mlle. de Scudéry's novels into a joke when Magdelon indignantly rejects Gorgibus' insistence on marriage as a business matter: 'Mon Dieu, que, si tout le monde vous ressembloit, un roman seroit bientôt fini! La belle chose que ce seroit si d'abord Cyrus épousait Mandane, et qu'Aronce de plain-pied fût marié Clélie', 'Goddness, if everyone were like you, how soon a novel would be over! A fine thing it would be if Cyrus married Mandane right at the start, or if Aronce got married to Clélie straightaway'. But it was not just to ensure that *Le Grand Cyrus* continued to its full ten volumes that Cyrus did not marry Mandane directly; it was essential to an ideal of love in which marriage was not so much the happy ending as a necessary evil.

In the abstract, no doubt, many modern readers would sympathise with this ideal, in so far at least as its alternative was immediate marriage to a stranger enforced by a father as crudely authoritarian as Gorgibus. Could Molière really have intended us to be on the side of the brutal and tyrannic parent against the rebellious daughters? The traditional bias of comedy for the young against the old seems to make it unlikely. The perspective of *Les Précieuses Ridicules*, however, makes it impossible to respect Magdelon and Cathos as representatives of feminism revolting against masculine domination in marriage and it makes Gorgibus into an instrument of satire rather than a figure to approve or detest. For what we learn from Gorgibus indirectly is that the girls' abhorrence of men is hypocritical. He complains of their extravagance:

> Ces pendardes-là, avec leur pommade, ont, je pense, envie de me ruiner. Je ne vois partout que blanc d'oeufs, lait virginal, et mille autres brimborions que je ne connois point. Elles ont usé, depuis que nous sommes ici, le lard d'une douzaine de cochons, pour le moins, et quatre valets vivroient tous les jours des pieds de moutons qu'elles emploient.
>
> *Les Précieuses Ridicules* iii

A typical comic bourgeois father with adolescent daughters, grumbling about what they cost, indignant at their cosmetics. But we are aware, even before they enter, that Magdelon and Cathos are equivalently comic teenage girls, heavily made-up, and no doubt heavily flirtatious. If they complain about the shocking idea of marriage it is not because they have any objection to men, but that they want more time to attract more men. This is the cynical view of the *précieuses*, that they are prudes only because they are coquettes at heart.

Magdelon explains to her father, with the peculiarly patronising tone used in addressing obtuse parents:

> Mon père, voilà ma cousine qui vous dira, aussi bien que moi, que le

mariage ne doit jamais arriver qu'après les autres aventures. Il faut qu'un amant, pour être agréable, sache débiter les beaux sentiments, pousser le doux, le tendre et le passionné, et que sa recherche soit dans les formes,   *Les Précieuses Ridicules* iv

Magdelon wants a lover who will do everything according to the book and her long speech, which follows the lines quoted here, is a spoof of the typical novelistic progress of a romance – a parody similar to those of Jane Austen's juvenilia. For the would-be fashionable cousins the fact that La Grange and Du Croisy have missed out the whole elaborate progress of courtship, have 'taken the novel by the tail', is unforgiveable. This is not only a standard comic situation of romance being applied literally to life. The *précieuse* idea of the pursuit of love, with its refined charades and repeated frustrations, is for those who view it as crudely as Magdelon and Cathos, a titillating ritual which they look forward to with a full-blooded enthusiasm not at all *précieuse*.

This, of course, is one of the ironies of the appearance of 'le marquis de Mascarille', that the cousins are almost immediately floored. As against the *précieuse* ideal of feminine aloofness, only gradually won to an expression of feeling, it needs the bare name of a marquis and a couple of remarks from Mascarille, and they are convinced:

> *Magdelon.* Ma chère, c'est le caractère enjoué.
> *Cathos.* Je vois bien que c'est un Amilcar.
>
> *Les Précieuses Ridicules* ix

Their periphrastic language, so far from delicately avoiding suggestive subjects, actually betrays their eager state of mind. Cathos entreats Mascarille to be seated: 'Mais de grâce, Monsieur, ne soyez pas inexorable à ce fauteuil qui vous tend les bras il y a un quart d'heure; contentez un peu l'envie qu'il a de vous embrasser'. 'I beg you, Monsieur, do not be merciless to that chair which has been holding out its arms to you for the last quarter of an hour; give some satisfaction to its desire to embrace you'. (Sc. ix) The conceit is delightfully absurd in itself, but the emotion is so plainly transferred from the speaker to the chair that the invitation appears positively seductive. It is at once a travesty of *précieux* language and a revelation of how far Magdelon and Cathos are from true *précieux* attitudes.

To understand the effect of the scene with the mock-marquis, we need to bear in mind the nature of Mascarille as a theatrical figure. As with Sganarelle in the doctor plays, Mascarille was for the audience a blatant imposter from the start. Molière had been playing Mascarille parts in *L'Etourdi* and *Le Dépit Amoureux* throughout the year 1658–9 before the creation of *Les Précieuses Ridicules* and the spectators at the Petit Bourbon theatre would have known just what to expect once the name was mentioned. The moment at which Marotte announces 'le Marquis de Mascarille' must have been a gag-line in the theatre. He may or may not have been masked, but he would certainly have been quite identifiable enough to make his appearance in the guise of a marquis a howling absurdity. (His partner Jodelet had his face whitened in clown style.) Once again, as with Sganarelle, Molière as star *farceur* is using his *commedia* role as the mainspring of the comic situation. The measure of the girls' credulity is that they should take Mascarille – Mascarille who everyone can see is a comic servant – for a fashionable aristocrat.

The joy of watching Mascarille is that he plays his part at once so very well and so very badly. He is the first in the line of Molière's comic 'marquis', empty-headed and incurably vain, with fashionable literary pretensions. The recital of the poem, for example, is a rehearsal for Oronte's performance in *Le Misanthrope*. Like all gentlemen writers of the period, he is proud of his amateur status – 'Tout ce que je fais a l'air cavalier; cela ne sent point le pedant', 'Tout ce que je fais me vient naturellement, c'est sans étude'. 'Everything I do has that cavalier air to it: it has nothing of the pedant about it', 'Everything I do comes naturally, unstudied'. He apes all sorts of aristocratic manners, combing his wig in public, having himself carried by his chairmen right up into the house he is visiting. In all of this he is recognisably what he claims to be. But no real marquis, presumably, ever had quite Mascarille's sublime self-satisfaction, as he invites admiration for his poem or directs the girls' attention to the various items of his dress. Utterly unwarranted self-confidence was to become the standard trait of Molière's 'marquis', but none of them play the part with the gusto of Mascarille. For instead of the languid foppishness of the real thing he has a boastfulness much more crude and vigorous, much more alive.

Mascarille's various subjects of conversation are strung together like the sketches of a stand-up comedian. From his 'impromptu', both recited and sung, he turns to the theatre, allowing Molière to satirise the Parisian claques and his rivals 'les grands comédiens'; then, just as abruptly, to his clothes. Finally, à propos of nothing at all, he accuses Magdelon and Cathos of an unfair double attack upon his heart. This is, of course, the cue for his supporting partner Jodelet to appear, to even up the numbers. With both of them on stage the comedy becomes steadily cruder and more explicitly sexual. Mascarille's solo performance as fashionable gentleman of letters shifts to an outrageous *miles gloriosus* turn for two, in which he and Jodelet vie with one another in displaying their wounds. As they prepare for an impromptu ball, Mascarille's language too is in *déshabillé*: 'Moi, je dis que nos libertés auront peine à sortir d'ici les braies nettes' – a grotesque mixed metaphor which is difficult to translate and which Molière's editors are inclined to leave without comment, 'I tell you, our liberties will find it hard to get out of here with their pants clean'. When La Grange and Du Croisy interrupt the ball, Magdelon and Cathos are virtually on the point of being seduced by the disguised valets.

This is not merely *Les Précieuses Ridicules* reverting to its origins in crude farce. The sexual comedy is perfectly consonant with the literary satire. Cathos originally protested at the shocking idea of marriage with the famous comic line, 'Comment est-ce qu'on peut souffrir la pensée de coucher contre un homme vraiment nu?' 'How could one bear the thought of sleeping beside a wholly naked man?' The girls' preoccupation is with clothing, both literal and metaphorical, with the ribbons and feathers of Mascarille, and with the *précieux* periphrases which are their literary equivalent. What Magdelon wants, above all, is the appearance of being in the know:

> On sait à point nommé: 'Un tel a composé la plus jolie pièce du monde sur un tel sujet; une telle a fait des paroles sur un tel air . . .' C'est là qui vous fait valoir dans les compagnies; et si l'on ignore ces choses, je ne donnerois pas un clou de tout l'esprit qu'on peut avoir.
>
> *Les Precieuses Ridicules* ix

The love pursuits of the *précieux* novels are for Magdelon and Cathos a sort of emotional strip-tease. It is because we are led to suspect them of such hypocrisies that we find it so funny when Mascarille and Jodelet begin their comic business of undressing to show off their scars. And it is this, also, which makes the final stripping of the imposters an appropriate form of comic justice.

For, at first sight, it might seem as though this was an unnecessary piece of brutality. Mascarille and Jodelet have presumably been suborned by their masters to carry out the trick and it would seem to be taking the joke rather too far to beat and humiliate them for their success. Most often in comedy this sort of imposture is rewarded with the indulgent laughter of everyone on stage and off and one might expect from La Grange and Du Croisy a wink and a pat on the back rather then the violent punishment they inflict. It is, however, a part of the whole mocking show which they ruthlessly play out in revenge against the *précieuses*. The exposure of the pretended marquis and vicomte is a double ignominy for Magdelon and Cathos, who have believed in their rank. The full irony of the situation is that Mascarille and Jodelet have dressed in their masters' clothes, and it was to La Grange and Du Croisy's unlover-like dress that the disdainful cousins objected most strenuously. With these borrowed plumes removed, La Grange can leave behind the valets, if not 'vraiment nus', at least in their underclothes, with the final deadly insult to the girls: 'Maintenant, Mesdames, en l'état qu'ils sont, vous pouvez continuer vos amours avec eux tant qu'il vous plaira; nous vous laissons toute sorte de liberté pour cela, et nous vous protestons, Monsieur et moi, que nous n'en serons aucunement jaloux'. 'Now, Mesdames, in their present state, you may continue your courtship with them as long as you like; we shall leave you all possible freedom for it, and as for Monsieur and myself, we assure you that we shall be in no way jealous'. This is indeed brutal stuff. Mascarille's parting line is a better joke, and serves as ironic moral for the whole play: 'Allons, camarade, allons chercher fortune autre part: je vois bien qu'on n'aime ici que la vaine apparence, et qu'on n'y considère point la vertu toute nue'. 'Come on, friend, let us go and take our chance somewhere else; I can see that here only vain appearance is admired, and no consideration is given to naked virtue'.

Les Précieuses Ridicules may be seen as anti-literary as *Le Malade Imaginaire* or *The Alchemist* could be seen as anti-scientific. We have here a similar sort of comic mood. Where medicine or alchemy were exposed as quackery, dishonest imposture upon the credulous layman, the disingenuous motives detected behind the *précieux* fashion are sexual. Preciosity was very vulnerable to this line of attack, for the *précieuses* were always preoccupied with the subject of love, even while they professed to be trying to refine and etherealise it. As Paul Benichou points out, they were condemned from two opposite quarters, as often for their corrupting obsessiveness with sexual relations, as for their over-spiritual affectations.[10] From the comedian's viewpoint, precosity becomes a form of sublimated or concealed courtship display. Gorgibus cannot see that far; he only known that the girls' 'notions' get in the way of the orthodox bourgeois marriage and opposes them blindly. He offers us a comic view of the activities of the *précieuses* but we laugh at his stupidity from the comfortable detachment of another level of irony. To us it is immediately apparent that Cathos and Magdelon are husband-hunting butterflies whose literary affectations are pure flummery. Their exposure by means of the exhibitionism of Mascarille confirms us in the reductive, even brutal, sense of reality which underlies the play. We are invited to share an almost scornful amusement at the vagaries of adolescence, very unlike the relatively sympathetic and indulgent attitude of, say, *A Midsummer Night's Dream*. This is comedy bent on exposing fraud, on unmasking literary masqueraders, with some indignation at the liberties they take with language and the reality that language should reflect. It is this indignation which accounts for the harshness of the play's ending where the fashionable forgers are stripped and pilloried to vindicate a principle of truth.

LOVE'S LABOUR'S LOST

The 'academe' of *Love's Labour's Lost* is roughly comparable to the *précieuse* school in so far as it represents a deliberate alternative to the normal way of the world in love and marriage. It is also, however, related to any number of opening situations in comedy where an irrational law blocks progress towards sexual fulfilment. At its most absurd we find it in the anti-flirtation laws of Titipu; at its most grimly real, it is the legislation re-activated by Angelo in the Vienna of *Measure for Measure*. For those interested in establishing anthropological or psychological origins for comedy, such a law naturally invites interpretation. If the ur-function of comedy was to propitiate fertility deities or to enact the cycle of natural growth, then the community dominated by the irrational law represents the winter kingdom of barrenness which must be transformed. But, however it may have originated, the essential hypothesis of this sort of comic scenario is that the law will be proved unworkable. Titipu is saved from depopulation only by the ridiculous expedient of making one of the condemned Lord High Executioner; as Pompey, who also goes from convict to hangman's assistant, puts it succintly – 'Does your honour intend to geld and splay all the youth of the city?' In *Love's Labour's Lost* the outcome of the King's oath is quite as inevitable. Navarre cannot long remain in the unnatural state of celibacy which its ruler proposes, and in fact we are not out of the first act before the first breach of the anti-sexual ordinance is reported.

What differentiates the situation in *Love's Labour's Lost* from other instances of the law against love is that it is initiated by the young lovers themselves. Whereas normally the arbitrary statute is the edict of a tyrannic ruler (the Mikado) or the inheritance of some dim and harsh period of history (the long-forgotten legislation of Vienna), here we actually see the young men self-censored. This, of course, makes it all the more unlikely that the oath will be sustained, for in comedy any self-assertive act of will tends to be suspect. What is more, one of the courtiers taking the oath sees all too clearly how it will end:

> Necessity will make us all forsworn
> Three thousand times within these three years' space;
> For every man with his affects is born,
> Not by might master'd, but by special grace.   I i 148–51

In fact, well over half the opening scene, in which the purpose of the academe is explained, is given over to Berowne's eloquent objections. We may well be suspicious when it emerges that the rule against the presence of women at court will be broken as soon as it is made. When Berowne reminds the King of the embassy of the French Princess, he exclaims unconvincingly, 'What say you, lords? why, this was quite forgot'. Was it, indeed? The academe looks increasingly like a charade which is not only unrealistic but disingenuous. The King and his courtiers are in that phase of immaturity in which austere good resolutions are made only to be abandoned, made partly in order to be abandoned. Self-abnegation of this sort is a form of self-display, and at some level, the King may not be as innocently unaware of the approach of the Princess as he claims.

What is going to happen to the King's academe is prefigured in the second scene of the play with the appearance of Armado. The King in his opening speech has vain-gloriously addressed his followers as

> brave conquerors – for so you are,
> That war against your own affections
> And the huge army of the world's desires,   I i 8–10

But Armado, the familiar *miles gloriosus*, makes ridiculous just this image as he confesses his love.

> If drawing my sword against the humour of affection would deliver me
> from the reprobate thought of it, I would take Desire prisoner, and
> ransom him to any French courtier for a new-devised courtesy.
> I ii 55–9

As with the Captain of *commedia del arte*, to whom he is related, Armado's soldiership becomes no more than a means of inflating the prestige and value of his love. From the enormous height of his military grandeur he condescends to love the 'base wench' Jacquenetta. He takes comfort from his Page Moth by aligning himself with the great soldier/lovers of antiquity, Samson and Hercules. The irony, that their loves were disastrous, is evident to us and to Moth, but not to Armado, who is busy comparing heroic prowess: 'O well-knit Samson! strong-jointed Samson! I do excell thee in my rapier as much as thou didst me in carrying gates. I am in love too.' (I ii 69–71). The boastful soldier's manly independence is established only to be transformed by love, so that it is no suprise when the 'brave conquerors that war against their own affections' become 'affection's men-at-arms'. It is a volte-face as natural as it is comically inevitable.

The joke of the King and Armado's postures is their lack of self-awareness. But throughout the play there are flanking spectators who comment cynically and satirically on the mock battle of the sexes. Moth fulfils the usual page-boy function of being wiser than his master, laughing up his sleeve at the Spaniard's pretensions, deflating them with sardonic *double entendres*. In a different way Costard's plain speaking undercuts Armado's periphrases: when accused of 'sorting and consorting . . . with a child of our grand-mother Eve', he replies simply, 'Sir, I confess the wench'. However much the protagonists may evade the sexual aspect of their relations there are always those who can remind them of it. Boyet, in his view of the Princess's embassy, is an almost pimp-like figure.

> Now, madam, summon up your dearest spirits:
> Consider who the king your father sends,
> To whom he sends, and what's his embassy:
> . .   . .
> Be now as prodigal of all dear grace
> As Nature was in making graces dear
> When she did starve the general world beside,
> And prodigally gave them all to you.   II i 1—11

This is no doubt conventional courtier's stuff but there is no mistaking the knowingness of his conclusion after the first meeting of King and Princess:

> I'll give you Aquitaine, all that is his,
> An you give him for my sake but one loving kiss.   II i 247—8

As Maria puts it, Boyet is an 'old love-monger' and can see that the most potent argument in the diplomatic negotiation over Aquitaine will be the Princess's beauty.

In this, of course, Boyet is well ahead of the story. The Princess herself deftly disclaims the implications of his remarks — 'Come to our pavillion,' she says to her ladies, 'Boyet is dispos'd' (to jest understood). But the intial meeting between the opposing groups of France and Navarre does set the pattern for the war of courtship which is to continue through the play — a pattern of alarums and excursions, sorties and retreats. Boyet comes back from his preliminary parley with an amused account of Navarre's celibate court:

> Marry, thus much I have learnt;
> He rather means to lodge you in the field,
> Like one that comes here to besiege his court,
> Than seek a dispensation for his oath,
> To let you enter his unpeopled house.   II i 84—8

Navarre then enters himself, with all the rhetorical forms of a general treating with an enemy power:

> Fair princess, welcome to the court of Navarre II i 90

But his antagonist will have none of this, and replies in blunt prose:

> Fair I give you back again; and welcome I have not yet: the roof of this court is too high to be yours, and welcome to the wide fields too base to be mine. II i 91–3

Navarre's attempt to apologise for his oath, which is in fact a form of boasting, is sharply cut down. The Princess outwits the King by refusing to play his game. She is like Rosalind interrupting the mannered wooing of Silvius and Phoebe with a brusque and down-to-earth scolding. The Princess's retorts to the King may well seem indecorous and she herself apologises for them. This is a comedy of love, however, and she is here not so much the daughter of the King of France on an important diplomatic mission as the type of comic heroine whom Shakespeare virtually invented, witty, direct, with an assertiveness which just stops short of aggression.

After this one burst of fire, however, the Princess turns to business and a business-like manner. From this point on, indeed, she and her party resolutely refuse to interest themselves in the court of Navarre and its doings and in a later scene we hear the Princess making most efficient plans for leaving directly the documents which will clinch the negotiations have arrived. And, of course, it is this indifference which provokes the interest of the courtiers. If, at some level, we may feel that the King and his band hoped to make themselves objects of attention by their oath of isolation, the ladies effectively play the antithesis of that game by letting them severely alone.[11] We see them creeping back one by one with feigned casualness to enquire the names of the several ladies whom they have singled out. This pattern is repeated again in the magnificent discovery-scene where each, unaware of eavesdroppers, emerges to confess his love and where finally they re-form as a company to charge the enemy – 'Saint Cupid and soldiers to the field'. Their joint sortie, however, in their Russian disguise is no more successful and when they separate to encounter hand-to-hand they are ambushed by the stratagem of the ladies. The King and his men, by the end of the play, have been as thoroughly discredited as any boastful soldiers in comedy.

Language is the most luxuriant vegetation of the King of Navarre's park. Even when not engaged in the war of words which is the central action of the play, both sides spar among themselves with elaborate word-games. Boyet exchanges innuendoes with the ladies to the point where the Princess has to restrain them from so misplacing their energies: 'This civil war of wits were much better us'd On Navarre and his book-men, for here 'tis abus'd'. The King and his men twit Berowne with his love for the dark Rosaline in the obscure terms which have made possible the detection of the hidden school of night. Later on in the play, Sir Nathaniel and Holofernes add two more ludicrous word-mongers to the cast. Words provide the source of endless assertive dispute and self-congratulation, whether the subject is the precise form of deer the princess shot, the aptness of Armado's metaphors, or Dull's ancient riddles. Holofernes's complacent pride in his 'extemporal epitaph on the death of the deer' is typical: 'This is a gift that I have, simple, simple; a foolish extravagant spirit, full of forms, figures, shapes, objects, ideas, apprehensions, motions, revolutions'. It is a spirit common to nearly all the characters of *Love's Labour's Lost* at their various mental levels, from the King down to Dull and Costard.

For the lovers, language is display. When in succession the King, Longaville, and Dumain read aloud their sonnets, we laugh at them less for their fashionable conceits than for the state of mind which they indicate in the writers. Self-preoccupied and self-deceived, the lovers express their natural feelings in grandiloquent and pretentious form. Berowne comments cynically on Longaville's sonnet:

> This is the liver vein, which makes flesh a deity;
> A green goose a goddess; pure, pure idolatry.   IV iii 71−2

Just as the *précieuses* tried to etherealise what is from the comedian's point of view a largely biological impulse, so Navarre and his courtiers are afflicted with the disease incident to their time of life. They are in Jacques' third age of 'the lover, sighing like furnace, with a woeful ballad made to his mistress' eyebrow', using verse as a means of giving themselves false dignity rather than communicating meaning. Dumain is even inclined to send a prose gloss to accompany his verse:

> This will I send, and something else more plain,
> That shall express my true love's fasting pain.   IV iii 118−19

The naive exhibitionism of the lovers is evident throughout the play, above all in the masque and antimasque of the Russians and the Nine Worthies.[12] The visit of the Russians is in the tradition of the Tudor entertainments from which the masque originated and may be a specific imitation of the Gray's Inn Muscovites of 1594. But the comedy enables us to see in it also the childish antics of disguising and the earnest attempt to impress. The ladies, of course, thwart this attempt by refusing to be impressed and instead make puncturing jokes like unkind adults at a children's pantomime, 'dashing it like a Christmas comedy'. Literal-minded puns, in particular, are used to make fools out of the cavalier aims of the lovers:

> *King.* Say to her, we have measur'd many miles
> To tread a measure with her on this grass.
> . . . .
> *Rosaline.* It is not so. Ask them how many inches
> Is in one mile: if they have measur'd many,
> The measure then of one is easily told.   V ii 184—90

The whole art of the masque depends upon an audience prepared to accept its hyperbolic conventions. It is therefore very easy to guy it by an ungracious reception.

Yet the reaction of the Princess's party to the Russians is much less unkind than that which the Navarre courtiers give the show of the Nine Worthies. Critics have been shocked at how boorish and brutal the behaviour of the King's men is in this scene, and have been inclined perhaps to sentimentalise the pathos of the derided actors. Would an Elizabethan audience have seen real dignity in what may seem to us the dignified rebuke of Holofernes, 'This is not generous, not gentle, not humble'? The Princess comments at his exit, 'Alas, poor Maccabeus, how he hath been baited' but after all baiting of one sort or another was still a sport in the sixteenth century. We are surely not intended to feel for the humiliation of Armado when he is forced to reveal that he has no shirt, as Bobbyann Roesen suggests we should.[13] Yet the incessant and often rather silly barracking of the King and his courtiers throughout the 'anti-masque' does seem remarkable. Berowne provides one explanation when he urges that the performance should go on — 'tis some policy To have one show worse than the King's and his company'. Having suffered through the discomfort of having their own play heckled, the courtiers feel that they may now at least show to more advantage when heckling the worthies. But their aggressive wisecracking in fact shows only for what it is, the strident effort to win admiration for themselves from the ladies. We find similar exaggerated high spirits from the lovers at the mechanicals' play in *A Midsummer Night's Dream*, though there the women join in as well. To contrast with this behaviour the Princess in *Love's Labour's Lost*, just like Duke Theseus, presents the proper gracious attitude towards such amateur theatricals:

> That sport best pleases that doth least know how.
> Where zeal strives to content, and the contents
> Dies in the zeal of that which it presents;
> Their form confounded makes most form in mirth,
> When great things labouring perish in their birth.   V ii 512—16

The lovers cannot let the natural absurdity of the Worthies alone, but feel they have to make the laughter more hilarious with their own witty comments. The tone has the shrill and forced quality of a student party where too many people are trying to be too loudly clever.

Throughout the play the behaviour of the King and his party may be characterised as immature, an immaturity which shows itself above all in their lack of self-awareness. Their solemn oath and their rapid perjury, their verbal airs and graces, their puppyish egoism, all set them up for our amused mockery. But what then of Berowne, who is certainly self-aware and who is significantly different from the others at each stage of the play's development? What is his function in the comedy? He has what is almost a choric role in several scenes, as, for example, at the beginning when he predicts what will happen to the academe:

> I'll lay my head to any good man's hat,
> These oaths and laws will prove an idle scorn.   I i 299—300

This and his protests earlier in the scene make it clear that he subscribed to the oath without any serious belief in the whole project. And yet he, rather than the others, seems more genuinely taken aback when he does fall in love:

> What! I love! I sue! I seek a wife!
> A woman that is like a German clock,
> Still a-repairing, ever out of frame,
> And never going aright, being a watch,
> But being watch'd that it may still go right.   III i 184—8

Love does not make him abandon his cynical judgement of his beloved's attractions:

> A whitely wanton with a velvet brow,
> With two pitch-balls stuck in her face for eyes;
> Ay and by heaven, one that will do the deed
> Through Argus were her eunuch and her guard.   III i 191—4

(It is interesting that the sexual aspect of love in the play is most often associated with Berowne and Rosaline). But in spite of such cynicism it is Berowne who gives the magnificent panegyric of love with which the oath is formally annulled. Berowne seems to occupy the role which in later plays Shakespeare was to give to Rosalind or Benedick; a figure who believes in real love, yet with sceptical reservations about lovers' cant. In this play, where so few of the court of Navarre are capable of irony, Berowne with his shrewd perceptions and lively wit looks very much like a *raisonneur* perhaps even a protagonist.

And yet the play's ending does not treat him as such. He is given his punishment of servitude with the others, a particularly gruesome one indeed.

> You shall this twelve month term from day to day
> Visit the speechless sick, and still converse
> With groaning wretches; and your task shall be
> With all the fierce endeavour of your wit
> To enforce the pained impotent to smile.   V ii 842–6

There is here a strict comic justice, but all the same for those of us who have on the whole enjoyed Berowne's wit throughout the play it seems a severe sentence. Once again, as with the humiliation of Mascarille, we may feel that there is an unexpected lack of generosity in the comic ending where we so often look for a spirit of indulgence. But then the changed atmosphere of the dénouement, the King of France's death, and the outcome indicated by the play's title, all infringe conventional notions of the way comedy should end. And it is Berowne who points out the deliberate indecorum:

> Our wooing doth not end like an old play;
> Jack hath not Jill: these ladies' courtesy
> Might well have made our sport a comedy.   V ii 866–8

There can be little doubt of the theatrical effectiveness of the change of tone introduced by the messenger Marcade. (Shakespeare's hint for a lighting direction – 'The scene begins to cloud' – has been picked up by many modern producers). Why, though, in terms of the action we have watched, should we be denied the usual multiple marriage of Shakespearean comedy? Marriages, after all, are made elsewhere in apparently much less propitious circumstances – witness *Much Ado, All's Well,* or *Measure for Measure.* A great deal has been written about the ending of *Love's Labour's Lost,* much of it emphasising the symbolic importance of the songs of Spring and Winter with which we are moved out from the play-world into a world of everyday reality. [14] There is certainly at the end of the play an insistence on reality as something other than the mannered antics we have watched throughout. Reality is death and disease, facts of our lives which make them homely, painful, or sordid – greasy Joan, or the cuckoo twitting the jealous husband. In contrast with all this, the court games of love are stigmatised as false, wordplay is counterfeiting. Such puritan disapproval of frivolity may seem paradoxical when the frivolities of the play are so evidently enjoyed and enjoyable. Berowne solemnly renounces the 'taffeta phrases' in which all the characters have flounced about, but he does it in a witty and stylish way which reminds us how graceful those taffeta phrases have been. Unlike *Les Précieuses Ridicules*, Shakespeare's satire on linguistic affectation is thoroughly benign, positively delighting in what it mocks.

Yet, although Shakespeare is indulgent where Molière is more sharply critical, the final attitudes of the two plays are comparable. We may laugh more or less kindly at the extravagances of adolescent love, but in the end we return to an adult recognition of reality which is insistently down to earth. Many comedies allow demonstrably silly heroes and heroines to pair off, with the implied assumption that maturity will come after marriage, or that the ceremony itself will bring sobriety. *A Midsummer Night's Dream*, with its contrast of the relationship of the older couple Theseus and Hippolyta with the young lovers, is a striking case in point. But in both *Love's Labour's Lost* and *Les Précieuses Ridicules* it is understood that young people who are still shadow-flirting like Cathos and Magdelon or the King and his men are not ready for marriage. They must learn to accept the responsibilities of real experience, to distinguish between meaning and display. Words, the value and significance of words, are crucial in both cases, for it is in the dysfunction of language that we most clearly see the comic inadequacies of the characters. Berowne must visit the 'speechless sick' to find that there is human experience beyond transformation by a witty tongue, where his brilliant rhetoric will have to be laid aside. If the silly *précieuses* seem scarcely capable of becoming more reasonable, they have certainly had a spectacular demonstration of the bare truth beneath their linguistic pretensions.

Such a conclusion may make it sound as though these two plays are heavily moralistic, dourly insisting on a drab reality and vindictively punishing those who deny it, and of course this is not the case. Molière's brief farce by its very form and tone eschews any suggestion of a didactic purpose. *Love's Labour's Lost*, with its equivocal attitude to what it mocks, half satiric, half celebratory, is certainly not a stern and kill-joy tract. We must go carefully here, as throughout this study, for the tactful implications of comedy may be totally falsified by being stated in crude abstract form. Yet it is striking how different the comic contract is in *Love's Labour's Lost* or *Les*

Précieuses Ridicules from that of plays we looked at earlier, *As You Like It, A Midsummer Night's Dream*, or *L'Ecole des Femmes*. There the absurd games of love were a preparation for reality, were indeed transformed into reality; here they are its opposite. Molière and Shakespeare are postulating in *Les Précieuses Ridicules* and *Love's Labour's Lost* a different sort of adult attitude, a different view of adolescence. We watch the *précieuses* and the courtiers as people who may be amused and entertained but who themselves 'have put away childish things'.

6 Monstrous Regiment

Meredith argued that one of the pre-conditions for an era of great comedy was that there should not be 'a state of marked social inequality between the sexes'.[1] The historical evidence would scarcely seem to bear this out as a general proposition. Comic playwrights from Aristophanes on have made capital out of sexual inequality as the social norm. The idea of the women taking over in *Lysistrata* or *Ecclesiasuzae* would not be funny if it were not seen as a fantastic aberration from normality. Women enforcing a peace treaty, women voting in the Assembly, these are spectacles as remote from the actual as Cloudcuckooland or the comic Hades of *The Frogs*. The idea of assembly or congregation, for legislative or educational purposes, is understood to be an essentially male activity, and the banding together of women is the basis of comic works as different as Erasmus's colloquy *Senatulus* and Gilbert and Sullivan's operetta *Princess Ida*. To take an example from a minor play, interesting principally as a source for Molière, the feminist call to arms of Emilie in Chappuzeau's *Académie des Femmes* is intended as typically absurd:

> Ils [les hommes] ont, pour s'établir, sénats, académies,
> Cours, diètes, conseils; nous seules, endormies
> Nous seules, sur le point de nous voir accabler,
> Ne songeons point qu'il est temps de nous assembler.[2]

It is on this basis, too, as instances of 'monstrous regiment' that we are asked to laugh at the Collegiate women of Jonson's *Epicoene*, and the *précieuse* circle of *Les Femmes Savantes*.

It may well be hard for us in the twentieth century to retain our sense of humour over plays such as these. Jonson and Molière seem to be appealing to social prejudices which many of us now deplore – the concept that women are naturally incapable of public or professional life, that any attempt to escape their domestic situation is necessarily laughable. Some critics of Molière, such as Antoine Adam, have been obviously appalled at the apparent anti-feminism of *Les Femmes Savantes*:

Moliere, to whom all fanaticism was alien, had no reason to attack the learned ladies . . . All his work, from *L'Ecole des Maris* on, exalted the idea of freedom, preached emancipation . . . Was Molière, for the first time in his life, going to take a hostile attitude to women's efforts towards a personal life?[3]

The only explanation which Adam can offer for this lamentable lapse of taste and judgement is that the play was a part of a personal feud against a literary enemy, the Abbé Cotin. Even so, he is inclined to write off *Les Femmes Savantes* as Molière's worst play, and remarks that 'it is only with difficulty that the lover of Molière can recognise him in it'.

But surely one only fails to recognise Molière in *Les Femmes Savantes* if one is bent on looking for a liberal humanist Molière, a Molière expressing consistently enlightened views on social issues from a twentieth century point of view. Though *Les Femmes Savantes* or *Epicoene* appear to uphold conservative attitudes, this may not be their main *raison d'être*. The traditional comic image of the women's revolt can be put to a variety of social or political purposes. The satire of Aristophanes is directed against the men in his society who have so misused their authority as to make the usurpation of the women necessary. With his vision of women as militant peace-makers and proto-communists, he might perhaps be taken for a forward-looking radical thinker. Such a reading would be misplaced, not only because of Aristophanes's known conservatism, but because what is essential to the comedy is the fantastic image itself rather than the ideological inferences which might be drawn from it. Jonson and Molière may be no more anti-feminist than Aristophanes is pro-feminist. They, like him, invite us to explore a world in which normal sexual roles are inverted but their purpose is not necessarily to challenge or confirm our usual social views on sexuality. Instead they build up from within the attitudes which they expect their audience to adopt. The success of the plays is to be judged, finally, on the internal coherence of these attitudes and the comic skill and energy which they are embodied.

EPICOENE

The Silent Woman, Jonson's sub-title for *Epicoene*, which seems quite early on to have become the name by which it was known, certainly appears to encourage an attitude of cynical anti-feminism in its audience. Like any number of play-titles of the period — *More Dissemblers Besides Women*, *A Woman is a Weathercock*, *Women Beware Women* — which depend upon proverbial jokes about female qualities of infidelity, fickleness, or treachery, *The Silent Woman* provokes the question: could there be such a thing? And the answer, of course, is no. The moment Epicoene, the 'silent woman', is married, she finds tongue and in her volubility stands revealed to her horrified husband as 'a manifest woman'. But the attack upon women in *Epicoene* goes much further than standard jokes about feminine talkativeness. From the very start of the play we are made aware of female sexuality as something grotesque and perverse. Clerimont's page-boy describes his reception at the house of Lady Haughty:

> The gentlewomen play with me and throw me o' the bed, and carry me in to my lady, and she kisses me with her oiled face, and puts a peruke o' my head, and asks me an' I will wear her gown, and I say no; and then she hits me a blow o' the ear and calls me innocent, and lets me go.   I i 13–17

Long before we meet the Ladies Collegiates, and Jonson delays their entrance until the middle of Act III, we are shown that the main title of the play, *Epicoene*, is indicative not only of the name and implied sex of the hero (ine), but of the amphibious sexual character of all the women in the play. As E. B. Partridge points out in his perceptive study, seventeenth century uses of the word 'epicene' suggested the abnormal no man's land (and no woman's land, too) between the normal male and the normal female',[4] and it is this no man's land with which the play is concerned.

Truewit describes the College to Clerimont, who has just come from Court and has not heard of it:

> A new foundation, sir, here i' the town, of ladies that call themselves the Collegiates, an order between courtiers and country-madams, that live from their husbands and give entertainment to all the Wits and Braveries o' the time, as they call 'em, cry down or up what they like or dislike in a brain or fashion with most masculine or rather hermaphroditical anthority   I i 67–73

The concern of the College with the judgement of dress recalls the women's senate set up by the Emperor Heliogabulus to deliberate on questions of taste and fashion. Although they are supposed, also, to concern themselves with the Wits as well as the Braveries, literature as well as modes of dress, we see relatively little of them in this blue-stocking role, which is dominant in *Les Femmes Savantes*. Presumably if Sir John Daw is their idea of a Wit it is not surprising that the subtleties of literary discussion are not much in evidence. The concept of the College is exploited in the play not so much for its associations with scholarship or learning, but simply as it suggests the masculine prerogative of single-sex congregation. The ladies live apart from their husbands, they gather together like the unmarried fellows of a college, they take upon themselves the function of authoritative judgement – in all of this they are 'hermaphroditical'.

It is significant that the three principal collegiates are introduced en masse in Act III sc. vi. (We have already met Mrs. Otter, who appears to hold something less than a full fellowship in the college). Jonson in *Epicoene*, as in his other comedies, normally takes care to identify his characters one by one: in the opening scenes, for example, Clerimont, Truewit, and Dauphine are each established individually, and later the comic fools – Sir John Daw, Sir Amorous La-Foole, Tom Otter – all appear separately before appearing together. But with the College it is their group presence rather than their several identities that is important. In context they represent a major crescendo in the growing volume of noise to which the unfortunate Morose is subjected, and the fact that they arrive in concert makes the intrusion all the more spectacular. More generally, however, the Collegiates present an image of monstrous female sexuality, rampant and insatiable. Their names, as many critics have pointed out, suggest their nature: Lady Haughty needs no comment, Lady Centaure's name derives its force from the proverbial lustfulness of the half-horse half-man and E. B. Partridge supplies us with a useful gloss on Mistress Mavis from Florio's Italian dictionary (1611) – "maviso", for "malviso", an ill face'.[5]

The defense of polyandry which they present to the supposed novice Epicoene, with the aid of Daw and La-Foole, is certainly repulsive enough:

> *Haughty* . . . Why should women deny their favours to men? Are they
> the poorer, or the worse?
> *Daw.* Is the Thames less for dyers' water, mistress?
> *La Foole.* Or a torch for lighting many torches?
> . . .   .
> *Centaure.* They are empty losses women fear in this kind.
> *Haughty.* Besides, ladies should be mindful of the approach of age, and let
> no time want his due use. The best of our days pass first.
> *Mavis.* We are rivers that cannot be called back, madam: she that now
> excludes her lovers may live to lie a forsaken beldam in a frozen
> bed.   IV iii 31–41

The obscenity derives partly from the way that Jonson localises the passage from Ovid's *Ars Amatoria* on which this is based. The 'vast waters' of the sea in the original become the revoltingly polluted Thames; Ovid's image of one lamp used to light another in La Foole's version has the customary Elizabethan innuendo about venereal disease.[6] Even more, though, it is hearing the Ovidian sophistries in the mouths of women which makes this passage grotesquely comic. The vision of a loveless old age in a cold bed:

> Tempus erit quo tu, quae nunc excludit amantes,
>   frigida deserta nocte iacebis anus.
> The time will come when you, who now keep out lovers,
> Will lie in bed at night, an old woman, cold and forsaken.

is an appropriate terrorist technique in the lover's campaign to reduce the woman's defenses and as such it is commonly employed by Renaissance love-poets. The same words spoken by a Mistress Mavis have the ludicrousness of the woman pre-empting the man's role.

The final attack of the 'mankind generation' upon Morose comes in the divorce scene. Their reaction when he confesses to impotence as a pretext to have his marriage annulled is voiced in a comic chorus of indignation:

> *Morose.* I am no man, ladies.
>   *All.* How!
> *Morose.* Utterly unabled in nature, by reason of frigidity, to perform
>   the duties of any of the least offices of a husband.
>   *Mavis.* Now, out upon him, prodigious creature!
> *Centaure.* Bridegroom uncarnate.
> *Haughty.* And would you offer it, to a young gentlewoman?
> *Mrs. Otter.* A lady of her longings?   V iv 40—7

Mrs. Otter even goes so far as to suggest that they should strip him to make sure that he is telling the truth. The image of the man at bay, unable to defend himself against the voracious sexual demands of a pack of women, is a fantastic comic scene which Wycherley was to use again in a very different context. Horner's plot to deceive husbands succeeds only too well and the laugh is on him as he stands on stage panting and desperately fending off insistent requests for more 'china'. What Wycherley and Jonson bring out is the comic discrepancy between the supposed female ignorance and modesty about sex and their actual outrage at the idea of an impotent man. 'Filthy French beast' says Lady Fidget. If one myth about women involved romantic idealisation or disincarnation, another equally available tradition was the devouring and insatiable female. In *Epicoene* Jonson obtains a part of his comic effect by bouncing one off the other.

The men, however, hardly come off much better than the women. Sir

John Daw and Sir Amorous La Foole are suitable intimates for the Collegiates, half-men to their half-women. Clerimont comments on Sir Amorous after his first appearance, 'Did you ever hear such a wind-fucker as this?' This is apparently an alternative name for what Hopkins made famous as the windhover. The kestrel was presumably so called for the same reason that the O.E.D. gives for 'windhover' — 'from its habit of hovering or hanging in the air with its head to the wind'. 'Windfucker', with all its associations, is Sir Amorous La Foole, (and Sir John Daw for that matter) to the life. With them both, as with Don Armado in *Love's Labour's Lost*, the pretension to learning, to valour, or to fashion, are all linked to sexual boastfulness. They are windbags, all talk and no performance. The baiting of the pair of them involves a double exposure of both forms of their vainglory. First there is the blind-man's buff scene in which they are dishonoured as cowards before the unseen audience of the ladies. Then they are lured on to confess that they have both enjoyed the favours of Epicoene: they politely defer to one another as to which of them had the honour of her maidenhead. In the final scene, when it is made clear that Epicoene had no maidenhead to lose, they are utterly disgraced with the contemptuous dismissal of Truewit:

> You are they that, when no merit or fortune can make you hope to enjoy their bodies, will yet lie with their reputations and make their fame suffer. Away, you common moths of these and all ladies' honours.
>
> V iv 210—13
>
> Exeunt windfuckers, disconsolate.

If *Epicoene* needed to be defended against the charge that it was conventionally anti-feminist, the best evidence to produce would be the attitudes expressed by the men, the he-fools of the play. Sir John Daw's madrigal is funny for reasons other than the awfulness of the verse:

> Silence in women is like speech in man,
>   Deny't who can.
>   Nor is't a tale
> That female vice should be a virtue male,
> Or masculine vice, a female virtue be:
>   You shall it see
>   Proved with increase
> I know to speak, and she to hold her peace.   II iii 111—19

Sir John's speech throughout the play is hardly such as to commend it as a masculine virtue, and his praise of female silence is enough to discredit an attitude common in the period — remember *King Lear*. His gloss on the lines, however, turns them into a still grosser parody of the male chauvinist role:

> *Daw* . . . Do you conceive me gentlemen?
> *Dauphine.* No faith; how mean you "with increase", Sir John?
> *Daw.* Why "with increase" is when I court her for the common cause of mankind, and she says nothing, but *consentire videtur*, and in time is *gravida*.   II iii 120—5

The egregious self-satisfaction of Sir John's vision, its monstrous egoism, is a splendid satire on the ideal of mute sexual submissiveness. Tom Otter's view of marriage, when his wife is absent and he has taken on enough courage from his bull, bear, and horse, is similarly primitive. 'Wife', he says, 'there's no such thing in nature. I confess, gentlemen, I have a cook, a laundress, a house-drudge, that serves my necessary turns, and goes under that title' (IV ii 49—51). If the main comedy of this scene is to watch the menial wife so described appear and batter the unfortunate Captain Otter for his insolence, it reveals also the inherent absurdity of the part of lord and master which he is trying to play.

It is of central significance that Morose subscribes to an ideal of wifely submission related to that caricatured through the speeches of Daw and Otter. Morose examines Epicoene as he might consider a purchase in the market — 'He goes about her, and views her' is Jonson's stage direction.

> She is exceeding fair and of a special good favour; a sweet composition or harmony of limbs; her temper of beauty has the true height of my blood. The knave [Cutbeard] hath exceedingly well fitted me without; I will now try her within.   II v 15—18

He goes on to test her out on possible defects of character, courtly manners, flirtatiousness, interest in fashion. Her deferential submissiveness — 'I leave it to wisdom and you, sir' — has him in ecstasies. He decides immediately that this is 'her whom I shall choose for my heifer'. He anticipates possible objections from his adviser, or rather supplier, Cutbeard:

> I know what thou woulds't say, she is poor and her friends deceased; she has brought a wealthy dowry in her silence, Cutbeard, and in respect of her poverty, Cutbeard, I shall have her more loving and obedient
> II v 78—81

Arnolphe, we remember, had a similar point of view.

En femme, comme en tout, je veux suivre ma mode.
Je me vois riche assez pour pouvoir, que je croi,
Choisir une moitié qui tienne tout de moi,
Et de qui la soumise et pleine dépendance
N'ait à me reprocher aucun bien ni naissance.   I i 124–8

Morose's desire to conceal himself, to hide away from the noise of the public world, is related to a posessiveness like Arnolphe's, a desire to have absolute control over what is his.

Ian Donaldson has pointed out that the invasion of Morose's house by strangers is a sort of *charivari*, the cacophanous and insulting ceremony commonly performed 'under the window of an old dotard married . . . unto a young wanton, in mockery of them both'.[7] A list of other occasions of the *charivari* given by E. K. Chambers, which Donaldson also cites, makes it clear that it was used to deride a whole variety of forms of marital disharmony or incongruity – 'a hen-pecked husband or a wife-beater, a shrew or an unchaste woman'.[8] It is, of course, ironic that those taking part in Jonson's *charivari* would many of them be suitable objects of this type of mockery themselves; the Ladies Collegiates, and particularly Mrs. Otter, would certainly qualify as shrews. The punishment of Morose, however, is appropriate just because he has tried to make his marriage a private secret affair; he has assumed that he can take a wife as he might make a bargain, behind closed doors. This is a denial of marriage as a social institution and society takes its revenge. In place of the public celebration which Morose would not have, he gets the public pillory of the *charivari*. A similar principle is being illustrated here as in the end of *L'Ecole des Femmes*: marriage and taking in marriage is never merely the acquisition of private property, and the Arnolphes and Moroses who work on this hypothesis are given exemplary comic punishment.

The tone and attitude of *Epicoene*, however, is very different from that of *L'Ecole des Femmes*. Arnolphe's tyrannical male egoism was steadily out-manoeuvred and ultimately defeated by the growth of a love which, as we saw in an earlier chapter, came to be recognised as naturally admirable and socially desirable. In *Epicoene* there is no such positive force of normality to set against the variety of perverse sexual attitudes which the play comically embodies. In place of Agnès, indeed, we find Mistress Epicoene, as sexually ambiguous as most of the rest of the characters. The part of Epicoene is surely one of the most interesting uses made by a Renaissance playwright of the boy-actor. Just what effect did Jonson intend by having his plot turn on a boy, played by a boy, disguised first as a modest maid, then as a termagant wife? There is Pepys's fascinating testimony about the effect of Kynaston, one of the last boy-actors, in the part in an early Restoration production:

> . . . to the Theatre and there saw *The Silent Woman*, the first time that
> ever I did see it and it is an excellent play. Among other things here,
> Kinaston the boy hath the good turn to appear in three shapes: 1, as a poor
> woman in ordinary clothes to please Morose; then in fine clothes as a
> gallant, and in them was clearly the prettiest woman in the whole house —
> and lastly, as a man; and then likewise did appear the handsomest man in
> the house.[9]

A standard complaint of the Puritan anti-theatre lobby throughout the
Elizabethan and Jacobean period was the lewdness and immorality of the
boy-actors playing women. Whether or not Jonson intended *Epicoene* to be
as bisexually attractive as Kynaston seems to have played her/him, there
can be little doubt that the play makes capital out of his/her epicene
nature.

Disguise plots with the boy-actors playing girls playing boys are of course
common enough to the drama of the period. Outside of Shakespeare, Lyly's
Gallathea, played like *Epicoene* by a children's company, supplies a situation
with complex layers upon layers of irony. What makes *Epicoene* to some
degree exceptional is partly that it has sexual perversity as its explicit theme
and partly that the disguise is kept as a secret from us, the theatre audience, as
well as from the characters on stage. The contrast with Shakespeare's boy-
girl-boy roles is striking. Rosalind's feminine nature is well-established
before she assumes her masculine disguise. Her pert page-boy cynicism
about women, when she is schooling Orlando out of love, is always offset by
her outbursts of emotion as soon as her lover leaves. 'O, coz, coz, coz, my
pretty little coz, that thou didst know how many fathom deep I am in love'.
The old cliché about Shakespeare's use of disguise-plots to make the
heroine's parts easier for boy-actors has now been thoroughly discredited.[10]
The Elizabethan boy-actors were evidently trained to play quite convincing
women, and when Shakespeare has Rosalind, Viola, or Portia appear in
masculine disguise, it was to add another dimension to their femininity
rather than to allow them to appear as the boys they actually were. If
anything, Shakespeare seems to have created deliberately difficult situations
to show the virtuosity of his 'boy-actress', as in the audacious lines in *Antony
and Cleopatra* —

> I shall see
> Some squeaking Cleopatra boy my greatness
> I' the posture of a whore.

In Jonson, the boy-actor plays at first an unnaturally submissive 'silent woman'; then he plays an equally exaggerated flighty wife, the sort of female caricature which Rosalind produces for the therapeutic benefit of Orlando. But what emerges finally as the truth is not a mean between the two, an ideal feminine nature like that of the undisguised Rosalind or Viola, but a boy who has been able to parody the different female roles.

Jonson has been criticised for the suprise ending of *Epicoene*, but its effect is more than that of a sensational *coup de théâtre*. It has an important function in the exposure and humiliation of the comic butts: Sir Amorous and Sir John's sexual pretensions are exploded by it, as we have seen, and the Collegiates are mortified to discover that their 'mysteries' have been revealed to a young gentleman. Epicoene has been the cuckoo in several different nests. Even more signally, however, it calls in question attitudes towards sexual roles which we in the audience have been encouraged to adopt through the play. We have laughed along with Morose's gullibility in supposing that the silent woman could be genuine. We have seen Epicoene growing into an immodest virago like her associates the Collegiates. But 'she' was a boy not a woman all along. In so far as our assumptions through the play have been based on traditional concepts of what is normally masculine and feminine, this final revelation must undermine those assumptions altogether. What may have looked to begin with like a reactionary anti-feminist vision, has turned into a much more radical scepticism about the nature of sexuality itself.

'*Epicoene*', E. B. Patridge tells us, 'is a comedy about nature, normality, and decorum'. He goes on to add:

> though the play offers no final answers, it suggests throughout that the various answers dramatised in the physical and verbal action of the play are comic in so far as they violate certain standards of what is masculine and what is feminine, as well as what is natural and what is artificial in dress, behaviour, and beauty — standards which, presumably, the spectators bring to the theatre with them.[11]

This is cautiously phrased to avoid the impression that Jonson's intentions are crudely didactic, yet it confirms what has become the orthodox critical view of the moral vision underlying Jonsonian comedy. Many critics, of whom Partridge is one of the most outstanding, have taught us to read Jonson's plays as deliberate grotesque distortions of the traditional moral and spiritual ideals of his audience, confirming those ideals by satiric parody. There can be no doubt that the comedy of a play such as *Epicoene* does derive from the violation of norms, as Partridge suggests, but whether, as he presumes, these norms are the ordinary standards brought to the theatre by the spectators seems more questionable. The danger of this sort of argument has always been that it assumes too direct an equation between the normal moral views of the audience, and the implied attitudes which the comedian invites them to share within the play.

The problem of this approach becomes particularly clear when we turn our attention to the characters in *Epicoene* who would seem to be there to represent a normal viewpoint, Clerimont, Truewit, and Dauphine. Critics have disagreed in trying to identify the authoritative Jonsonian spokesman among this trio. Jonas Barish is in no doubt that it is Truewit who is central and contrasts his intellectual poise with the shallowness of Clerimont and Dauphine.[12] Robert Knoll, on the contrary, argues that Truewit is to be judged critically against the standard of the urbane and courtly Dauphine.[13] E. B. Partridge suggests that none of the three are exempt from satire: 'The play's ironic exposure extends to the young gentlemen as well as the old.'[14] We have encountered this critical game of 'hunt the *raisonneur*' before in connection with *Bartholomew Fair*, but in *Epicoene* it seems more appropriate, as Dauphine, Clerimont, and Truewit are certainly Jonson's satiric presenters in a way in which Quarlous and Winwife are not, in spite of the superficial similarity of their position as gentlemanly onlookers. The distribution of audience approval among the wits of *Epicoene* is a matter of genuine importance in the structure of the play.

Jonson's technique, in fact, appears to involve never allowing his audience to settle into a confirmed preference for one of these three over the other two. The play opens with Clerimont dressing and his conversation with his page boy first sets the tone for our attitude towards the Collegiates. His song 'Still to be Neat' is an epigrammatic statement of the ideal of simplicity against feminine artifice. When Truewit retorts with a defense of cosmetics, borrowed like so much else in the play from Ovid's *Ars Amatoria*, the effect is that of outrageous irony.[15] Clerimont here takes on the role of straight man to Truewit's clown; they share the same satiric attitude and the mock dispute of nature versus art is only a strategy for its comic expression. When Dauphine enters, however, and even more after Truewit leaves, it seems as though there is a discrimination between Dauphine and Clerimont, the gentleman courtiers, and Truewit, whose social level would seem to be nearer to that of the bourgeois Collegiates. Truewit is not let into the secret of Dauphine's plot and Clerimont is reproached for blabbing to an outsider even though 'Truewit's a very honest fellow'. The result is Truewit's comic blunder when he tries to dissuade Morose from the very marriage which Dauphine has contrived for him. After this has been cleared up, however, Truewit, in his determination to make good his mistake, virtually takes control of the plot and stage-manages the whole series of tricks and gullings that follow. Clerimont and Dauphine appear no more than his assistants. Yet when the secret of Epicoene's sex is revealed, which Dauphine has kept back from Clerimont as well as Truewit, the latter acknowledges: 'Well, Dauphine, you have lurched your friends of the better half of the garland, by concealing this part of the plot', (V iv 199–200). But even as Truewit resigns his role as master-wit, he launches into the final speech of the play in which he dispenses comic judgement on all the fools, and invites the audience to approve with applause.

There is, indeed, a good deal to puzzle us in this shifting pattern of prominence among the wits if we are trying to pin down a definitive Jonsonian position which his audience would have shared. The emphasis on the ideal of gentlemanly urbanity in Dauphine and Clerimont is unusual in Jonson, though it was no doubt the reason why Dryden and the Restoration comedians so distinguished *Epicoene* with praise and imitation. We might possibly seek an explanation in the circumstances of the play's production in a private theatre, and therefore, perhaps, for a rather different audience from King's Men plays such as *Volpone* and *The Alchemist*. Yet the tradition of comic knights is so strong in Jacobean comedy, public and private, – Sir Politic Would-be, Sir Epicure Mammon, Sir Petronel Flash in *Eastward Ho* – that it is surely remarkable to find Sir Dauphine Eugenie apparently to be approved specifically for his knighthood. At least it seems reasonable to make the assumption that because Morose detests him for being a knight and expends considerable jealous venom on the contemplation of his rank, we in the audience are expected to think well of him for it. It is certainly not like the title which Sir Amorous La Foole acquired in the notorious wholesale knightings of Essex's Irish expedition (I iv 53). There can be little doubt that, with a name which means 'well-born heir', a knighthood is an appropriate title, not the meaningless handle which the Jacobean inflation of honours had made such a laughing-stock.

Yet if Dauphine was intended as a model of aristocratic behaviour, why does he 'fall in love' with the Collegiates? Even his friends protest at his confession that he is enamoured of all the ladies at once. 'Out on thee! We'll keep you at home, believe it, i' the stable an' you be such a stallion' (IV i 123–4). With one of Dauphine's spiritual descendents in Restoration comedy there would be no need for an explanation, since it is a regular hypothesis that the Restoration rake's appetite is limitless, however coarse the fare. But in *Epicoene* the repulsiveness of the ladies is so lovingly established that it is hard to imagine any normal man wanting to possess them, especially not if he were supposed to have delicate or fastidious tastes. We may well wonder why so much trouble is taken to transfer the collegiates' affections from Daw and La Foole to Dauphine, since their favour is a dubious honour, to say the least.

Problems such as these necessarily arise if we attempt a comparative moral evaluation of the three wits as standards of behaviour. Some of them disappear as problems if we see that all three are used as part of a comic strategy, not one rather than the others. Jonas Barish is probably right in pointing to the central function of Truewit in this respect, but that centrality is not achieved by contrast with his two companions. Truewit's attitude is exemplary only in so far as he enunciates self-consciously the view of life which is more or less common to all three. His opening speeches to Clerimont are half-serious, half-spoof reflections on time:

> O, Clerimont, this time, because it is an incorporeal thing and not subject to sense, we mock ourselves the fineliest out of it, with vanity and misery indeed, not seeking an end of wretchedness, but only changing the matter still.   I i 47–50

Clerimont will have none of Truewit's 'stoicity', and Truewit resigns himself with a shrug to joining in the foolish frivolities of society 'for company'. From then on, his object is to make himself and others sport by drawing out the absurdities of the men-women and the women-men. It is in this sense that he is the true wit, the man who can make satiric amusement for himself out of the idleness of society. And in this Clerimont and Dauphine are seen to be with him. Truewit may have a firmer sense of the limits of practical joking – he is shocked at Dauphine's proposal that they actually cut off one of Daw's limbs: 'How! Maim a man forever for a jest? What a conscience hast thou!' – but neither the proposal nor the reproof is entirely serious. He is the purer jester in that he is disinterested where Dauphine has an end to gain and he is therefore the appropriate person to give the final comic address to the audience. But Dauphine and Clerimont, as much as Truewit, are *agents provocateurs* leading the fools on to betray themselves. This is the point of Dauphine's 'love' for the Collegiates which Barish complains of as 'fatuous'. So it would be if we took it literally. In fact it is one more plot, one more scheme, to expose by assuming a protective camouflage of fatuity the fatuousness of the wits' social companions.

Ian Donaldson has tried to align *Epicoene* with the tradition of festive comedy and points out that its action takes place on the day that Sir Amorous La Foole is holding his 'quarter-day feast'.[16] This is perhaps less prominent than the anti-festivity of the *charivari*, which he also discusses. *Epicoene* is not like *Bartholomew Fair* in centering its comic structure round a specific holiday occasion. Yet the play's form does provide limits which suggest that the abnormality of its action is fantastic or exceptional. The perversion of sexual roles which we find in *Epicoene* is not a direct satire upon Jacobean London of 1609, though L. G. Salingar is no doubt right to alert us to the verisimilitude of the background of metropolitan life. [17] Instead Jonson invites us to join in for one day in a world in which women band together in monstrous regiment over their husbands, in which men are impotent and inadequate, in which marriage is a mating made preposterous by the interchangeability of the sexes. In case anyone in the audience were inclined to assume an attitude of moral outrage towards this spectacle Jonson asks us to share the stance of gentlemen wits, involved voluntarily with the epicene fools for the purposes of amusement, yet detached by their superior culture and ironic intelligence.

LES FEMMES SAVANTES

Les Femmes Savantes has very often been considered in relation to Molière's earlier comedy against preciosity and one critic has argued that it was first conceived not long after *Les Précieuses Ridicules*. [18] There can certainly be no doubt about the connections between the two plays. *Les Femmes Savantes* begins with Armande adopting the anti-matrimonial position of the earlier *précieuses*, although she expresses it more eloquently and elegantly. The very word marriage, she tells her sister, is nauseating:

> Ne concevez-vous point ce que, dès qu'on l'entend,
> Un tel mot à l'esprit offre de dégoûtant?
> De quelle étrange image on est par lui blessée?
> Sur quelle sale vue il traîne la pensée? I i 9– 12

She does not make this explicit as the cruder Cathos did – 'comment est-ce qu'on peut souffrir la pensée de coucher contre un homme vraiment nu' – but it is clear that this is the 'étrange image' which she has in mind. For Henriette marriage and its physical consequences have no terrors:

> Les suites de ce mot, quand je les envisage,
> Me font voir un mari, des enfants, un ménage;
> Et je ne vois rien là, si j'en puis raisonner,
> Qui blesse la pensée et fasse frissonner. I i 15– 18

Armande urges on her sister a marriage to philosophy, by which she may submit her animal appetites to the restraint of reason. Henriette protests that temperaments differ, and what suits her sister would not suit her.

> Habitez, par l'essor d'un grand et beau génie,
> Les hautes régions de la philosophie,
> Tandis que mon esprit, se tenant ici-bas,
> Goûtera de l'hymen less terrestres appas.   I i 63–6

In comedy, we tend to be sceptical about renunciations of marriage and we are prepared to be suspicious of Armande's professions of celibacy, as we were with those of Magdelon and Cathos or of the academe in *Love's Labour's Lost*, especially when it is revealed towards the end of the scene that all of Armande's lofty reproaches of her sister are related to the fact that Clitandre, formerly her lover, has transferred his affection to Henriette. What started out as an apparently philosophical debate over the value of marriage ends as a sisterly slanging-match of the 'He's mine!' 'He's mine!' variety.

Armande is shown throughout the play to be that species of prude-coquette whose coquetry is even less forgivable than that of Cathos and Magdelon in that she wants to hold on to those whom her beauty attracts, while granting them neither love nor marriage. *Les Femmes Savantes*, however, is unlike *Les Précieuses* in that it is not principally concerned with the vagaries of adolescent girls before marriage. Armande forms one of a company with Philaminte, her mother, and Bélise, her aunt, who together represent a cabale equivalent to Jonson's Collegiates. If the play does not show us a whole society taken over by women, it gives us at least that typical Molièrean microcosm for society, the bourgeois household, in chaotic feminist insurrection. In Molière, as in Jonson, the idea of the association of women is crucial. Philaminte has plans for an academy to display the ability of women:

> Et je veux nous venger, toutes tant que nous sommes,
> De cette indigne classe où nous rangent les hommes,
> De borner nos talents à des futilités,
> Et nous fermer la porte aux sublimes clartés.   III ii 853–6

The academy of *femmes savantes* is planned to discuss philosophy and grammar, whereas the College in Jonson is no more than an ironic courtesy title. In both plays, however, the point is not the ostensible purpose of the league of women, but the challenge to sexual norms represented by the league itself.

Looking through the cast-list of *Les Femmes Savantes* given in the

Répertoire of 1685 it comes as something of a surprise to discover Philaminte listed with the men's parts.[19] The part was, in fact, almost certainly created by Hubert, the actor in Molière's company who specialised in 'les rôles d'hômmes en femme'.[20] Molière's editors warn us against making the assumption that because Philaminte was played by a man, Molière intended a crude masculine caricature.[21] Hubert, who also played Mme. Jourdain in *Le Bourgeois Gentilhomme*, was no doubt as capable of a convincing performance as a woman as the boy-actor who took on Epicoene. But the comedy of Philaminte who wears the trousers in Chrysale's household would have been enhanced by the knowledge that she was impersonated by a male actor. Philaminte is in the tradition of comic shrews; she is Mistress Otter in her treatment of her husband, as well as Lady Haughty in her leadership of the *femmes savantes*. We first meet Philaminte when Chrysale is trying to persuade her to revoke her sentence of dismissal on the maid Martine. She there pursues the time-honoured shrew's technique of indignant reproach – 'Quoi? vouz la soutenez? . . . Prenez-vous son parti contre moi?' – 'What? are you supporting her? . . . Are you taking her part against me?' – so that it takes the unfortunate Chrysale half a scene to discover what sin of solecism Martine has committed, and by then he is too demoralised to question her decision. Philaminte is the supreme authority of the family:

C'est elle qui gouverne, et d'un ton absolu
Elle dicte pour loi ce qu'elle a résolu.   I iii 209–10

When Henriette appears deliberately to challenge that authority Philaminte resolves to teach her a lesson:

Je lui montrerai bien aux lois de qui des deux
Les droits de la raison soumettent tous ses voeux.
Et qui doit gouverner, ou sa mère ou son père
Ou l'esprit ou le corps, la forme ou la matière.   IV ii 1127–30

Part of what makes this funny is that 'corps' and 'matière' are so obviously the appropriate terms to describe the materialist Chrysale. But also there is the reversal of the traditional commonplace, deriving from Aristotle, by which the man was considered to supply form in procreation, the woman only matter. Philaminte not only usurps her husband's position as head of the family, she takes over the argument which normally justifies that position.

Bélise, the stupidest and most gloriously comic of the *femmes savantes*, represents a different sort of parody of the conventional female role. Molière apparently found in *Les Visionnaires* of Desmarets de Saint-Sorlin a character that suggested the *manie* of Bélise, continually imagining men in love with her. The systematic misconstructions of Bélise are made possible by the *précieuse* convention of mute platonic love which can never be directly expressed. She cuts off Clitandre in what she assumes is going to be a declaration of love to herself:

> Ah! tout beau, gardez-vous de m'ouvrir trop votre âme:
> Si je vous ai su mettre au rang de mes amants,
> Contentez-vous des yeux pour vos seuls truchements,
> Et ne m'expliquez point par un autre langage
> Des désirs qui chez moi passent pour un outrage   I iv 276—86

But if plain-speaking is ruled out, then disavowal is also impossible, as Clitandre finds out to his cost when increasingly desperate attempts to convince Bélise that he is not in love with her are all interpreted as adroit moves in the *précieuse* charade. For Cathos and Magdelon, as we saw in the previous chapter, the prolonged and indirect courtship of the *précieux* tradition was the pretext for endlessly renewed flirtation. With Bélise, presumably past the time of life for flirtation, it enables her to maintain her delusion of being universally desired.

The decorum of Molière's theatre would not have allowed him to suggest the sexuality of his *femmes savantes* with the explicitness Jonson uses in *Epicoene*. Yet he did manage to undermine the ethereal hyperboles of *précieux* language with involuntary sexual associations. By transferring a language of the passions to aesthetic experience, the *précieuses* left themselves open to the sort of comic innuendo which reverses the transference. Philaminte, Armande, and Bélise implore Trissotin to begin his reading:

> *Philaminte.* Ne faites point languir de si pressants désirs.
> *Armande.* Dépêchez.
> *Bélise.*   Faites tôt, et hâtez nos plaisirs.   III i 717—8

The absurdly exaggerated urgency of the demands turns this into a comic chorus of desire. The reading of the sonnet is punctuated with cries of enthusiasm and ecstasy culminating in the reaction when it is over:

> *Bélise.* Ah! tout doux, laissez-moi, de grâce, respirer.
> *Armande.* Donnez-nous, s'il vous plaît, le loisir d'admirer.
> *Philaminte.* On se sent à ces vers, jusques au fond de l'âme,
>   Couler je ne sais quoi qui fait que l'on se pâme.
>   III ii 776—9

One critic has traced Philaminte's 'je ne sais quoi' half way across Renaissance literature to illustrate the full range of its resonances.[22] What is perhaps most immediately relevant is that it is a phrase used again and again by Corneille and others to evoke the uncontrollable passion of love. It would be an indelicate overstatement to say that what Molière here gives us is a group orgasm, but he certainly contrives to suggest that sexual energies have a part in the delight the ladies express.[23]

This partly erotic reaction is made all the more ludicrous by the inadequacies of its object. The Abbé Cotin, whose sonnet and epigram Molière borrowed, evidently wrote some bad poetry, but Trissotin, the caricature of Cotin, is not only ridiculed as a poetaster. His first lines, mock-modestly deprecating the verse he is entreated to read, are as absurd as the poetry itself:

> Hélas! c'est un enfant tout nouveau-né, Madame.
> Son sort assurément a lieu de vous toucher,
> Et c'est dans votre cour, que j'en viens d'accoucher. III i 720–2

The metaphor of composition as giving birth is so conventional that we would not notice it, if it were not for Trissotin's insistence on extending it to the lengths of parturition in the salon. One is reminded perhaps of the coarser, but comparable, speech of the constipated Blepyros in *Ecclesiasuzae*, calling on the goddess of childbirth to relieve his pangs. The dubious masculinity of Trissotin is appropriate to his position as idol of the *femmes savantes*. His deferential feminism marks him as the tame man of the female cabale:

> Pour les dames on sait mon respect en tous lieux;
> Et, si je rends hommage aux brillants de leurs yeux,
> De leur esprit aussi j'honore les lumières. III ii 863–5

Trissotin and Vadius are much less gross caricatures than Sir Amorous La foole and Sir John Daw, but they occupy a similar position as the 'servants' of the ladies. In both plays intellectual and creative impotence is expressed partly through sexual inadequacy.

One of the major perversions of the *femmes savantes* is the attempt to marry off Henriette to Trissotin. It is not only an indication of the *entêtment* of Philaminte, willing to sacrifice her daughter to her feminism, as Argan wants to sacrifice his to his hypochondria, or Orgon his to his religious mania. Trissotin's lack of all lover-like feeling is apparent in the scene in which Henriette pleads with him to give up the idea of marriage. Henriette is driven to hint that forced marriage might lead to cuckoldry, but Trissotin is unmoved:

> Un tel discours n'a rien dont je sois altéré
> A tous événements le sage est préparé;
> Guéri par la raison des foiblesses vulgaires,
> Il se met par-dessus de ces sortes d'affaires,
> Et n'a garde de prendre aucune ombre d'ennui
> De tout qui n'est pas pour dépendre de lui.   V i 1543–8

A fascinating speech this, because we last heard this line of reasoning about cuckoldry from Molière in the mouth of Chrysalde, the *raisonneur* of *L'Ecole des Femmes*. In the earlier context, it was presented as a preferable attitude to that of the horn-obsessed Arnolphe. Here Trissotin's claim to despise the prospect of cuckoldry seems the ultimate indication of his lack of decent manly feeling; he can pretend to philosophical indifference about marital dishonour because marriage is for him a matter of material advantage, not of real emotional fulfilment. No passage in Molière illustrates better the dangers of attempting to work out a consistent set of Molièrean principles on the basis of the views his characters express in different plays.

Within *Les Femmes Savantes* itself, in fact, there might be room for doubt as to who is Molière's spokesman against the ridiculous bluestockings. It is certainly not Chrysale. The very fact that his part was played by Molière in the original production would be enough to confirm our view of the blustering hen-pecked husband as a comic butt. As with Tom Otter, the comedy of Chrysale derives largely from his show of bravado when not in the face of the enemy, followed by total collapse of stout party when she appears. He says grandly of Clitandre's suit to Henriette, 'Je réponds de ma femme, et prends sur moi l'affaire', 'I answer for my wife, and take the matter on myself', but when he actually meets Philaminte he never even gets round to mentioning it. In philosophical terms, Chrysale is a comic anti-Cartesian. Where the ladies, accepting Descartes' mind-body dualism, insist on the primacy of mind –

> Le corps, cette guenille, est-il d'une importance
> D'un prix à mériter seulement qu'on y pense . . .?   II vii 539–40

Chrysale retorts that it certainly is:

> Oui, mon corps est moi-même, et j'en veux prendre soin.
> Guenille si l'on veut, ma guenille m'est chère.   II vii 541–2

Chrysale's exasperated materialism is understandable and delightfully funny in context, but the Philistinism of the man who orders all the books in the house to be burned except for 'un gros Plutarque à mettre mes rabats', 'a fat Plutarch to press my collars', is quite as ludicrous as his wife's intellectual pretensions.

Chrysale's loyal aide-de-camp is Martine, the maid who makes mincemeat of the grammatical rules of Vaugelas. Molière's comic maids are very often enlisted on the side of the *raisonneurs*, supplying a viewpoint of pragmatic commonsense to support the higher ideal of reason. This is the function most notably of Dorine in *Tartuffe* or Toinette in *Le Malade Imaginaire*. But Martine is not as intelligent as Dorine or Toinette. Molière's Parisian audience would no doubt have laughed at her thick local-yokel dialect, even though they laughed as well at Philaminte and Bélise trying to school her in Vaugelas. Martine's closest relatives elsewhere in Molière are not the sharp wisecracking Toinettes and Dorines, but the slow-witted servants of *L'Ecole des Femmes*, Alain and Georgette. Bussy-Rabutin complained that this characterisation of Martine was not sustained consistently and that when she reappears later in the play to support Chrysale against Philaminte she is allowed some perfectly well-turned speeches.[24] It is true that Molière does largely drop the thick accent and the obvious solecisms, but the effect is no less comic for that. The whole situation is funny, with the maid arguing and the master solemnly nodding his head in agreement – 'C'est parler comme il faut', 'Fort bien', 'That is the way to talk', 'Very good' – but the views which Martine puts forward, including the approval of wife-beating, are grotesquely absurd. The speech which contains the lines Bussy-Rabutin thought too elegant is particularly delightful:

> Les savants ne sont bons que pour prêcher en chaise;
> Et pour mon mari, moi, mille fois je l'ai dit,
> Je ne voudrois jamais prendre un homme d'esprit.
> L'esprit n'est point du tout ce qu'il faut en ménage;
> Les livres cadrent mal avec le mariage;
> Et je veux, si jamais on engage ma foi,
> Un mari qui n'ait point d'autre livre que moi,
> Qui ne sache A ni B, n'en déplaise à Madame.
> Et ne soit en un mot docteur que pour sa femme.   V iii 1662–70

Substitute 'femme' for 'mari' throughout this speech, and what one would have would be the standard Arnolphe position on the ideal *Kinder, Küche, Kirche* wife. Martine, by her advocacy of the illiterate husband, involuntarily exposes the ridiculousness of the traditional male desire for an illiterate wife. What presumably most disturbs critics such as Adam who find *Les Femmes Savantes* disturbingly illiberal, is that Henriette and Clitandre seem to uphold seriously the view of male superiority and female deference in marriage, and the play apparently demands that we agree with them. Here, as always in Molière, we have to be careful to bear context in mind. The mock humility of Henriette, for instance, when she claims that her mind is only capable of down-to-earth matters such as marriage and a home, is used as part of an ironic strategy against her sister. (There was surely a further theatrical irony, whether intentional or not, in the fact that Henriette was played by Molière's wife, Armande, who was not exactly an example of the quiet stay-at-home type.) It is to Clitandre, however, rather than Henriette, that Molière gives the more explicit statement on women's learning:

> Je consens qu'une femme ait des clartés de tout;
> Mais je ne lui veux point la passion choquante
> De se rendre savante afin d'être savante;
> Et j'aime que souvent, aux questions qu'on fait,
> Elle sache ignorer les choses qu'elle sait;
> De son étude enfin je veux qu'elle se cache,
> Et qu'elle ait du savoir sans vouloir qu'on le sache,
> Sans citer les auteurs, sans dire de grands mots,
> Et clouer de l'esprit à ses moindres propos   I iii 218–26

At first sight this might seem pretty hard for a modern audience to stomach. The idea that women should be allowed a certain amount of knowledge, provided that they decorously conceal it (in male company implied), is likely to make the blood of even a moderate feminist boil. It scarcely helps to point out, as some critics have, that Mlle. de Scudéry, the greatest *précieuse* of them all, might have agreed with Clitandre.[25] Such information is not likely to make us agree with either of them.

Yet Clitandre's speech is not so egregiously male chauvinist as it might at first seem. His objection is not to feminine learning but to a certain sort of ostentatious display. The indecorum of a woman constantly parading her knowledge is as much a matter of ordinary social tact as it is of womanliness. This becomes clear when we see the very similar terms in which Clitandre condemns Trissotin later in the same scene:

> Je vis, dans le fatras des écrits qu'il nous donne,
> Ce qu'étale en tous lieux sa pédante personne:
> La constante hauteur de sa présomption

Cette intrépidité de bonne opinion,
Cet indolent état de confiance extrême,
Qui le rend en tout temps 'si content de soi-même   I iii 251—6

This sort of ostentatious self-congratulation is socially offensive whether in man or woman. Paul Benichou[26] is surely right to point out that the standards by which Clitandre judges here are those of the court, as is clear from his later defense of it against Trissotin:

elle [la cour] a du sens commun pour se connoître à tout;
. . . chez elle on se peut former quelque bon goût;
Et . . . l'esprit du monde y vaut, sans flatterie,
Tout le savoir obscur de la pédanterie.   IV iii 1344—7

It is against a courtly ideal of learning subordinated to graceful manners that both the *femmes savantes* and the *littérateurs* are found wanting.

Yet we need not accept Benichou's argument that Molière, throughout his work, upholds a point of view identifiably aristocratic. In his defense of court tastes in *Les Femmes Savantes*, as in *La Critique de L'Ecole des Femmes*, Molière probably wrote what he knew would be gratifying to the court audience whose support was so necessary to his plays. But the author of *L'Impromptu de Versailles*, *George Dandin*, or *Le Bourgeois Gentilhomme* was quite as capable of mocking the inanity and unscrupulousness of the aristocracy as of the bourgeoisie who aped them. Molière's use of the gentlemanly Clitandre in *Les Femmes Savantes* is no more indicative of a general pro-courtly point of view than Jonson's use of Clerimont and Dauphine in *Epicoene*. In both cases the comic strategy demands that we identify with an urbane and sophisticated persona, an 'honnête homme' in both meanings of the phrase, as audience sponsor and as gentleman. This does not mean necessarily that the two plays were directed up-market at the more aristocratic members of Jonson or Molière's audience. Rather the attitude of Clitandre or of the wits in *Epicoene* is generalised away from a recognisably class position — no great emphasis is laid on the aristocracy of these figures — to the point where it can be shared by an audience as a whole from whatever social group outside the theatre.

The audiences for *Les Femmes Savantes* and *Epicoene* are by implication urbane and sophisticated, just as for *Love's Labour's Lost* and *Les Précieuses Ridicules* they are mature and rational, for *The Alchemist* and *Le Malade Imaginaire* intelligent and commonsensical. The strategy in each case is to assign to the audience a vantage-point of superiority appropriate to the object of satire in the play. This may involve the assumption of attitudes which cannot simply be identified with their real-life counterparts: enjoying Molière's medical satires was not incompatible with believing in seventeenth century medicine; laughing at *Love's Labour's Lost* did not preclude the appreciation of florid Elizabethan poetry. And, similarly, joining in the mockery of the Collegiate Ladies or the *femmes savantes* was not necessarily a matter of endorsing a traditional anti-feminist position. The superiority of the comic audience is not merely an extension of a normally assumed masculine superiority. Although the satire of *Epicoene* and *Les Femmes Savantes* may rest upon assumptions about the normal roles of men and women within seventeenth century society and deride specific aberrations from that norm, we are encouraged finally to be sceptical about the whole range of sexual attitudes – those which were socially normal as well as those which were abnormal, male possessiveness as well as female assertive independence. Our final stance is not that of conservative anti-feminists reassured by a satiric parody of the monstrous regiment of women, but of detached observers delighting in the absurd and grotesque comedy of the sexes.

7 Follies and Crimes

Jonson gives us what is the entirely orthodox neo-classical theory deriving from Aristotle when he tells us in the Prologue to *Every Man in his Humour* that it is the function of comedy 'to sport with human follies not with crimes'. It is a definition which still influences the general idea of comedy, which, most people would feel, should be limited in the seriousness of its concerns, unless it is self-consciously 'black comedy'. What then of Jonson's own play *Volpone*: fraud, perjury, prostitution, conspiracy to murder, attempted rape – are these merely follies? *Volpone* has made many of Jonson's critics uneasy and uncertain of its classification. E. B. Partridge's comments are representative:

> Comic masks are not entirely appropriate for a play which creates such a profound sense of evil that the tone seems closer to tragedy than comedy . . . Is it satire, burlesque, farce, comedy of humour, melodrama? . . . all of these critical terms have some validity, but none is wholly justifiable.[1]

Similar problems of classification have arisen with Molière's *Tartuffe*, where equally the seriousness of the subject-matter seems to take the play outside the limits of comedy. The folly of Orgon becomes overshadowed by the crimes of Tartuffe. Is *Tartuffe* a *drame* rather than a comedy, as Brunetière suggested?[2] *Volpone* and *Tartuffe* may be taken as test-cases for the general question of how seriously comedy may threaten basic norms of order and truth. Does the comedian always have to pull his punches in order to retain his comic status? Does comedy always have to concern itself with minor human misdemeanours, or can it show more extreme forms of wickedness and evil and remain comedy?

VOLPONE

There can be no doubts from the opening moments of *Volpone* that we are being introduced into a corrupt and distorted world. It has become a critical commonplace to observe the perversion of religious language in Volpone's opening address to his gold.[3] But it is worth remarking also that it is the language of Catholicism which is being perverted. 'Open the shrine that I may see my saint . . . every relic of sacred treasure in this blessed room . . . Dear Saint . . . The price of souls; even hell, with thee to boot, Is made worth heaven' (I i 2—25). Presumably these are terms of which a Protestant audience of 1606 would be suspicious anyway, even without their being transferred blasphemously to material rather than heavenly things. From an English Protestant viewpoint, idolatry would have been idolatry, whether the object idolised was gold or saints' relics. It may be that the impression which this speech conjured up was less a sacrilegious inversion of traditional standards, as most critics have maintained, than a general sense of Italianate decadence in which religion and corruption were normally associated.

It is certainly the familiar picture of Italy in Renaissance drama which is evoked indirectly in this scene, a land of social and commercial as well as religious corruption. The means of making a living which Volpone eschews are significant: he has 'no mills for iron, oil, corn, *or men*, to grind 'em into powder'. Mosca takes up the theme.

> No, sir, nor devour
> Soft prodigals. You shall ha' some will swallow
> A melting heir as glibly as your Dutch
> Will pills of butter, and ne'er purge for't;
> Tear forth the fathers of poor families
> Out of their beds, and coffin them, alive,
> In some kind, clasping prison, where their bones
> May be forthcoming, when the flesh is rotten.
> But your sweet nature doth abhor these courses;
> You loathe the widow's or the orphan's tears
> Should wash your pavements, or their piteous cries
> Ring in your roofs, and beat the air for vengeance   I i 41—51

There was nothing un-English about the devouring of melting prodigals — Middleton's city comedies are about almost nothing else. Yet the imagery here, burial alive, flesh rotting from the bones, has the melodramatic strident quality which the Elizabethan dramatists so often associated with the exotic wickedness of foreign parts. Needless to say, the 'sweet nature' of Volpone may be viewed ironically. The purpose of the speech is to evoke the atmosphere of Volpone's environment rather than to establish him as an outstanding exception to it. We can see exactly where Mosca's flattery is leading when, at the end of the next speech, he adroitly begs something for himself from the 'bright heap' of gold Volpone has been adoring.

The monster show of Nano, Androgyno, and Castrone is also often taken to contribute to the play's special atmosphere of distortion. E. B. Partridge again makes the point eloquently:

> What these fools are is as functional as what they say. A eunuch, a dwarf, and an hermaphrodite — all are unnatural beings in whom the equipoise of body and soul has been disturbed. They are the living emblems of the perverted culture of this mean world.[4]

Harry Levin in an ingenious and influential article suggested that metempsychosis, the subject of the fools' playlet, gave the key to the central theme of *Volpone*, the degeneration of human beings into beasts.[5] All of this is true and illuminating. Yet it seems necessary to make some qualification to this sort of argument. The fool, eunuch, and hermaphrodite are no doubt grotesque degenerates, but they are also, or were certainly intended to be, entertaining. It is not so much that we have to be reminded that a Jacobean audience would have found them funny; the 1977 National Theatre production, for example, made it clear that even a modern audience could thoroughly enjoy their performance. In the original context, however, there was also the enjoyment of the stylistic parody, the old doggerel verse which was used by the early Tudor playwrights and which Jonson loved to take off. For the relatively sophisticated audience of the Globe (and perhaps for Jonson) there was surely an element of nostalgia in the mocking recollection of these primitive forms. No doubt the whole show is representative of Volpone's perverse tastes in entertainment, yet the audience in the theatre would have been entertained too, rather than sitting back in a mood of censorious disgust, as the tone of so many critics would lead us to believe.

It is always extremely difficult to assess this enjoyment of the repulsive and the grotesque. There can be no doubt that the central image of the beast fable in *Volpone* is disturbing with its monstrous, scarcely human, predators. And yet Voltore, Corbaccio, and Corvino, the human scavengers circling over the supposed dying fox, are extraordinarily funny. The successive visits of the three in the first act is a magnificently structured piece of comic theatre. Combined with the virtuoso skills of Volpone as dying invalid and Mosca who can modulate his sychophant's part to suit each different visitor, there is the self-revelation of the predators themselves. Voltore stands and smiles complacently as Mosca ironically describes the lawyer's art which has won him Volpone's esteem:

He ever liked your course, sir; that first took him.
I oft have heard him say how he admired
Men of your large profession, that could speak
To every cause, and things are contraries,
Till they were hoarse again, yet all be law;
That, with most quick agility, could turn,
And re-turn; make knots, and undo them;
Give forked counsel; take provoking gold
On either hand, and put it up.   I iii 51—9

Then Corbaccio —

A wretch who is indeed more impotent
Than this can feign to be, yet hopes to hop
Over his grave.   I iv 3—5

Jonson uses the simple gag of Corbaccio's deafness to excellent comic effect,
but the full grotesque humour of the scene is the wonder that a human being
so near total helplessness as Corbaccio should manage to retain so much
active greed and malevolence. Corbaccio's almost transparent unscrupulousness — he comes prepared to poison Volpone — is contrasted with the
conventional timidity of Corvino the 'spruce merchant' who comes next.
When Mosca boisterously suggests that they smother Volpone, he shies back
nervously. Yet this represents no real reluctance to commit the crime, only a
fear of being an accessory: 'Do as you will, but I'll be gone'. He has joined
happily with Mosca in the revolting barrage of insults which they fling at the
apparently insensible Volpone.

   Voltore, Corbaccio, and Corvino are utter monsters, far more extreme
caricatures than, say, the humour characters of Jonson's earlier plays, or even
than the various gulls in *The Alchemist*. Yet it is their very monstrous nature
which, in the context of the play, makes them funny. It is tough and pitiless
laughter. We share it with Mosca and Volpone as their allies in the deception
of the beasts of prey, yet this implies no more emotional identification with
them than we have for the fox or the crow in one of Aesop's fables. The
whole situation, the whole scene is distanced by its fantastic and grotesque
images. Volpone makes the identification of the beast-fable explicit and
overt for us:

Now, now, my clients
Begin their visitation! Vulture, kite,
Raven, and gorcrow, all my birds of prey,
That think me turning carcass, now they come.   I ii 88—90

(The kite would seem to be an anticipation of Lady Would-be, although Volpone does not yet know of her enrolment amongst his suitors.) He himself is 'a fox Stretched on the earth, with fine delusive sleights Mocking a gaping crow'. There is no question here of a representational comedy of manners with names merely hinting natures; these characters are all clearly labelled as half-animal, and the theatrical tradition of playing them with stylised beast costumes is surely justified by the text. The fact that they are all thus included in the beast-allegory removes them from the normal area of audience identification and we can laugh at them all, Volpone and Mosca included.

Sir Politic Would-be, who appears for the first time in Act II, seems a feeble and anomalous figure in this world of grotesques. Theatrical producers have tended to cut him out as an excrescence, and for years the critics had little more time for him. Since Jonas Barish pointed out that, as Sir Pol, he could be identified as a parrot and thus assimilated into the animal schema,[6] a variety of critical arguments have been advanced to support his integral function in the play. It may well be that Jonson introduced the abbreviation Sir Pol with the parrot-like features of chattering and mimicking in mind, but it seems unnecessary to pursue too far this line of interpretation, with Peregrine the hawk preying on Pol the parrot. (Do peregrines pursue parrots?) It seems clear that Sir Politic and Peregrine, whose name surely just means 'traveller', are intended to be distinct from the other characters, and to try to integrate them too closely with the main plot may be to miss their point. For, theatrically, their detachment from the Venetian setting, their Englishness, may have been important to Jonson's comic strategy.

From Act I to Act II we move out from the interior of Volpone's treasure-chamber into the piazza where Politic and Peregrine meet. They are fellow Englishmen abroad discussing the purposes of travelling. After a moment's puzzlement Peregrine identifies Sir Politic for what he is.

> *Peregrine.* (Aside) – This fellow, Does he gull me, trow? or is gulled? –
> Your name, sir?
> *Sir Politic.* My name is Politic Would-be.
> *Peregrine.* (Aside) – O, that speaks him –   II i 23 – 5

Sir Politic Would-be is as clear a designation as Volpone or Voltore. In a later aside Peregrine comments,

> O, this knight,
> Were he well known, would be a precious thing

> To fit our English stage. He that should write
> But such a fellow, should be thought to feign
> Extremely, if not maliciously.   II i 56–60

This is the sort of extra-dramatic joke with the audience which the Elizabethan and Jacobean dramatists used all the time, particularly in plays set abroad. It is a nudging reminder of the presentness and immediacy of the play in the theatre – alienation from the world of the play, but reaffirming direct communication with the world of the audience.

The general function of Sir Politic, in fact, may be as a sort of bridgehead for the English audience into the exotic and fantastic Venetian setting. The like of Sir Politic would presumably have been very familiar to them. All the topical allusions to the gossip of the time in Sir Politic's conversation would have acted like the constantly up-dated political jibes in a modern satirical revue. The familiar and banal is elaborated into the fantastic, as when Politic produces baroque details of the spying career of the well-known London clown Stone. Sir Politic is a home-grown idiot, quite different in comic character from the Venetian predators. Jonas Barish is surely right to emphasise the distinction between English folly and Italian vice in differentiating the two plots of *Volpone*. The joke is not so much that Politic mimics the role of Volpone the manipulator, it is that he is such a hopelessly inept mimic. To set up for a Machiavel in Italy, the land of Machiavelli, is ridiculous in any case; intrigues exported from England are real coals to Newcastle. But Sir Politic is so evidently and so thoroughly timid and law-abiding – 'I hope you travel, sir, with license? . . . I dare the safelier converse' – that his pretensions to politicking are ludicrously pathetic, and his comic punishment, pursued for his supposed treasonable practices, the more appropriate. In the genuinely corrupt world of Italy, he is a preposterously unaware, almost innocent, outsider. The English audience could scarcely have congratulated themselves on being countrymen of Sir Politic, yet in his relatively harmless imbecility he might have been reassuring. Italian vice was undoubtedly more interesting, more exciting than English folly, yet one might be a little relieved to be living among a nation of Sir Politics rather than a society of Volpones.

The mountebank scene which follows the introduction of Sir Politic could be used as a classic example of multiple dramatic irony. The revelation of Sir Pol's foolishness continues. Though Peregrine may never have been in Italy before, he can tell a charlatan when he sees one. Sir Politic assures him, we may feel partly out of a spirit of contradiction and a need to maintain his position of knowledgeable authority, that Scoto di Mantua and his like are 'the only knowing men of Europe'. For the original audience Scoto, who was a real mountebank of the sixteenth century and had been to England in 1576, would have been a familiar name, a byword for skilful deception.[7] They would no doubt have enjoyed his virtuoso display of rhetorical nonsense with the interspersed songs of the fools. Yet any audience will be aware that Scoto is not Scoto but Volpone, and the scene affords him a chance to exercise his acting powers in an energetic and lively part, the very opposite of his role as dying invalid. We know also that there is a purpose behind this piece of impersonation, and when Celia appears at the window, the question as to why Scoto should have chosen this particular place for his act is answered. The moment at which Celia drops her handkerchief is the climax of the scene, the moment which we, with Volpone, must have been hoping for, the reward for his skilful performance.

The entry of Corvino abruptly ends Volpone's act with a slapstick beating, and we move indoors again from the entertaining public show as witnessed by the uncomprehending Sir Politic, to the closeted atmosphere of Italian intrigue. Volpone is desperate for the favours of Celia; Corvino is just as desperate at the thought of cuckoldry. The hysterically jealous attack upon Celia is, as Corvino himself indicates, a characteristic display of Italian temperament:

> I am a Dutchman, I!
> For if you thought me an Italian,
> You would be damned ere you did this, you whore!   II v 24—6

The violence of language in this scene is not far from the jealous ravings of Ferdinand in *The Duchess of Malfi*.

> What couldst thou propose
> Less to thyself than in this heat of wrath,
> And stung with my dishonour, I should strike
> This steel into thee, with as many stabs
> As thou wast gazed upon with goatish eyes.   II v 30—4

But we are not left long to imagine that we have strayed into a tragedy rather than a comedy, for Mosca arrives on cue to explain to Corvino the need for 'some young woman . . . lusty and full of juice' to sleep with the supposedly comatose Volpone. It takes relatively little manoeuvring from Mosca before Corvino is prepared to offer Celia. The readiness to sacrifice his honour to his greed would not be so funny if we had not just seen him give such a bravura performance as jealous husband. Celia is confronted with a bewildering volte-face:

Corvino. . . . Come I am not jealous.
Celia.   No?
Corvino. Faith I am not, I, nor never was;
           It is a poor unprofitable humour.   II vii 5—7

Corvino, whose avarice is stronger than his jealousy, is perhaps an even more repulsive character than such as the pathological Ferdinand, but by contrast there is no doubt that he is a character of comedy.

The third act in *Volpone*, as in *The Alchemist*, is the act in which all the deceivers' schemes seem to begin to get out of hand. Too much happens too quickly, and even the talents of Mosca as quick-change artist look insufficient to control events. The act starts with Mosca's magnificent soliloquy in which he congratulates himself on those talents.

> I fear I shall begin to grow in love
> With my dear self and my most prosp'rous parts,
> They do so spring and burgeon; I can feel
> A whimsy i' my blood. I know not how,
> Success hath made me wanton.   III i 1—5

Mosca communicates his own delight in his virtuosity to an audience, yet this speech sounds very like a symptom of comic *hubris*. We may expect Mosca's pride to be dashed. However, he succeeds in giving an excellent display of his powers in the encounter with Bonario, whose suspicions of him he allays. When he returns to the house he finds his patron Volpone in dire need of his managing skills, for instead of the beautiful Celia he has been visited by the 'beauteous Lady Would-be'. The comedy of Lady Would-be is cognate to that of her husband; as he sets up as an Italian Machiavel, she sets up for a cultured Italian lady. Her guidebook knowledge of Italian literature, her 'tires and fashions and behaviour' sedulously imitated from Venetian courtesans, all contribute to a devastating portrait of the English lady-traveller. What is funniest of all is the very unaphrodisiac effect of all this upon Volpone, who in Act I had been anticipating her arrival with a lecherous leer:

> 'Fore heaven, I wonder at the desperate valour
> Of the bold English, that they dare let loose
> Their wives to all encounters!   I v 100—2

Some wives, it seems, can be safely let loose anywhere, even among the randy Italians.

Mosca swiftly disposes of Lady Would-be, and the stage is clear for Celia. Well almost – Bonario has to be tucked somewhere out of the way first. Jonson leaves us unclear what to expect from Celia in this situation. She is given very few lines in Act II, we have only seen her drop her handkerchief to Volpone, and then attempt to defend her action to Corvino. Might she not now be expected to give in to the proposals of Volpone? Her situation, with her own husband forcing her in with her seducer, is akin to that of the ironically named Lucrezia, the heroine of Machiavelli's *Mandragola*, whose adultery is promoted by all the guardians of her honour, her husband, her mother, her confessor. Corvino's language in urging her to prostitution is even more violent than it was when accusing her of betraying him:

> Death! I will buy some slave
> Whom I will kill, and bind thee to him, alive;
> And at my window hang you forth, devising
> Some monstrous crime, which I, in capital letters,
> Will eat into thy flesh with aquafortis,
> And burning cor'sives, on this stubborn breast.   III vii 100–5

If this is comedy, it is comedy for strong stomachs. Yet theatrically it can well be funny, with the ultimate absurdity of Corvino's wheedling tone following immediately after this threat:

> Pray thee sweet;
> Good faith, thou shalt have jewels, gowns, attires,
> What thou wilt, think and ask. Do, but go kiss him.
> Or touch him, but. For my sake. At my suit.
> This once.   III vii 111–13

We all know the efficacy of stick and carrot, but Corvino is unaware that one cannot convincingly pretend to be at once an ogre capable of monstrous revenge and a sweet and loving husband begging for one small favour.

Is not, then, Celia's rhetorical question bewailing her fate as she is abandoned by her husband, well answered by Volpone?

> Celia. O God, and his good angels! whither, whither,
>   Is shame fled human breasts? that with such ease
>   Men dare put off your honours, and their own?
>   Is that, which ever was a cause of life,
>   Now placed beneath the basest circumstance,
>   And modesty an exile made, for money?

Volpone. Ay in Corvino, and such earth-fed minds,
        (*He leaps off from the couch.*)
        That never tasted the true heaven of love.
        Assure thee, Celia, he that would sell thee,
        Only for hope of gain, and that uncertain,
        He would have sold his part of Paradise
        For ready money, had he met a cope-man.   III vii 133—44

The leap from the bed adds to the éclat of this as an opening gambit for courtship. The language of religion is met by the religion of love, a transition which we shall see attempted again by Tartuffe. Here Volpone would seem to have a great deal working for him. His description of the pandering husband we have just seen is so wittily exact that we might expect it to win sympathetic assent from Celia. If indeed shame has fled human breasts, if one is living in a world of Corvinos, why not accept this opportunity for some compensating pleasures? Such are the arguments which finally convince Machiavelli's Lucrezia to accept adultery in spite of her virtue. Yet Celia remains unmoved, indeed repulsed. Why?

There are several different ways of playing this scene, depending on how attractive one feels Volpone should be. Is he what he pretends to be,

        As hot, as high, and in as jovial plight
        As when in that so celebrated scene
        At recitation of our comedy,
        For entertainment of the great Valois,
        I acted young Antinous, and attracted
        The eyes and ears of all the ladies present,
        T'admire each graceful gesture, note and footing.   III vii 158—64

Or is he a ludicrous old roué trying to conjure up the spirit of past conquests of which he is no longer capable? Perhaps the most convincing Volpone, theatrically, might be somewhere between these two, an aging epicure, still full of energy and desire, but needing the stimulus of imagination to fend off the fear of approaching impotence. Yet however attractive or unattractive Volpone may be, it makes no difference to Celia. Hers is not the relativist morality of so much comedy in which the youth and beauty of the lover palliates the sin of illicit love; she speaks the absolute language of Christianity.

        Good sir, these things might move a mind affected
        With such delights; but I, whose innocence

Is all I can think wealthy, or worth th'enjoying,
And which, once, lost, I have nought to lose beyond it,
Cannot be taken with these sensual baits.   III vii 206–210.

The effect of the scene between Volpone and Celia is partly that of a
comedy of cross-purposes. They do not speak the same language. When
Celia shrinks from Volpone's advance with a modest exclamation, he
reassures her:

> Nay, fly me not.
> Nor let thy false imagination
> That I was bed-rid, make thee think I am so:
> Thou shalt not find it.   III vii 154–7

Volpone imagines that Celia is like the ladies in *The Country Wife* and that
her horror is aroused by his supposed impotence. Celia promises to pray for
him, to 'report, and think you virtuous', if she is allowed to escape with her
honour intact, but this is an insult to Volpone:

> Think me cold,
> Frozen, and impotent, and so report me?
> That I had Nestor's hernia thou wouldst think.
> I do degenerate and abuse my nation
> To play with opportunity this long   III vii 260–4

What for Celia is honour, chastity, and holiness, for Volpone is dishonour,
impotence, a betrayal of the reputation of Italians for hot-blooded lechery.
The lack of any shared scale of values, any terms which would make
communication possible provides a comic angle to this scene, however
apparently uncomic the situation.

The weakness of the characterisation of Celia and even more her rescuer
Bonario, has been an outstanding problem for those who read the play. Why
should Jonson have made the only demonstrably good characters in the play
seem so wooden and unconvincing in comparison with the sharply etched
caricatures which surround them? The problem stems surely from their total
isolation, the very fact that no-one else shares their point of view. Celia's
situation is poignant, pathetic:

> If you have ears that will be pierced, or eyes
> That can be opened, a heart may be touched,
> Or any part that yet sounds man about you;

If you have touch of holy saints, or heaven,
Do me the grace to let me 'scape.   III vii 240–4

But an appeal to Volpone's manhood, as we have seen, means something quite different to him, and there is no-one, nothing in the whole world of the play, to verify or realise these ideals of holy saints, heaven, or grace. Celia ends up sounding hollow and melodramatic, using language indeed not unlike that of her husband in its violence: rather than dishonour her, she begs Volpone to

> punish that unhappy crime of nature
> Which you miscall my beauty: flay my face,
> Or poison it with ointments for seducing
> Your blood to this rebellion.   III vii 251–4

Bonario's cry when he leaps from his hiding-place –

> Forbear, foul ravisher! libidinous swine!
> Free the forced lady, or thou diest, imposter –   III vii 267–8

may seem more absurd than intended to modern audiences who hear in it the accents of Victorian melodrama. Yet these words do seem ludicrous because they can take no purchase on the reality of the play. In *Volpone* it goes without saying that everyone is an imposter; to call the foul ravisher a 'swine' loses its point in a world where all the characters are seen to be beasts. The profound cynicism invited by the comic contract in *Volpone* pre-empts the indignation of Bonario which can only therefore sound foolish.

Whatever the tone of his language, the action of Bonario seems to mean certain exposure for Volpone.

> I am unmasked, unspirited, undone,
> Betrayed to beggary, to infamy –   III vii 278–9

For the first time in the play we see the arch-plotters Volpone and Mosca in complete dismay, unable to do anything but bewail their misfortunes and wait fearfully for the appearance of the Saffi to hale them off to justice. What follows is a comic theatrical anti-climax, as instead of the menacing officers of justice the doddering Corbaccio totters on to the stage. Without a moment's hesitation Mosca, who has been apparently floored a minute ago, is back into his stride lying as effortlessly and as plausibly as ever. We cannot but admire his skill as, first for Corbaccio and then for Voltore, he invents stories to retrieve the disaster. The predators are as willing as ever to believe what they want to believe, and to go along with whatever intrigues Mosca may propose to further their supposed interests. By the end of Act III, although the situation is left uncertain, Volpone and Mosca are on their way back to control.

In Act IV the management of deception is developed to a new level of art. As Mosca waits for the judges to appear in the courtroom, he enquires of his witnesses:

> Is the lie
> Safely conveyed amongst us? Is that sure?
> Knows every man his burden?   IV iv 3−5

What follows is indeed a marvellous part-song of lies, with each of the birds of prey croaking his own cacophonous entry in the total harmony. Voltore, indeed, the main soloist, is mellifluous enough as he vindicates the reputation established for him in Act I as one of those who 'could speak To every cause, and things mere contraries, Till they were hoarse again, yet all be law'. But Corbaccio and Corvino positively go over the top in their anxiety to perjure themselves. Bonario, according to his father, is a 'monster of men, swine, goat, wolf, parricide'. Corvino, earlier so sensitive to the possibility of cuckoldry, now proclaims it to the world:

> This woman, please your fatherhoods, is a whore
> Of most hot exercise, more than a partridge
> Upon record −   IV v 117−19

'There is no shame in this now, is there?' he asks Mosca complacently. Most striking of all perhaps is the part of Lady Would-be in the chorus of perjury. A casual lie told her by Mosca earlier has sent her off on a hunt for her supposed unfaithful husband. After first identifying the unfortunate Peregrine as the suspected paramour in disguise, she is gathered up into the intrigue by Mosca who assures her that it is in fact Celia who was seen with her husband. Her performance before the justices is so transparently brainless, so spontaneous and genuine in all its absurd affectations, that no one could doubt it as testimony. When even this idiotic outsider can contribute towards the success of Mosca's plot, nothing can withstand it.

The appearance of Volpone, once again in his role as dying invalid, finally convinces the court. Bonario and Celia, as we know, the only innocents in the court-room are condemned as shameless creatures. We have been shown, step by step, the process by which black has been changed to white before our eyes. When the Avocatori first appeared they were entirely convinced by Bonario and Celia's story:

> *1st Avocatore.* The like of this the Senate never heard of
> *2nd Avocatore.* 'Twill come most strange to them when we report it.
> *4th Avocatore.* The gentlewoman has been ever held
> Of unreproved name.
> *3rd Avocatore.*   So the young man.
> *4th Avocatore.* The more unnatural part, that of his father.
> *2nd Avocatore.* More of the husband.
> *1st Avocatore.*   I not know to give
> His act a name, it is so monstrous!   IV v 1−7

But as the ingeniously orchestrated deception moves forward, they are as easily won over as Mark Antony's listeners in the Forum. It is noticeable that Bonario's outspoken indignation does not help his cause. He accuses Voltore of corruption − 'This fellow, For six sols more would plead against his Maker' (IV v 96−97). True, no doubt, but one is not allowed to say things like this of a barrister in a court of law, and Bonario is reprimanded by the first Avocatore, as he would be by any magistrate: 'You do forget yourself'. One critic has argued that Jonson set *Volpone* in Venice because of the high reputation for integrity of Venetian justice.[8] In view of the total credulity the Avocatori show in this scene it seems an extraordinary argument. As with *Julius Caesar*, what we witness here is the power of language used unscrupulously to sway the minds of an audience, and the justices here, whatever their dignified status and their high reputation in Elizabethan travel literature, are as gullible as Shakespeare's Roman plebs. We are convinced once again, if we needed convincing, that in Volpone's Venice simple truth is powerless, not to say meaningless, so fluent and so pervasive are the arts of deception.

But nemesis, though it is delayed, comes in the end. The fifth act begins with the humiliation of the suitors, when Volpone pretends at last to be dead. They arrive in the same order as in Act I, Voltore, Corbaccio, Corvino, Lady Would-be, only to discover Mosca ensconced as heir. It is the pay-off of the earlier comedy, with Volpone enjoying it unseen. It retains the perfect symmetry of farce to the end as Lady Would-be, Corvino, Corbaccio, Voltore are denounced and expelled by Mosca in reverse order to that of entry. This is punitive comedy at its simplest. What is happening at a more complicated level in Act V is the working out of the relationship between Volpone and Mosca. It is in a spirit of pure fantasy that Volpone installs the parasite, his creature, in his own habit of *clarissimo*. The joke on the predators will be all the funnier when they discover how outrageously unsuitable an heir Volpone has actually chosen in preference to them all. Voltore's indignation is representative:

> Outstripped thus, by a parasite! a slave,
> Would run on errands, and make legs for crumbs?   V vi 1−2

Yet Mosca in possession begins to look much less grotesquely inappropriate than Volpone had imagined.

There is a repeated pattern of partnership in Jonson's plays: Subtle and Face in *The Alchemist*, Sejanus and Tiberius in *Sejanus*, Catiline and Caesar in *Catiline*. In each case the front-man, the eponymous protagonist of the play, is ultimately undermined and left exposed by his more shadowy accomplice. Mosca, too, emerges gradually through the action from his position as Volpone's tool to an independence which can threaten if not completely defeat his master. Though we admire his skills in Act I, they are self-effacing skills, and Act II is entirely devoted to the acting of Volpone. It is only with the soliloquy at the beginning of Act III that Mosca moves out into centre stage, just as at an equivalent moment of *Sejanus* Tiberius steps out from behind the bogey image of Sejanus. Mosca's challenge to Volpone is never direct in the earlier acts, but there are signs that it is there. This is partly a matter of age and energy. Mosca thrives on acting; the tighter the corner, the more complicated the intrigue, the more dazzling is his performance. Volpone is much more easily tired and frightened, and Mosca doesn't let him forget it. As they are congratulating themselves on their victory in court, Mosca slips in,

> 'T seemed to me you sweat sir.
> *Volpone.* In troth, I did a little.
> *Mosca.*   But confess sir;
> Were you not daunted?
> *Volpone.*   In good faith, I was
> A little in a mist, but not dejected.   V ii 37−40

As Ian Donaldson has remarked in a fine essay, 'with the gentlest of touches, Jonson manages to suggest at points throughout the play Volpone's increasing fear of physical affliction'.[9] The younger and more physically self-confident Mosca with tiny pin-pricks plays upon this fear.

It is not, then, altogether a surprise when Mosca double-crosses Volpone. It is in a sense the obvious comic dénouement − the rogues fall out among themselves. What is alarming is how nearly Mosca brings it all off. Once again he seems on the point of hoodwinking the justices, even though at first he had the eloquent Voltore against him. Money and rank count for a lot in Venice, as we can see from the changing attitude of the Avocatori.

> *4th Avocatore.*   We have done ill, by a public officer
> To send for him, if he be heir.
>
> *2nd Avocatore.*   For whom?
>
> *4th Avocatore.* Him that they call the parasite.
>
> *3rd Avocatore.*   'Tis true
> He is a man of great estate now left.
>
> *4th Avocatore.* Go you, and learn his name, and say the court
> Entreats his presence here, but to the clearing
> Of some few doubts.   V x 36–42

By the time he arrives in court, Mosca is already being considered as an eligible match for a daughter of one of the justices. There seems, in fact, nothing to stop the whole façade of deception from hardening into reality, except, of course, what ultimately precipitates the dénouement – Mosca's greed and Volpone's pride. The rogues over-reach themselves finally, when no-one or nothing else could have defeated them.

The severity of the play's ending has worried many readers, and Jonson himself was aware of the difficulty, as he showed in his prefatory Epistle:

> though my catastrophe may in the strict rigour of comic law meet with censure . . . I desire the learned and charitable critic to have so much faith in me to think it was done of industry: for with what ease I could have varied it nearer his scale (but that I fear to boast my own faculty) I could here insert. But my special aim being to put the snaffle in their mouths that cry out: We never punish vice in our interludes, &c. I took the more liberty . . .   *Epistle* 104–11

Conceivably some of the Puritan critics of the theatre might have been silenced – it seems unlikely – but is the ending of *Volpone* positively edifying in the way Jonson suggests? We surely cannot regard Bonario's triumphant comment without irony – 'Heaven could not long let such gross crimes be hid'. It has scarcely been a play to support an audience's faith in Providence. The pious moral drawn by one of the Avocatori after the event, 'If this be held the highway to get riches, May I be poor', adds to the effect of ironic satire. We notice that Mosca, who so nearly fooled the justices in the habit of a *clarissimo* bears the first brunt of their indignation:

> You appear
> T'have been the chiefest minister, if not plotter,
> In all these lewd impostures; and now, lastly,
> Have with your impudence abused the court,
> And habit of a gentleman of Venice,
> Being a fellow of no birth or blood. V xii 107–12

The Avocatori have no more moral standing than the Mikado, devising punishments to fit the crime as a 'source of innocent merriment'.

This is, indeed, perhaps, the attitude of the play's ending, however much fiercer than Gilbert and Sullivan it may be. The punishments do represent comic justice: Mosca the parasite condemned to forced labour, Corvino given the public shaming of a cuckold, Corbaccio dispossessed in favour of his son. It is Volpone himself who suggests the attitude the audience may be expected to adopt. Given his sentence, that his goods be 'confiscate to the hospital of the Incurabili' and he himself 'to lie in prison, cramped with irons, Till thou be'st sick and lame indeed', he comments wryly, 'This is called mortifying of a fox'. It is a wittily apt remark, the mortification of the flesh being at once a spiritual punishment and the literal process of decomposition. This is indeed savage humour, but the self-awareness of it, the direct allusion to the fable, indicates that it is intended to be comic.[10] It points the way towards the traditional comic epilogue:

> The seasoning of the play is the applause.
> Now, although the fox be punished by the laws,
> He yet doth hope there is no suff'ring due
> For any fact which he hath done 'gainst you.
> If there be, censure him; here he doubtful stands.
> If not, fare jovially, and clap your hands.

In a sense this lets the audience off, reassures them that they live in a world outside that of the play, in a community of good-humoured enjoyment of the performance. Yet it does not impinge upon the integrity of the play's comic image, nor qualify the unremittingly ironic view of human society as a battle of monstrous predators in which positive moral sanctions are meaningless. We must enjoy that grotesque spectacle from a vantage point unrepresented on the stage.

TARTUFFE

In *Tartuffe*, by contrast, the representatives of audience values throng the opening scene. Five characters – Dorine, Mariane, Damis, Elmire, Cleante – make up a group with whom we are directly identified. We make their acquaintance through the distorted view of Mme. Pernelle, who ticks them off one by one as an impertinent servant (Dorine), a stupid good-for-nothing (Damis), a sly contriver (Mariane), an extravagant and irresponsible housewife (Elmire), and a libertine apologist (Cléante). Though each of these descriptions is founded upon some feature of their real characters, and acts to that extent as an explanatory introduction, we know from the tone and manner of Mme. Pernelle that they are caricatures. From the very beginning we are oriented towards a view of domestic normality upset and inverted by the intrusion of Tartuffe and the monomaniacal passion of his disciples Mme. Pernelle and Orgon. The sanity of the majority defines itself by contrast to the palpably distorted vision of the comically deranged.

In one way, therefore, no play of Molière's would seem to give a more reassuring sense of the normality of reason and good sense than *Tartuffe*. If the bourgeois family represents a comic microcosm in Molière, in few of his plays, except possibly *L'Avare*, is the source of disruption so restricted and isolated. In *Les Femmes Savantes* the family is divided down the middle, the feminists and the anti-feminists in about equal numbers. In *Le Bourgeois Gentilhomme* and *Le Malade Imaginaire*, M. Jourdain and Argan introduce assistants for their passions into the household. But in *Tartuffe*, every single major character in the play can see the hypocrite for what he is, with the two central exceptions. The image here would seem, therefore, the exact opposite of that in *Volpone* where only Celia and Bonario stood out among the universe of freaks and monsters. In *Tartuffe* we start with numbers at least on the side of order and normality. However disturbing it may be to see the life of the family undermined by the infatuation of its head, the substance of that life is soundly and solidly established.

But a seventeenth century French bourgeois family was not a democracy in which moderate common sense might outvote extremism; it was a despotism, benevolent or tyrannical as the case might be. And if Orgon's seems an exceptionally harmonious and consistently sensible family in itself, it will only go to show what an extraordinary degree of damage the comic tyrant can do. Yet even before the spiralling effect of disorder caused by Orgon's folly has started, we are given doubts as to the capacity of the forces of reason to prevail. Outside and beyond the comfortable and reassuring circle of the family there are off-stage figures, malicious gossips and prudes mentioned in passing by Cléante and Dorine, who restrict the sense that the attitudes of those on stage are representative of the society as a whole. Mme. Pernelle's total imperviousness to argument, which foreshadows that of Orgon, starts the play in an atmosphere of frustration. None of her opponents are allowed more than three words before they are denounced, and then when they do manage to put their case, they are accused of talking all the time. The combination of not listening and interrupting, familiar enough in Molière's monomaniacs, is used by Mme. Pernelle to set aside what she refers to contemptuously as 'tous ces raisonnements'.

We remarked in Chapter Three on the practical ineffectiveness of the *raisonneur*. In *Tartuffe* this is particularly striking. 'Raisonnements', for Orgon, as for Mme. Pernelle, have nothing to do with the case. We first see Orgon's absurd fixation on Tartuffe as exposed by Dorine in the famous scene of 'le pauvre homme'. Yet although we laugh with Dorine here and later in the play at Orgon's distorted view of reality, there is no hope that Dorine any more than anyone else can make him see sense. Indeed it is largely his complete imperviousness to reason which makes him so funny. Dorine shares with Cléante the function of *raisonneur*. The cynical pragmatic arguments – if Orgon insists on marrying off Mariane to Tartuffe he can expect her to cuckold him etc. – are given to the low comic servant; Cléante, whose respectability as the spokesman for true piety was very important to Molière in the public controversy over the play, is given nothing but the most high-minded points of view. Where Dorine, like so many of Molière's *soubrettes*, argues the case from the vantage-point of natural commonsense, Cléante appeals to an ideal of reason.

Cléante's long speeches in Act I, scene v, defining the true religion against which it is evident that Tartuffe's is hypocritical, have been the centre of endless analyses to establish where precisely Molière stood on the question of the 'dévots'. Whatever we may think on this controversial issue, there can be no doubt that Cléante represents, in Guicharnaud's phrase 'la norme selon la pièce',[11] the implied audience standpoint of the comic contract. Yet as another critic has pointed out, 'his role is purely forensic, not dramatic and actual'.[12] However much we may concede the reasonableness of Cléante's argument, it is hardly persuasive from Orgon's point of view. After a tirade against the 'faux dévots' of over 20 lines, he comes to a peroration:

> Les hommes le plupart sont étrangement faits!
> Dans la juste nature on ne les voit jamais;
> La raison a pour eux des bornes trop petites;
> En chaque caractère ils passent ses limites;
> Et la plus noble chose, ils la gâtent souvent

Pour la vouloir outrer et pousser trop avant.
Que cela vous soit dit en passant, mon beau-frère.   I v 339—45

With the inept attempt to pass off this chunk of moralising as a few casual remarks in parenthesis, it is perhaps understandable that Orgon should reply with heavy sarcasm:

Oui, vous êtes sans doute un docteur qu'on révère
Tout le savoir du monde est chez vous retiré.   I v 346—7

Cléante's statement seemed for a whole generation of critics the classic affirmation of the *juste milieu*, the ideal of moderate reason. Yet when we look closely at it, what it actually suggests is the irredeemable irrationality of 'la plupart des hommes' judged by this ideal. We in the audience, included with Cléante in this rational stance, see with him not how abnormal but how typical of human nature Orgon's behaviour is, and in nothing more so than his unwillingness to be told at length just what he is doing wrong.

When he preaches at his brother-in-law, Cléante gets barbed and sarcastic retorts; when he presses Orgon on the practical matter of Mariane's marriage to Valère, Orgon simply rolls himself up like a hedgehog and refuses to respond. So much for reasoning. The marriage which the tyrannic father obstructs is the common comic symbol of desirable normality. In this case it also represents the basic family order which Orgon's mania has interrupted; it was agreed on in the traditional bourgeois way before the arrival of Tartuffe. In attempting to marry Mariane to Tartuffe instead of Valère, Orgon is going back on his word and, as Dorine points out to him in no uncertain terms, making a very bad bargain:

que vous apporte une telle alliance?
A quel sujet aller, avec tout votre bien,
Choisir un gendre gueux?   II ii 482—4

Yet Orgon can do it, will do it, in spite of all Dorine's mockery, in spite of Mariane's dismay. Certainly when we see the young lovers together we can hardly imagine Valère and Mariane exercising a very powerful or effective opposition to the will of Orgon. The beautifully choreographed scene of the lovers' quarrel is an almost detachable piece of theatre, which critics have often condemned as a filler added by Molière in his expansion of the play from its original three-act form. Yet in its ironic view of the stereotyped pair of young lovers it adds to the growing sense of the weakness of the anti-Orgon/Tartuffe forces in the play. The ingénue Agnès and the naive

Horace, in their very innocence, were constantly able to outwit Arnolphe. We can have no such confidence in Valère and Mariane.

Who then will bell the cat? Who can match the cunning of Tartuffe and counteract his influence on Orgon, to bring about the restoration of family order? After the first two acts all hopes must rest on Elmire and we are prepared for the great scene of confrontation which follows soon after Tartuffe's long delayed appearance on the stage. The scene occupies exactly the same central structural position in *Tartuffe* as the Volpone–Celia scene in *Volpone*, and it is interesting to compare the two. Tartuffe like Volpone uses the metaphoric language of the religion of love — 'de vous dépend ma peine ou ma béatitude' — but whereas Volpone's epicureanism was offered as an alternative creed to Celia's orthodoxy, Tartuffe is parodying his own language of devotion. The specious pseudo-Platonic rhetoric by which Tartuffe attempts to reconcile his devout pose with his sexual desires —

L'amour qui nous attache aux beautés éternelles
N'étouffe pas en nous l'amour des temporelles . . .   III iii 933–4

gives us a comedy of ironic self-revelation quite different in effect from Volpone's grandiose and forthright sensuality. What is more striking, however, is the difference in reaction between Celia and Elmire. There are no exclamations of outraged virtue from Elmire, but rather cool retorts — the famous 'Que fait là votre main?' — and a dryly ironic rebuff. She is content to draw Tartuffe out, rather than wringing her hands in horror like Celia.

Elmire's behaviour in this scene has been the subject of controversy. Some critics have seen in the slight coquetry of her attitude a trace of an earlier version of the play in which Elmire was more *complaisante*. This sort of speculation, however, is founded on hypotheses which can hardly be proved. At the theatrical level of *vraisemblance* Molière needs to have Elmire fairly cool in this scene in order to enable her to take in Tartuffe with her supposed change of heart in Act IV. She herself claims that a respectable married woman can afford to laugh at such proposals, that such is the proper contempt with which to treat them. But Elmire is also pursuing a political strategy. She listens to Tartuffe's wooing because it may give her a weapon against him. The scene between them ends as she is attempting to put pressure on him into allowing the marriage between Valère and Mariane, in exchange for not revealing his attempted seduction to Orgon. Against Tartuffes you need to use Tartuffe-like strategies, such seems to be the lesson of this scene. After the high-minded but ineffective reasoning of Cléante, the crude but equally ineffective jibes of Dorine, it seems sobering to realise that

the best chance of defeating Tartuffe may be the lady-like use of blackmail.
We never get a chance to find out how successful Elmire's strategy might
have been — perhaps not very, in view of Tartuffe's adeptness as a political
tactician — because the hot-headed Damis can contain himself no longer in
his concealment in the 'petit cabinet'. He comes storming out just like
Bonario in *Volpone*:

> Non, Madame, non: ceci doit se répandre.
> J'étois en cet endroit, d'où j'ai pu tout entendre;
> Et la bonté du Ciel m'y semble avoir conduit
> Pour confondre l'orgueil d'un traître qui me nuit.   III iv 1021 — 4

This is the high language of neo-classical tragedy, and the audience might be
expected to be amused at the element of hyperbolic parody. What is more, in
Tartuffe we can hardly take unironically allusions to the ways of Providence,
and the influence of 'le Ciel', since these are the catch-words of the imposter
and his dupes. This in itself makes us doubtful of the success of Damis' frontal
attack upon Tartuffe. Elmire's instinct 'not to make a scene' seems well-
founded, and though we cannot foresee what in fact happens, the very
loudness and self-righteousness of Damis' exclamations prepares us to see
him outwitted.

What occupies almost the whole of Act IV of *Volpone*, the elaborate
intrigue by which the swindler's mask is replaced after the ignominious
exposure of Act III, all this is accomplished in the space of one short scene in
Tartuffe, in some 20 lines. The accusation is made, the testimony is there,
Tartuffe is asked to answer the charge.

> Oui, mon frère, je suis un méchant, un coupable,
> Un malheureux pécheur, tout plein d'iniquité . . .   III vi 1076 — 7

What is so marvellous about Tartuffe's tactic is that it is so elegantly simple
and unplanned. He does not attempt denials or excuses; in a sense he may
even be playing for time in mouthing his empty self-accusations. But it is
their very emptiness on which he can count, a vacuum into which Orgon's
overflowing faith is inevitably drawn. Orgon is so used to the meaningless
rhetoric of humility that he assumes it amounts to a protestation of
innocence, and it is against Damis rather than Tartuffe that he turns in rage.

> Ah! traître, oses-tu bien per cette fausseté
> Vouloir de sa vertu ternir la pureté?   III vi 1087 — 8

In *Tartuffe*, as in *Volpone*, innocence is not enough. The skills of a Tartuffe, a Mosca, Voltore, Volpone, are such that the most clear and unequivocal honesty can be made to seem its opposite. The protestations of outraged virtue from Bonario or Celia, or here Damis, are dismissed as hypocritical performances by the dupes of the swindlers. We laugh partly at the skill of the deceivers, partly at the naiveté of the champions of truth, but overall at the way of the world where appearance and reality are so consistently interchanged.

The simple device which Tartuffe employs here is as characteristic of his method, as the elaborate schemes of Volpone and Mosca are of theirs. Where they take pleasure in displaying their Machiavellian talents, Tartuffe never once shows that he has a specific end in mind. He is essentially an opportunist, seizing psychological advantages where he can. By pleading with Orgon on Damis' behalf, by imploring his patron to allow him to leave to ensure family peace, he secures not only the banishment of Damis but, what he can surely not have banked on, the disinheritance of the son in his favour. His attitude is one of accepting reluctantly what is forced upon him – 'God's will be done', 'La volonté du Ciel soit faite en toute chose'. It is surely this quality which makes Tartuffe such a sinister figure, as he moves forward inexorably, but apparently without premeditated design, towards the ruin of the family. There is in the play, as Jacques Schérer has pointed out, a technique of escalation by which we are carried on from one danger to another, each more serious than the previous one.[13] The disinheritance of Damis marks an important point of transition from the regular comic obstacle of the tyrannic father blocking the young people's marriage towards a more wide-reaching disorder. We are moving beyond the sphere of the single family, in which the father's rights are unquestioned. It is the business of a paterfamilias to marry off his daughters as he may see fit, but when he cuts off the line of succession to his son, though legally within his rights, broader principles of social order seem in question. With Orgon, as with Corbaccio in *Volpone*, the disinheritance of the natural heir is a signal instance of unnatural and anti-social behaviour.

At the beginning of Act IV Cléante tries to point this out to Tartuffe:

> le vrai zèle a-t-il quelque maxime
> Qui montre à dépouiller l'héritier légitime?   IV i 1237–8

But Tartuffe is armed against any such arguments, and when he has no reply left, he can always excuse himself by saying that it is time for prayers. (There is a story of Boileau's that it was with exactly the same excuse that Lamoignon, who had ordered the second prohibition of *Tartuffe* in 1667, cut short the protests of Molière.[14]) The logic of Cléante is as ineffective with Tartuffe as it was with Orgon. Once again in Act IV as in Act III, the situation (now much more serious) seems irretrievable unless Elmire can retrieve it. It is now a point of honour with Orgon to go ahead with the destruction of his family – he braces himself against the pitiful pleas of Mariane – and he allows Elmire to attempt her demonstration not because he has any doubts of Tartuffe, but because he is certain that he will be vindicated.

Some critics have felt it necessary to explain why Tartuffe should have been so easily taken in by Elmire in their second interview. It is psychologically well prepared – Elmire's lack of violent reaction in the earlier scene, the skill of her argument here, making herself out a coquette feigning indifference in order to win greater passion, all contribute to convincing Tartuffe of what he wants to believe in any case. But Tartuffe's attitude here is in fact very different from that in the earlier scene. He is cautious and suspicious of Elmire's supposed change of heart:

> Ce langage à comprendre est assez difficile
> Madame, et vous parliez tantôt d'un autre style.   IV v 1409–10

He is now more directly and more coldly rapacious than before. The sensuality of Tartuffe in the earlier scene had the comedy of the involuntary urge overcoming the will, but here will and desire are unequivocally at one. Tartuffe wants proof, wants a guarantee of Elmire's words:

> je ne croirai rien, que vous n'ayez, Madame,
> Par des réalités su convaincre ma flamme.   IV v 1465–6

The unfortunate Elmire, who was very much in control of the earlier interview, finds herself forced into a defensive position in which it is all she can do to stop herself being seduced to satisfy the disbelief of Tartuffe and the incredulity of her husband. It almost seems as though Elmire will become an involuntary Angélique – 'Vous l'avez voulu, George Dandin.' And if she is saved finally it is perhaps because Tartuffe at last hurt Orgon's pride rather than because the seduction of his wife would have convinced him. It is Tartuffe's comments on his credulity which bring him out of his *cachette*:

> C'est un homme, entre nous, à mener par le nez;
> De tous nos entretiens il est pour faire gloire,
> Et je l'ai mis au point de voir tout sans rien croire.   IV v 1524–6

Orgon might well not have believed his eyes, but he cannot forgive Tartuffe for saying so. When he denounces his rejected idol, to retain his self-respect he has to claim that he was on to Tartuffe all the time:

> J'ai douté fort longtemps que ce fût tout de bon,
> Et je croyois toujours qu'on changeroit de ton.   IV vii 1547–8

Orgon, undeceived, is as self-deceiving as ever.

Act V of *Tartuffe* necessarily raises the problem of Molière's revisions of the play. Did the original three-act version end with the present Act IV, and were Acts II and V later additions, as John Cairncross has argued?[15] What had Molière in mind when he expanded the play, if in fact the final text does represent an expansion of a version complete in three acts? Molière scholars have analysed the evidence minutely to try to establish the facts. If indeed the original play did end with Tartuffe exposed, without the complications of the deed of gift or the *cassette*, then it would seem as though the addition of Act V was a deliberate attempt to blacken Tartuffe further, to take the sequence of events beyond the sphere of domestic comedy. Though it is often felt that the business of the incriminating *cassette* is very awkwardly introduced, Schérer is surely right to point out that the introduction of a new and still greater danger at this stage is quite consistent with the rhythm of the action.[16] Each time it looked as though Tartuffe was defeated, or at least contained, he escaped from the apparent impasse and re-emerged as a still more threatening figure. The use of the deed of gift and the *cassette* is entirely in line with the way in which the hypocrite rides the unpredictable waves of events through the play. What is more, it follows out the logic of escalating gravity by which Tartuffe's power spreads outward from the single bourgeois family to the society as a whole. His establishment as Monsieur Tartuffe, the master of Orgon's house, is like the appearance of Mosca in the habit of a Venetian *clarissimo*. It represents not only a supreme example of the deceiving skills of an imposter, but a basic threat to the security of a hierarchical society.

In Jonson's Venice only some very dubiously just justices stood for the security of the society. Molière by contrast, had the King as the ultimate and supreme arbiter of truth to reinstate the principle of order. Yet the fact that he is only invoked *in extremis*, when all the logic of the play's action has seemed to lead inevitably to the triumph of Tartuffe and the ruin of Orgon's household, makes the tone and effect of the miraculous dénouement problematical, to say the least. Obviously one way of seeing it is that Molière needed to end the play with a public acknowledgement to the King for his support against the *cabale*, but this is virtually to write off the ending as an excrescence. It is equally possible to claim that Molière was using quite seriously the image of the King as the fountainhead of truth in the society, as Jonson tried to use Elizabeth at the end of *Cynthia's Revels.* Louis is all that Orgon is not. As Jacques Guicharnaud says, 'Against the corrupted father/head of household (on the comic level of the bourgeois family) Molière sets up, at the highest level, the example of the enlightened and just king.'[17] One might say that in the terms of Descartes' argument in the *Meditations* Louis is God to Tartuffe's deceiving demon. Yet Tartuffe has been so successful as deceiving demon that it may be hard for an audience to find their faith again with the reinstatement of the deity.

Are we intended to see ironically the disparity between arbitrarily imposed dénouement and reality? 'The audience', argues Georges Pholien, 'has every reason to believe that if the ending is happy, it is only because the genre demands it; whereas, in the mind of the author, the normal order of things would demand the opposite'.[18] This is elaborated into a general view of Molièrean comedy in the influential essay of Jules Brody, who claims that in *Tartuffe*, as elsewhere in Molière, there is a self-conscious awareness of the contrast between the perfection of aesthetic form and the unreliable and uncertain nature of social reality.[19] Certainly at the end of *Tartuffe* there seems to be a pointed conjunction of the emotions of relief and delight aroused by the sudden *coup de théâtre*, and the attitude of sceptical disillusion which the play as a whole seems to invite. Made explicit in Gay's *Beggar's Opera*, and still more in Brecht's *Threepenny Opera*, it becomes knowing and overt irony: we give you happy endings, Brecht and Gay tell us, because we know that is what you want, not what these characters would in fact be likely to get. It is not nearly as aggressive or cynical as that in Molière. But we are unusually aware that we are watching the end of a comedy where the exceptional may be allowed to intervene to avert the ultimate catastrophe, even when the folly of the fools and the knavery of the knaves make catastrophe seem unavoidable.

'Heaven be praised', 'Que le Ciel soit loué', exclaims Dorine as Tartuffe is led off to prison. There is surely a final irony in giving this speech to Dorine, the most earthbound of the characters in *Tartuffe*. It is the first time we have heard her use the word 'Ciel' — so often in the mouths of all the others — and we associate her with a robust doctrine of self-help rather than resignation to Providential intervention. It would not be hard for an actress playing Dorine to give this line an explicitly ironic inflection, remembering how constantly Tartuffe used 'le Ciel' as authority for his actions. Yet such an interpretation leads on inevitably to the most controversial of Molière controversies: is Molière satirising the language of religion in *Tartuffe* or, as he claimed, merely the language of hypocrisy? For if 'le Ciel' by the end of the play has come to seem the debased rhetorical device of a conman, that would seem to imply a serious if oblique attack on seventeenth century French orthodoxy in which 'le Ciel' was the conventional and accepted synonym for the divine will. The most convincing arguments of twentieth century critics would suggest that Molière's position on religion in *Tartuffe* was that of the court '*mondains*' opposed to the rigorism of the '*cabale des dévots*'.[20] Cléante's doctrine of a 'dévotion humaine et traitable' was entirely consistent with the unenthusiastic religion of the court, which from the point of view of the '*dévots*' was no religion at all. Lionel Gossman puts the case most bluntly when he claims that Molière 'has no interest or understanding of the religious point of view as such, since he regards it, from his Courtly point of view, as an idiosyncracy to be tolerated when kept out of sight and eliminated when it becomes a social reality and a social challenge.'[21] Even if we do not go as far as this, it seems clear that the opponents of *Tartuffe* had legitimate grounds for complaint. As Raymond Picard, among others, has shown, many of the attitudes ridiculed in Tartuffe and Orgon as fanaticism were widely taught as the orthodox doctrine of the Church.[22] Without making Molière into a libertine polemicist, it is possible to see him as related to the gradual 'désaffection de la morale religieuse' which was an underlying current in France from the mid-seventeenth century on.[23]

Yet it may not be necessary thus to specify the attitude towards religion in historical terms. It is true that Cléante's view of devotion is a highly secular one, which seems to exclude any real understanding of a fervent spiritual life. But comedy frequently ignores this spiritual dimension in human behaviour and treats its characters as if they were purely social animals. It may be that Molière in *Tartuffe* was not so much adopting a specifically 'mondain' line with which his courtly audience might have been in agreement, but rather asking them to leave aside as temporarily irrelevant the consideration of absolute spiritual concerns. To refuse to go along with a comedian when he asks for such a temporary suspension of one part of our serious interests is to 'lack a sense of humour', and the opponents of *Tartuffe* showed themselves as outstandingly humourless. For a Bourdaloue or a Bossuet, just what was pernicious about Molière's comedy was that it set aside questions of absolute truth and concerned itself only with superficialities. Bossuet denounces 'la morale du théâtre qui n'attaque que le ridicule du monde, en lui laissant cependant toute sa corruption' — 'the morality of the theatre which attacks only the ridiculousness of society, while leaving all its corruption untouched'.[24] These are the reactions of those who opt out of the comic contract, who insist on re-introducing the attitudes which the comic structure excludes.

Tartuffe, then, is not a polemic attack upon religion, but it has no place for a genuine language of devotion. This is not only because Tartuffe with his hypocritical cant debases the currency; the basic attitudes we are encouraged to adopt in the comedy are incompatible with a reverent appreciation of ultimate truths. It is similar to the isolation and attenuation of Celia and Bonario's language in *Volpone*. In that case there was no question of hypocrisy — Celia and Bonario no doubt believe in the Christian ideals they proclaim. (So, for that matter, do Orgon and Mme. Pernelle). But in the atmosphere of universal dishonesty in Venice their rhetoric as much as the rhetoric of Voltore or Mosca falls under suspicion. Jonson and Molière ask us to adopt a generally sceptical attitude for the purposes of the comedy, whatever our (or their) ideological allegiances outside the theatre. (Jonson was still a Catholic when he wrote *Volpone*; it would be hard to discover it from the evidence of the play). Religious professions tend to be included among the many forms of posturing which in *Volpone* and *Tartuffe* are the masks of gulls and swindlers.

We started with the issue of whether comedy was necessarily limited to dealing with follies rather than crimes, minor rather than major human errors. The answer on the basis of this analysis of *Tartuffe* and *Volpone* would seem to be no. The grotesque monstrosity of the beast/men in *Volpone* is predicated in the very structure of the comic fable; what they do in the course of the play is only by way of illustration of the animal labels they bear. One action leads on to another without an essential change in perspective, so that there is no point at which we feel that comedy has been left behind. The same is true of *Tartuffe*. However menacing the hypocrite becomes, no stage of his rise to power is a sudden and unexpected twist, by its unexpectedness threatening the security of the comic viewpoint. The logic of the play, indeed, leads us to expect each new device by which Tartuffe escapes possible defeat and turns it into victory, though of course the nature of the device always comes as a surprise. We are theatrically satisfied by the progressive revelation of Tartuffe's dishonesty and unscrupulousness, rather than alarmed by them, just as there is a pure pleasure in watching the chorus of false witnesses in the first courtroom scene in *Volpone*. The hypotheses on which the comedies rest, that unscrupulous hypocrisy is all but invincible in society, or that the bestiality of man makes social ideals of justice or truth a mockery, are spectacularly confirmed. This is a comic contract to which we can subscribe with no more misgivings than to that of plays with triumphant happy endings such as *As You Like It* or *L'Ecole des Femmes*, which we looked at in Chapter Two. In comedy we may as readily assent to an idea of the overwhelming power of artifice and deceit as to the concept of the inevitable victory of natural truth.

8 Two Plays in Search of an Audience

Molière's *Dom Juan* and Shakespeare's *Troilus and Cressida* are the sort of plays for which the critical case-book might have been invented.[1] No-one can agree about anything in either of them, except that they are difficult to understand. They have every variety of problem on which criticism and scholarship thrive: textual problems, a peculiar stage-history, difficulties of authorial intentions and generic classification. Given that this study is based on a notion of the comic contract in which attitudes are agreed, these two plays which invite a bewildering range of different responses, would hardly seem suitable cases for treatment as comedies. It appears to be the outstanding feature of both *Dom Juan* and *Troilus and Cressida* to leave any audience doubtful of where they are intended to stand. Yet if we presuppose that Molière and Shakespeare intended us to stand somewhere, that the plays are not merely incoherent creative accidents, then it is worth trying to establish the sort of audience contract they imply.

Dom Juan and *Troilus and Cressida* could both be classified as experimental plays. This is the more surprising because the idea of an 'experimental play' is very much a modern one. In the Elizabethan theatre concepts of genre were simply too vague and too fluid for self-conscious formal experiment to have much meaning. When trying to classify *Troilus and Cressida* critics have been able to choose between the Folio editors' decision to place it among the tragedies, the 1609 Quarto's title-page which calls it a History, and the enigmatic Quarto preface which praises it among Shakespeare's comedies. But as a modern editor of the play argues, 'Nothing is really proved by this contradictory nomenclature except how casual the Elizabethan and Jacobean vocabulary was when it came to naming genres'.[2] Molière's contemporaries, if they had ever heard of experimental drama, would certainly have condemned it as anarchist rebellion against the 'règles'.

Yet for all its apparent anachronism, 'experimental' does seem the right adjective to describe the formal characteristics of *Dom Juan* and *Troilus and Cressida*. In both there appears to be a deliberate, even a wanton, dislocation of the normal principles of dramatic structure. As Richard Fly comments in an article on *Troilus and Cressida*, 'Our expectations of formal stability, symmetry, and coherent sequence are perpetually being frustrated, and we experience as we follow the play unfolding a growing sense of radical disorientation.'[3] This disorientation seems too consistent a technique to be accidental. Similarly with *Dom Juan*, as Jacques Schérer has pointed out,[4] Molière rejected the principles of causal relation between events which can be found in his sources. In Dorimon's and Villiers' version of the play, the various adventures are linked, however implausibly: Dom Juan is shipwrecked, *while* trying to escape from Spain, *in order* to avoid arrest *after* killing the Commander. In Molière all the traditional images are there, but Molière does not explain how or why one should follow another. Molière and Shakespeare were both working with stories familiar to their audiences, and in one sense they gave them the scenes which were expected. But those scenes are viewed from such unexpected angles, they are shown in such anomalous sequences, that the disparity between conventional image and dramatic reality seems deliberately developed for ironic effect. Rather than try to show that *Troilus and Cressida* and *Dom Juan* are definitively comedies, the purpose of this chapter is to follow up the idea of the contract with the audience, to isolate what there is of a comic attitude in the plays, and to see the effect it has when applied to what are largely non-comic forms and materials.

TROILUS AND CRESSIDA

Modern critics have become increasingly wary about assuming that we know what an Elizabethan or Jacobean audience thought, or what expectations they brought to the theatre. The more research is done on the background of the period, the less we feel we can risk those convenient generalisations about how 'the Elizabethans' — monolithic group — would have reacted to any given stage event or image. *Troilus and Cressida* provides an interesting example of this changing perspective. Earlier critics placed *Troilus and Cressida* firmly in a mediaeval tradition originating with Caxton, Lydgate and Henryson, which treated the Trojan story in a satiric and anti-heroic light.[5] Others differentiated between the Trojans, whom the Elizabethans admired, partly because of the legend of Brute, the Trojan prince, as founder of Britain, and the Greeks, who were bywords for various sorts of vice.[6] Yet, as Robert Kimbrough has shown, the tradition deriving from Caxton was ambivalent in attitude because Caxton used eclectically two sources, Dictys and Dares, one of which was pro-Trojan and one pro-Greek. Examining the range of attitudes towards the Troy story of

Elizabethan literature and drama, Kimbrough illustrates 'the wide variety, contradiction and stereotypes prevalent in the Trojan literary tradition'.[7] We are forced to the conclusion that there is no one fixed and stable received view of the Homeric material which Shakespeare was consciously following, or else deliberately parodying, but instead a malleable and shifting area of common knowledge to be used now one way, now another.

It is this which makes it so extraordinarily difficult to know what to make, for example, of the Greek council of war in the first act of *Troilus and Cressida*. Agamemnon and Nestor produce speeches which to most modern ears sound impossibly pompous and verbose, full of periphrases, repetition, and empty-sounding Latinate vocabulary. Would they have sounded that way to an audience in 1601–2? Is this a case of deliberate burlesque?[8] And if Shakespeare was sending up the huffing and puffing of the two senior Greek leaders, what of the third speaker, Ulysses, who is given one of the most famous speeches in all the plays, the oration on 'degree' which has so often been taken as the classic exposition of the 'Elizabethan world order'? Homer's characters are by no means unrecognisable in the versions Shakespeare gives us, but it would have been easy to play them in the theatre so that they parodied themselves, Agamemnon's majestic presence turned into ponderous self-importance, Nestor's venerable wisdom into prosy old age, and Ulysses' statescraft into the bromides of a tricky politician.

The text does provide evidence that some degree of irony was intended in this scene. Directly after the speeches of the three leaders, Ulysses relates how Patroclus burlesques them for Achilles' benefit. First the commander-in-chief:

> Sometime, great Agamemnon,
> Thy topless deputation he puts on,
> And, like a strutting player, whose conceit
> Lies in his hamstring and doth think it rich
> To hear the wooden dialogue and sound
> 'Twixt his stretched footing and the scaffoldage,
> Such to-be-pitied and o'er-wrested seeming
> He acts thy greatness in; and when he speaks,
> 'Tis like a chime a-mending, with terms unsquared,
> Which, from the tongue of roaring Typhon dropped,
> Would seem hyperboles.   I iii 151–61

No doubt this is a caricature of the Agamemnon we have just heard speak, but it is surely a recognisable caricature. Then Achilles calls for a performance of Nestor:

Now play me Nestor; hem, and stroke thy beard,
As he being dressed to some oration.   I iii 165—6

There is an easy laugh in the theatre at these lines if Nestor, whom we have seen 'dressed' to an oration, habitually strokes his beard before he speaks. Ulysses does not altogether let himself off either. Achilles, Patroclus, and the other disaffected members of the Greek camp, we are told, despise the qualities for which he is especially famous:

They tax our policy and call it cowardice
. . .   . . . The still and mental parts
That do contrive how many hands shall strike
When fitness calls them on, and know by measure
Of their observant toil the enemy's weight —
Why, this hath not a finger's dignity:
They call this bed-work, mappery, closet war.   I iii 197—205

Yet if there is irony here, it is not simply a matter of debunking the solemnity of the Greek high command. It is after all Ulysses who is acting out Patroclus' and Achilles' charades with as lively mimicry and as much scorn for their performance as they have for their superior officers:

At this fusty stuff
The large Achilles, on his pressed bed lolling,
From his deep chest laughs out a loud applause   I iii 161—3

It is a fairly satiric picture for our first glimpse of the legendary hero. The irony here and throughout much of the play works not in one pointed direction, but rather towards a more generally sceptical awareness of the disproportion between intended performance and actual effect. We see a further example of this, later in the scene, when Aeneas enters to present Hector's challenge to the Greeks. With an enormous number of flourishes Aeneas asks where he can find Agamemnon:

Aeneas.   How may
                A stranger to those most imperial looks
                Know them from eyes of other mortals?
Agamemnon.   How?
     Aeneas. Ay:
                I ask, that I might waken reverence,
                And bid the cheek be ready with a blush

> Modest as morning when she coldly eyes
> The youthful Phoebus.
> Which is that god in office, guiding men?
> Which is the high and mighty Agamemnon?
Agamemnon. This Trojan scorns us, or the men of Troy
> Are ceremonious courtiers.   I iii 224 – 34

The incident would suggest a rather insignificant looking Agamemnon, a little man whom Aeneas could not easily identify as 'that god in office, guiding men'. (The emphasis on 'high and mighty' and 'topless deputation' would make this an obvious theatrical joke.) Yet the laugh is surely as much against Aeneas, who is indeed a 'ceremonious courtier'. It is the neutral perception of the absurdity of a mistimed miscast performance on both sides.

Bathos and anti-climax are the play's characteristic techniques. No line of action, no argument ever actually goes anywhere, most of all not where we would expect it to go. This is most striking in the council-scene of the Trojans in Act II. In contrast to the Greeks who seemed to have called a council of war simply to discuss the general state of affairs, the Trojans at least have something to debate – an offer of peace on condition they give Helen back. (It is typical of the total disjunction of the play's plot that we never hear anything of this peace-offer on the Greek side.) The debate that results is a genuine and serious one in which basic issues of honour and right are argued out. Are the Trojans to accept Troilus's arbitrary evaluation of Helen – 'What's aught but as 'tis valued?' – or Hector's view of the 'moral laws of nature and of nations' which 'speak aloud to have her back returned'. As we all know, Hector wins the debate but loses the argument, and the sudden volte-face with which he gives in has been treated as one of the central cruxes of the play. What is remarkable, however, is not only that the most eloquent of the doves is transformed thus abruptly into the leader of the hawks, but that he reveals at the end of the scene, what we already knew from Act I, that he was committed to a hawkish attitude from before the scene began.

> I have a roisting challenge sent amongst
> The dull and factious nobles of the Greeks
> Will strike amazement to their drowsy spirits.   II ii 208 – 10

Even though the challenge was a 'friendly', so to speak, surely it makes nonsense in retrospect of the whole debate.

One of the reasons advanced to support the thesis that *Troilus and Cressida* was written for, or at least performed at, one of the Inns of Court, is the large number of legalistic arguments such as those for and against the keeping of Helen, which it is thought that the young lawyers would have enjoyed. Scenes such as the Trojan council certainly do seem to evoke a lawyer-like interest in debate for its own sake. Who wins or who loses in a court-case may be regarded cynically or fatalistically as a matter of luck; the superiority of one argument over another will not ensure the success of the cause it advances. Hector submits to what he recognises as the way of the world, whatever his opinion 'in the way of truth'. And yet the skill of the debaters and the force and elegance of the arguments can be admired in spite of their ultimate lack of relation to reality. It is important not to over-state the degree and quality of irony here. As Patricia Thomson has put it acutely, 'Ironies do not turn speeches into speechifying'.[9] If Shakespeare had wanted to mock the useless committee-room atmosphere of a council of war, he could easily have achieved his aim without writing the dense and eloquent poetry he gives to Hector and Troilus.

The same question of interpretation arises with Ulysses' two great speeches, on 'degree' (I ii 75–137) and on 'time' (III iii 145–89). Many critics have by now pointed out that there is an ironic disparity between the vast generalisations of these speeches and the specific political effect which Ulysses has in mind in each case. Moreover, there is another ironic dimension if the two are compared, for they imply wholly contradictory views of the universe. And yet once again it would seem, to say the least, uneconomical of Shakespeare to produce these magnificent lines as food for cynics. It may be that there is here a middle ground between idealism and disillusion which we as modern readers or audiences find hard to rediscover. We are accustomed to an idea of political rhetoric as entirely disingenuous inflated language with little or no meaning, only to be read for what it can signify between the lines. It is only the very unsophisticated who take at face value the clichés of the modern politician. But the cliché, to be a cliché, must once have had pretensions to originality. Ulysses' speeches on degree and time are based not on clichés but on commonplaces. An Elizabethan audience in recognising some of the most traditional and conventional attitudes of their time would not have sneered at them as fly-blown truisms, but would quite probably have been impressed by the eloquence with which the familiar arguments were expressed. And yet there can be no doubt that the situation in the play does ironically qualify that impressiveness while not necessarily denying it. What Shakespeare seems to be doing in *Troilus and Cressida* — and Molière may have been attempting something similar in *Dom Juan* — is to place his audience in the space between idea and action, argument and event, to make them continuously aware of a double reaction to both.

'This is and is not Cressid', Troilus calls out in anguish as he watches himself betrayed. But it is true of Cressida throughout the action, not just when she gives herself to Diomedes, and it is equally true of most of the other characters. What we see them do, what we see they are, is shadowed always by what we know they have become in the familiar legend. This is most striking with Troilus and Cressida themselves who, at the very moment when their love is about to be consummated, freeze themselves into their proverbial stereotypes, 'as true as Troilus', 'as false as Cressid'. This might be a tragic irony, but it is not, and not only because Pandarus weighs in with his prose identification of himself as the first 'pandar'. Rather than feeling the poignancy of this ironic declaration of what is to come, we experience what is to them the hypothetical future as our present. They *are* already what they prophesy they will be. And though they may not know it, their language does. This certainly is the effect of Troilus' desperate effort to deny Cressida's infidelity later:

Let it not be believed for womanhood!
Think we had mothers. Do not give advantage
To stubborn critics, apt without a theme
For depravation, to square the general sex
By Cressid's rule. Rather think this not Cressid.   V ii 129–34

Even as Troilus protests in the story-time when Cressida's unfaithfulness is first made manifest, he lives in the language-time when she is a banal example used by cynical misogynists.

Throughout *Troilus and Cressida* there are moments like this in which the present of the audience seems to overcome the stage present. It is one of the means by which Shakespeare flattens out and deadens the emotional responses which his play might otherwise arouse. Gervinus sums it up well:

It is very remarkable, but every reader will confess that this piece creates throughout no real effect on the mind. No one on reading the play will readily feel any sympathy or love for any character, any preference for any part, any pity for any suffering, any joy at any success; not even in the affair between Troilus and Cressida, which speaks to the heart more than any other incident in the piece.[10]

This is not to be dismissed as nineteenth-century sentimentalism; it is indeed an effect of the play, and one which Shakespeare seems deliberately to have cultivated. Troilus and Cressida are almost never allowed to appear alone together without the ironising presence of Pandarus. When they do briefly

have a moment to themselves in Act III scene ii — Pandarus has gone to get a
fire — the effect is striking, for suddenly in place of the lyrical verse which we
might expect from them, they speak Pandarus's prose. In a very cool and
unecstatic vein, Troilus debunks as monstrous,

> [lovers'] undertakings, when we vow to weep seas, live in fire, eat rocks,
> tame tigers; thinking it harder for our mistress to devise imposition
> enough than for us to undergo any difficulty imposed. This is the
> monstruosity of love, lady — that the will is infinite and the execution
> confined; that the desire is boundless and the act a slave to limit.   III ii
> 76—82

The sexual innuendo in 'will' is taken up by Cressida who answers with puns
on 'performance' and 'act' which place this conversation closer to the bawdy
repartee of Pandarus than anything else we hear from the lovers together. It
is as though the leering view of love supplied by Pandarus is a necessary part
of their relationship, which his presence usually spares them from voicing
themselves. It is not only as a go-between that Pandarus is essential to them;
he is the catalyst which makes their love happen, and there could be no such
thing as a Pandarless affair between Troilus and Cressida.

It was once said of someone that he had the Midas touch in reverse, he
turned everything he touched to tinsel. It should have been said of Pandarus.
Before ever we meet the legendary figures of the Trojan war, Hector, Paris,
Helen, Cassandra, we hear of them, in the bathetic anecdote of Pandarus,
laughing in an atmosphere of frivolous inanity at the white hair on Troilus'
chin. Not only does Pandarus hover round the lovers urging them into bed
with visible vicarious pleasure, but he burlesques the pathos of their parting:

> *Enter Troilus.*
>
> *Pandarus.* Here, here he comes. Ah, sweet ducks!
> *Cressida.* O Troilus! Troilus! [*embracing him*]
> *Pandarus.* What a pair of spectacles is here! Let me embrace too.
>   'O heart', as the goodly saying is,
>   O heart, O heavy heart,
>   Why sigh'st thou without breaking?

where he answers again,

>   Because thou canst not ease thy smart
>   By friendship nor by speaking.

There never was a truer rhyme. Let us cast away nothing, for
we may live to have need of such a verse. We see it, we see it.
How now, lambs!   IV iv 11 – 23

With Pandarus's absurd tag of popular song, Shakespeare seems to inoculate
us against a fully emotional response to some of the most beautiful, some of
the most purely lyrical, verse in the play which is shortly to follow:

Troilus. . . . We two, that with so many thousand sighs
Did buy each other, must poorly sell ourselves
With the rude brevity and discharge of one.
Injurious Time now with a robber's haste
Crams his rich thievery up, he knows not how:
As many farewells as be stars in heaven,
With distinct breath and consigned kisses to them,
He fumbles up into a loose adieu,
And scants us with a single famished kiss,
Distasted with the salt of broken tears.   IV iv 39 – 48

Here, as with the great speeches of Ulysses, we are left admiring the language
without reacting to what it actually says.

What Pandarus is to the love-plot of *Troilus and Cressida*, Thersites is to
the war. If we are rarely allowed a view of the romantic lovers without the
bathetic comments of Pandarus, Thersites is nearly as constant a presence in
the scenes devoted to the great Greek heroes. Each of them in turn is given his
Thersites label: Ajax is 'this lord . . . who wears his wit in his belly and his
guts in his head' or 'Mars his idiot'; Patroclus is 'Achilles' brach' or 'his
masculine whore'; Agamemnon 'has not so much brain as ear-wax'; as for
Menelaus – 'I care not to be the louse of a lazar, so I were not Menelaus'; and
finally we have 'that stale old mouse-eaten dry cheese, Nestor, and that same
dog-fox Ulysses'. Pandarus and Thersites are not only complementary in
their dramatic function of making ridiculous what would otherwise have
some claim to be thought sublime. They are anti-types, each the caricature
representative of his side in the war. G. Wilson Knight in *The Wheel of Fire*
identified the opposing values of Trojans and Greeks as 'intuition' against
'intellect' 'emotion' against 'reason'.[11] Pandarus, accordingly is a sen-
timentalist and vulgariser, travestying the value of love, whereas Thersites is
a denigrator, whose reductive cynicism masquerades as unvarnished truth-
telling.

If we recognise this parallel, it may not be so hard to detach ourselves from the point of view of Thersites, which has sometimes been taken to sum up the way we are to see the play. 'Lechery, lechery; still wars and lechery; nothing else holds fashion.' Thersites' temperamental need to call a spade a bloody shovel is as comically placed as Pandarus' pandering – and was for the Elizabethans nearly as proverbial.[12] Thersites' stage role as ironic commentator appears to leave him closer to the audience than he actually is. In the multiple eavesdropping scene in which Thersites watches Ulysses watching Troilus watching Diomedes and Cressida, the normal dynamics of irony would seem to place us with Thersites at the most inclusive level of awareness. Certainly Thersites' comments distance us from Troilus' emotion; on his anguished disbelief of what he sees Thersites remarks acidly, 'Will 'a swagger himself out on's own eyes?' Yet we, who have seen Troilus' Cressida before she became Diomedes', will view this scene differently from Thersites, or from Ulysses who categorised Cressida straight off as a 'daughter of the game', or indeed from Diomedes who treats her as such. If we do not share Troilus' shock of disillusion – an audience expects Cressida's infidelity *a priori* – we can perhaps see in her hesitant acceptance of Diomedes not just the whorish playing-hard-to-get which it is for Ulysses and Thersites, but the remnants of her loyalty to Troilus. There is some poignancy in her last brief monologue which begins:

> Troilus, farewell! One eye yet looks on thee,
> But with my heart the other eye doth see.   V ii 106–7

We are not identified with Thersites as the actor furthest downstage; rather we are given a panoramic irony which allows us to see both Cressida as she is, and the onlookers' various conflicting valuations of what she is and what she ought to have been.

The ultimate problem of the play, and particularly the end of the play, is what we are left with when the gap between expectation and reality is finally exposed. Ulysses thought that by his statesmanly skill he could manoeuvre Achilles back into the war; his 'policy . . . is not proved worth a blackberry'. When Achilles re-enters the war it is for quite different reasons. Hector believes in chivalrous principles of fair play which Troilus warns him are fool's play; and so he finds out when he is treacherously murdered by Achilles' Myrmidons. The death of Hector, the catastrophe of Homer's epic, is turned into something as meaningless as a gangland killing. In nothing are audience expectations fulfilled. The play ends with Troilus still alive, and not a glimpse of the ultimate degradation and punishment of Cressida which the Henryson tradition might have led an Elizabethan audience to expect. As

Philip Edwards says, 'the play is anti-art, because its very structure is a kind of defiance of the continuity, congruence and unity which the more usual kind of play will provide.'[13]

One main thrust of the play may be identified as iconoclasm, but when we try to establish just what sort or degree of iconoclasm we are back with the question with which we started – what kind of icons would Shakespeare have been trying to break and to what end? There can be no doubt, presumably, that his version of the death of Hector is a deliberate alteration of the normal story. In Caxton and Lydgate, it was Troilus who was killed in a treacherous ambush, and to transfer this death to Hector, who in all the other sources dies, as in Homer, in single combat with Achilles, suggests a definite desire to shock. But what is the point of the shock tactic? Is it to underline the inadequacy of Hector's ideals of chivalry in the reality of war, and if so what values are implicit in the terms 'chivalry' and 'reality'? For critics such as Wilson Knight there can be no doubt that Shakespeare intended us to see in Hector's death the savage destruction of an admirable and admired ideal order. Alternatively *Troilus and Cressida* can be seen as mock-heroic, not lamenting the death of love and honour as glorious ideals, but debunking the 'rant and cant' associated with both of them.[14] It appears virtually to be a case of paying our money and taking our choice which interpretation we elect.

The formal frame to the play may perhaps help here to determine the attitude which Shakespeare expected his audience to adopt. The tone of the Prologue many critics have found peculiar, and for some it has provided clear signs of a comic intention. The strangely overblown phrasing – 'the princes orgulous', 'disgorge their warlike fraughtage', 'corresponsive and fulfilling bolts' – interspersed with moments of brisk colloquialism – 'and that's the quarrel', 'tickling skittish spirits' – may be construed as knowing burlesque. The play ends with Pandarus' address to the audience bequeathing them his diseases, which seems like a deliberate parody of the normal ingratiating comic epilogue. Certainly no other tragedy of Shakespeare's is so framed at both ends, although *Romeo and Juliet* has of course its expository Prologue. But the formal frame is not so very different in tone from that used in the history plays, particularly in *Henry V*, the last of the chronicles written before *Troilus and Cressida*. If we have to choose a label for the play, à la Polonius, perhaps 'comical history' might be more appropriate than either 'comedy' or 'tragedy'.

There is a great deal in *Troilus and Cressida* to remind us of the history plays, particularly the two parts of *Henry IV*. Troilus' speeches in the council scene have the ring of Hotspur:

Nay, if we talk of reason,
Let's shut our gates and sleep. Manhood and honour
Should have hare hearts, would they but fat their thoughts
With this crammed reason.   II ii 46–9

The charades of Falstaff and Hal juxtaposed with the serious scenes they parody are like the antics of Achilles and Patroclus recounted by Ulysses. Thersites on the battlefield, at once the cowardly buffoon and the cynical war-correspondent, is a thin and bad-tempered version of Falstaff at Shrewsbury. It may be that in *Troilus and Cressida* Shakespeare turned to a different sort of history in order to pursue effects which in his English chronicles he could not fully explore. Many critics have noticed in *Henry V* the ironies which sit uneasily with the epic story of Agincourt as the Tudor myth of history compelled Shakespeare to write it. With the legend of Troy, which had much of the substantial weight of history but demanded no single orthodox interpretation, he was able to give these ironies freer play.

John Bayley, in one of the most illuminating of modern essays on *Troilus and Cressida*, stresses the way in which the enactment of the play in the present seems to deny the reality of the historical past:

> the game seems to be to deny that the famous and the legendary ever existed as time has reported them, or that we would ever find anything at any moment in history beyond scraps of idiotic dialogue and meaningless event.[15]

The play in this is as much anti-history as anti-art, rejecting the historian's claim to make shape and form out of the chaos of fact. Yet what we see is not only the incoherent reality behind the historical myth, but also the characters attempting to act out their historical parts with all the meaning normally attributed to them. They are not, like Stephen Dedalus, trying to awake from the nightmare of history but quite given over to their sleepwalking performances. It is we the audience who are awake, and who can watch with sceptical detachment the various postures adopted by these legendary figures. Or, at least, that seems to be the attitude the formal structure invites us to adopt. We may look again at whether this is its actual effect when we have considered the analogous case of *Dom Juan*.

DOM JUAN

The story of Dom Juan did not, of course, come to Molière with all the weight of centuries of tradition, nor did it have the semi-historical status of the Trojan war. It had originated with Tirso de Molina only some 40 years before Molière, and if we are inclined to think of it as a basic and universal legend it is mainly because of its widespread use since the seventeenth century. Yet already by Molière's time there had grown up what Jacques Schérer has called a *'folklore donjuanesque'*. Particularly for a Parisian audience in the 1660's, with two full-length French versions and an Italian *commedia* on the subject having been played within the space of a few years, the title *Dom Juan*, or rather *Le Festin de Pierre*, would have aroused the expectations of familiarity. They knew what they were to get, the spectacular scenes of picaresque adventure, the *lazzi* of a comic servant, and finally the morally edifying ending of 'l'athée foudroyé', the atheist struck down. It was unashamedly heterogeneous material, and though no doubt the Italian *commedia* actors played up the comic parts more than Dorimon and Villiers in their formal verse 'tragicomédies', the mixture is more or less the same in all of the different versions. Where we have lost the earlier Elizabethan play on Troilus and Cressida by Chettle and Dekker, we can follow minutely Molière's use of his immediate sources for *Dom Juan*. Astonishingly little in the play is in fact wholly original; the most striking scenes in Molière can nearly all be traced back to at least a suggestion in one of his predecessors.[16]

And yet it is not possible to accept, what was accepted by so many generations of critics, that the anomalies of the structure and tone in *Dom Juan* can be explained away as the inescapable features of a popular subject which Molière put together as a get-rich-quick play when short of money and time. The discovery of the contract for the provision of the sets, dated December 3rd, 1664, makes it clear that two and a half months before the first performance Molière must have been sufficiently well on with the play to know precisely the visual effects he wanted for each act.[17] With a man who could write, rehearse, and produce a play in less than a fortnight, this can not be classified as a piece written in haste. But in a way the violent reaction of *Dom Juan*'s opponents is the most convincing evidence that this could not be dismissed as just another popular version of a subject which, in all its mingling of sacred and profane, had never roused protests in its earlier treatments. Molière's *Dom Juan* bothered people, and has continued to bother people – not in itself necessarily a sign of a great work of art, but an indication that there is more to it than an ephemeral crowd-catcher.

Perhaps Molière's most striking general alteration of his sources is the substitution of words for action. It is a commonplace that in the course of the play the great seducer never actually succeeds in seducing anyone. The murder of the Commander, which both Dorimon and Villiers included, is relegated in Molière to a casual retrospect of an incident six months old.

Dom Juan's violent treatment of his father was a central feature of the earlier versions: both Dorimon and Villiers sub-title their plays *Le Fils Criminel*, have a scene in which he strikes his father, and depict him as a virtual parricide. Molière's hero politely offers his father a chair and waits until he has stormed out of the room before expressing his callous sentiments. Though Dom Juan may represent a principle of movement in the play, as Guicharnaud suggests,[18] it is rarely directed or purposeful movement. Dom Juan does very little, he talks a good deal, and he elicits even more talk from others. Sganarelle's opening tirade on snuff, from which he turns as though reluctantly to the business of exposition, sets the rhythm for the play as a whole – a series of discussions, conversations, quarrels, occasionally interrupted by action.

'Quoi que puisse dire Aristote et toute la Philosophie, il n'est rien d'égal au tabac' – 'Whatever Aristotle and all the philosophers may say, there is nothing like tobacco.' Much has been made of the thematic keynotes to be found in this speech, in particular the idea of contractual obligation and its relation to 'honnêteté'.[19] But at the simple level of comic technique it introduces the burlesque of ideas which it is Sganarelle's function to supply throughout the play. It is partly in imitation of his master, partly in rivalry, that Sganarelle loves to argue, and as so often with servant imitations in comedy, it comes out all wrong. At its crudest, reasoning ends up with slapstick, as when he is discoursing on the marvels of the mind's control over the body and trips. 'Voilà ton raisonnement qui a le nez cassé'. All Sganarelle's arguments end up with one sort of broken nose or another, and he can never win against the effortless skill of his master. At the end of Dom Juan's first virtuoso defense of his life-style, Sganarelle is simply stunned:

> Vertu de ma vie, comme vous débitez! Il semble que vous avez appris cela par coeur, et vous parlez tout comme un livre.   I ii

Some critics have tried to see this as ironically undercutting the sophistries of Dom Juan's philosophy of conquest, but surely the laugh is rather against Sganarelle who, in face of aristocratic spontaneity, can only think in terms of the rote-learning to which he attributes eloquence.

We laugh at Sganarelle's bafflement as he tries to formulate a reply to his master:

> Ma foi! j'ai à dire . . ., je ne sais que dire; car vous avez tourné les choses d'une manière, qu'il semble que vous avez raison; et cependant il est vrai que vous ne l'avez pas. J'avois les plus belles pensées du monde, et vos

discours m'ont brouillé tout cela. Laissez faire: une autre fois je mettrai mes raisonnements par écrit, pour disputer avec vous.　I ii

We have no doubt that Sganarelle is right: what Dom Juan has done is exactly to 'make the worse appear the better reason' according to the old sophist formula and Dom Juan himself is perfectly aware of this. What is comic is Sganarelle's touching belief in formal written argument, where we can see that it is exactly Dom Juan's capacity to think on his feet, to produce *ad hoc* verbal strategies, which makes him so unassailable. He delights in the very preposterousness of his point of view, as he makes out that his infidelity represents a policy of justice to all:

toutes les belles ont droit de nous charmer, et l'avantage d'être rencontrée la première ne doit point dérober aux autres les justes prétentions qu'elles ont toutes sur nos coeurs　I ii

The absurd egoism by which Dom Juan here in fact sets himself up as a prize for whoever can catch him, is made attractive by the self-conscious flimsiness of the rhetoric. Sganarelle will always lose in argument against his master however carefully he marshalls his ideas in advance because he is trying to argue for what he believes, whereas Dom Juan, who believes in nothing, is arguing for the fun of it.

Dom Juan represents in the play a spirit of pure negation, pure perversity. There has been a great deal of controversy over whether Dom Juan is an atheist (who does not believe God exists) or a libertine (who defies God), but in fact Dom Juan's only principle is to deny any consistent principle at all beyond the axiomatic certainty of his famous 2 + 2 = 4. This is why he is so adept at evading the various sorts of creditor, financial, moral, and spiritual, whose claims upon him occupy so much of the play.[20] He can always pay one in the money appropriate to another, for one currency is as valueless to him as another. In the first act, for example, when Elvire taxes him with infidelity, she expects the usual excuses of the gallant, and half satirically, half hopefully, she asks him why he does not proffer them.

Que ne vous armez-vous le front d'une noble effronterie? Que ne me jurez-vous que vous êtes toujours dans les mêmes sentiments pour moi, que vous m'aimez toujours avec une ardeur sans égale, et que rien n'est capable de vous détacher de moi que le mort? Que ne me dites-vous que des affaires de la dernière consequence vous ont obligé a partir sans m'en donner avis . . .　I iii

But Dom Juan answers not as the gallant she expects, but as a *dévot* who fears the wrath of Heaven for having taken her from a convent. The brazen insolence of this, in view of what we already know of Dom Juan's views on Heaven, is all too evident yet it is a strategy which completely out-manoeuvres Elvire. He uses the same technique, after his official conversion to hypocrisy in Act V, to head off the just demands of honour made upon him by Dom Carlos. As with Tartuffe, 'le Ciel' serves as blocking move against all attempts to make him pay up.

The juxtaposition of the visits of M. Dimanche and Dom Louis in Act IV brings out this technique strikingly. By that stage of the play Dom Juan is positively beseiged with duns of every sort. Where earlier he had led a picaresque life of easy escapes, in Act IV he is confined to his house, forced to meet all comers. The game by which he outwits M. Dimanche is well-known, and one of the most purely comic scenes in the play. His treatment of Dimanche as a friend and equal so flatters and bewilders the unfortunate bourgeois that he cannot remember his capacity as creditor. But in face of the much more serious demands of Dom Louis, Dom Juan uses exactly the same ploy: 'Monsieur, si vous étiez assis, vous en seriez mieux pour parler' (IV v) – 'Sir, if you were seated, you could talk more comfortably.' To offer M. Dimanche a 'fauteuil', the most honourable form of seating, in the presence of an aristocrat like himself, was an extraordinary compliment; to his father, in the context, it is a nicely veiled insult. To make the point in the theatre, it would almost certainly be the same 'fauteuil'. In the case of Dimanche, as Jules Brody has remarked, he 'raises a commercial relationship up to the social level', with Dom Louis he brings 'moral relationships down to the social level'.[21]

This alienating strategy of Dom Juan's raises similar questions of ironic interpretation to those we met in *Troilus and Cressida*. Dom Louis' speech of remonstrance is an eloquent expression of the ideal of nobility, a nobility of behaviour rather than of blood alone:

> qu'avez-vous fait dans le monde pour être gentilhomme? Croyez-vous qu'il suffise d'en porter le nom et les armes, et que ce nous soit une gloire d'être sorti d'un sang noble lorsque nous vivons en infâmes? Non, non, la naissance n'est rien où la vertu n'est pas.   IV v

The idea that aristocracy must be validated by virtue in every generation is attractive in itself, and Molière draws on respected classical commonplaces to give it weight and authority. But as with Ulysses' great commonplaces in *Troilus and Cressida*, does not the ironic context undermine the effect of the rhetoric? Is not Dom Louis' posture reduced to posturing by the simple device of Dom Juan, kicking the props from under him, or rather suggesting he needs props under him? A basic comic dynamic — some theorists would argue the most basic — is the humiliation of a figure of authority, and if that is what happens here, surely Dom Louis' argument lies in ruins.

The most crucial instance of this problem of interpretation in the play is the so-called 'scène du pauvre'. In spite of the fact that it may have been suggested by Dom Juan's encounter with a pilgrim in earlier versions of the story and a variety of other sources, the tone and effect of the scene are entirely original. It so worried Molière's contemporaries that it was altered after the second performance, and even after his death appeared in full only in pirated editions of the text published outside France. It is understandable that it should have been found so disturbing, not because it is an unequivocal victory of the atheist over the believer — after all the poor man does not blaspheme to win his louis, though a louis would have been a small fortune to him — but exactly because it is not an unambiguous victory for either.[22] If the poor man, in his staunch simplicity, is unmoved by Dom Juan's ironies which he cannot understand, the libertine nevertheless scores some important points against orthodox piety. The special credit of the poor man with Heaven which makes his prayers for the charitable a suitable exchange for alms,[23] is called in question by his miserable state of necessity. How, says Dom Juan ironically, can a man who spends his life praying to Heaven be anything but prosperous? When he throws the poor man the louis, 'pour l'amour de l'humanité', parodying the traditional almsgiving formula, 'pour l'amour de Dieu', does he succeed in turning the defeat, represented by the poor man's refusal to swear, into a libertine victory?

The line suits equally well every available view of Dom Juan. It can be seen, by those who are sympathetic to Dom Juan, as a rallying-cry for humanism against the tyrannies of religion. Or just the opposite, Dom Juan can be imagined flinging down the coin in spite, and trying to save his face with a sneering phrase. For those who argue that the play ultimately ridicules Dom Juan as well as his opponents, this line brings out, paradoxically, his inhumanity, his dogmatism of disbelief, which is as inflexible as its opposite.[24] The range of points of view on the play is made possible by the negativity of the protagonist. His refusal to be what any other character in the play wants him to be means that he is, as it were, free to represent what any audience or critic may want. Yet his perversity, his consistently ironic stance and the grace and elegance with which he carries it off, makes it hard to resist a measure of identification with Dom Juan. In his questioning of every ideal he is like an attractive version of Thersites and the principles of irony seem to work to ally us with him as the least deceived of the characters. What is more, there is always Sganarelle, like Pandarus, to parody the positions we might have adopted. When the converted Elvire begins her passionate and eloquent plea to Dom Juan in Act IV, Dom Juan looks with dry-eyed irony at his servant, 'Tu pleures, je pense'. Any tendency we might have had to be moved by Elvire's remonstrance is stopped dead by the (no doubt noisy) sobs of the grotesque clown. It is the same technique by which Pandarus' sentimentalism is used to chill our emotional response to Troilus and Cressida's parting. As Guicharnaud sums it up neatly, 'Sganarelle is the risk we run in condemning Dom Juan'.[25]

This is, of course, what made *Dom Juan* so shocking for Molière's contemporaries. The Prince de Conti and the Sieur de Rochemont, the play's two most vehement opponents, both complained (with justification) that the stupidity and ridiculousness of Sganarelle as the apologist of orthodoxy make him no match for the wit and intelligence of the libertine. The whole comic mechanism of the play depends on our delight in Sganarelle's repeated defeat in argument. And this delight is part of a more general anticipation that Dom Juan will go on undefeated to the end. Earlier Dom Juans had had their moments of anxiety or repentance; in Tirso's *Burlador* his final repentance, too late, is the point of the play. It is the basic *donné* of Molière's character that he should never for an instant swerve from his principleless principles. The opening of Act V, when Dom Juan has apparently been converted, is a moment of dramatic suspense in which we are afraid he has given in; we are immensely relieved when we discover that this is simply the last and most audacious of his poses. The progress of Tartuffe, or Volpone, as we saw in the last chapter, is viewed in somewhat the same way. But whereas in *Tartuffe* and *Volpone* the continuing success of the rogues went to validate a satiric hypothesis, the effect of Dom Juan's libertinism is rather different. He is closer, perhaps, to a Mr. Punch figure whose wilful and conscienceless defiance of all norms of social and moral order wins from an audience a scandalised and delighted assent to the wish-fulfilment liberation he represents.[26]

Yet there are two logics of audience expectation working through the play; we want Dom Juan to escape the repeated attempts to corner him, to pin him down, but we equally look forward to his final punishment. In many scenarios Punch outwits even the Devil at the end, but Dom Juan *must* be destroyed by the Statue. This is not merely a matter of a spectacular dénouement with which Molière was obliged to conclude his play whether it suited his artistic purpose or not. From the first appearance of the Commander, at the end of Act III, we recognise an opponent whose demands Dom Juan will not be able to set elegantly aside, and at some level Dom Juan recognises it too. Although he does not lose his nerve, the brusque 'Allons, sortons d'ici' to Sganarelle at the end of their first encounter with the

Statue, and even more the unconvincing attempt to find a naturalistic explanation for the Statue's nod — 'nous pouvons avoir été trompés par un faux jour' — suggest that Dom Juan is bothered by the supernatural, to put it no more strongly. It is for this reason, perhaps, that his temper becomes noticeably worse in the last two acts. Sganarelle's remonstrances are cut very short indeed with the threat of a whipping. We suspect that the earlier, more insouciant, Dom Juan would not have felt the need to abuse his father even behind his back; and the final assumption of hypocrisy has an element of wanton and defiant recklessness about it.

This is not to try to make the case, as some critics and stage producers have, for a Dom Juan who is a believer in spite of himself, who denies ever more stridently the God whom he is not sure does not exist. To Dom Juan all those who make demands upon him are nuisances, unless he can turn them into amusements. He senses very early on that the Statue will prove the greatest nuisance of the lot, but he tries valiantly to categorise him as an entertainment by the invitation to supper. The trouble is that in the Commander he has met not only a stronger, more implacable, will than his own, but a figure who can completely torpedo his jests. The ultimate in Dom Juan's bravado is to insist punctiliously on lighting the Statue home to his tomb after supper. The reply flattens the offer into trivial facetiousness: 'On n'a pas besoin de lumière, quand on est conduit par le Ciel' (IV viii) — 'One has no need of light, when one is led by Heaven.' The Statue is the only character in the play (if he can be called a character) who can have the last word over Dom Juan. He outwits the libertine before he destroys him.

All of this, on one simple theatrical level, could no doubt be successful enough. The first audiences of *Dom Juan*, to judge by the receipts of La Grange's Register, obviously loved it (for all the Sieur de Rochemont's report that few 'honnêtes gens' looked satisfied leaving the theatre).[27] They could enjoy both the witty audacity of Dom Juan and his spectacular punishment. Such double-thinking is the very stuff of popular theatrical entertainment, and the combination of exciting lawlessness and reassuring morality is the basis of the success of earlier Dom Juans, as it is of half Elizabethan drama. Yet the more closely we examine *Dom Juan* as a serious work, the more problematic it becomes, especially in relation to the dénouement. For what does the Statue represent? By what power is he enabled to take Dom Juan off to Hell? Dom Juan has been warned often enough that this moment will come, but the very monotonous frequency of the warnings, and the fact that they are most commonly uttered by Sganarelle, for whom werewolves and bogeymen are as meaningful terrors as 'le Ciel', has turned it into all but a comic gag-line. We are encouraged to adopt an attitude of scepticism towards the sanctions with which Dom Juan is threatened, the duties of marital fidelity, charity, filial obedience, financial probity, all underwritten alike by the monolithic system of 'le Ciel'. Yet finally a direct representative of the Heaven which we have been inclined to see as an unreal menace set up by self-interested parties, does indeed wreak vengeance on the sinner. This is a much more serious difficulty than that with *Tartuffe* or *Volpone*, where the arbitrariness of the dénouement could be reconciled with the satiric viewpoint of the whole play. With *Dom Juan* it is not surprising that contemporary opponents accused Molière of patching on a 'painted thunderbolt', or that modern critics have seen in the ending a deliberate assertion of the absurd, in which 'the problem is resolved by nothingness'.[28]

This it is which *Dom Juan* and *Troilus and Cressida* have in common, they leave us with an ideological vacuum. Both plays encourage us to see with ironic and sceptical detachment ideals of love, honour, and cosmic order which were to some extent the orthodoxies of their day. They do not deny to these ideals all their grandeur: Elvire and Dom Louis, Ulysses and Troilus, are eloquent spokesmen for the values they represent. But ironic ambushes are constantly being set for their deployed rhetoric. Even a nearly ideal representative of chivalry, Hector in *Troilus and Cressida*, Dom Carlos in *Dom Juan*, though not submitted to the same sorts of irony, ends up illustrating very little of the significance of his code. Yet the plays are not conventionally iconoclastic; they do not simply satirise the orthodoxies of the romantic or the pious. For the ironisers have no more final authority than those they mock. It would be as intolerable to be imprisoned within Thersites' view of the world as it is impossible to share Troilus'. If we run the risk of looking like Sganarelle in condemning Dom Juan, we must face the stone guest if we are to identify with him.

It is not surprising that both *Troilus and Cressida* and *Dom Juan* should have been twentieth century 'rediscoveries'. They disappeared almost totally from the stage after the seventeenth century, replaced in each case by later adaptations of Dryden and Thomas Corneille which were more to the taste of eighteenth and nineteenth century audiences. Astonishingly the first recorded performance of Shakespeare's *Troilus and Cressida* was in 1898, and even by the 1920s the Comédie-Française had only given some 80 performances of Molière's *Dom Juan* in the whole of its history (as against over 2,000 of *Tartuffe*). The background of two world wars helped to make *Troilus and Cressida* seem relevant as never before, the most 'modern' of Shakespeare's plays. In one of the most influential essays on the play, significantly published in 1945, Una Ellis-Fermor argued that the new understanding of the play derived from 'our actual experience of disintegration and disruption [which] has thrown light upon the nature and foundations of what we call civilisation'.[29] Since Louis Jouvet's production of *Dom Juan* in 1947, it too has been reinstated as one of Molière's major plays, and likewise admired for its modernity. The attitude of Joseph Pineau is representative: 'The moral heaven had to be swept clear by Freudianism and modern scientific thought before the full depth of Molière's *Dom Juan* could be understood.'[30] *Troilus and Cressida* and *Dom Juan*, according to such accounts, have had to wait some three centuries to find their real audiences.

Yet to see the plays as statements of moral nihilism or theatre of the absurd before its time necessarily involves an act of wilful critical anachronism. We need not perhaps share the indignation of Nevill Coghill, who roundly denounces 'the sick criticism of our sick century, that is perpetually seeking corroboration from Shakespeare for its cynicism and disillusion'.[31] We must see what we can from where we are. But a nihilist *Troilus and Cressida* or a Sadian *Dom Juan* does not solve the problem of what Shakespeare or Molière thought they were doing with the plays, for self-evidently the terms in which they are analysed by modern critics would have meant nothing to them or their audiences. The concept of a cosmic pessimism was of course available at the period of *Troilus and Cressida*, and one explanation for the tone of the play is the sense of approaching moral cataclysm at the end of Elizabeth's reign and the beginning of James'. Likewise no doubt there was a strain of advanced free-thinking already in the mid-seventeenth century in France, to which *Dom Juan* might be related. Yet such ideas are still far removed from their more radical modern equivalents, and the concept of the deliberate disjunction of form to express meaning, or rather to deny meaning, seems on the whole a modernist phenomenon. We are driven back towards pragmatic explanations of the historical circumstances which gave *Troilus and Cressida* and *Dom Juan* their anomalous, seemingly modern character: *Dom Juan* was a story inherited by Molière from a Baroque tradition which he found partly alien and only half succeeded in adapting to his own comic form;[32] *Troilus and Cressida* was Shakespeare's attempt to write in the new satiric style of the private theatres, compromised by his temperamental allegiance to the conventions and attitudes of the public tradition in which he normally worked.[33]

Could either or both the plays have been intended to imply the sort of agreed comic contract which we have been considering in earlier chapters? There is a strong body of critical opinion supporting the notion of *Dom Juan* as a comedy, and Alice Walker, the editor of *Troilus and Cressida*, saw in it a 'comprehensive comic purpose'.[34] If comedies, they are to say the least very peculiar comedies. We have noticed the curious parody of the comic epilogue in *Troilus and Cressida* with Pandarus insulting the audience rather than wooing them in the normal way. The ending of Molière's *Dom Juan* is equally at odds with tradition. Molière's predecessors had justified the 'comedy' part of their 'tragicomedies' by ending their plays with multiple marriages made possible by Dom Juan's removal. In Molière we have only Sganarelle shouting for his lost wages — a traditional *commedia* joke no doubt, but one which takes on a different tone when he is left as the sole survivor on stage. Dom Juan's fiery end, according to Sganarelle, pays every debt, satisfies everyone but him, yet it is hard to see that it has really settled anything and the last laugh, like the laughter Pandarus invites, seems the final touch of inconsequence in a disconcertingly inconsequential dénouement.

Shakespeare and Molière in *Troilus and Cressida* and *Dom Juan* seem to be asking us to detach ourselves from all ideological allegiances, positive or negative, to watch a sort of ultimate human comedy, in which even the most serious concerns of life and death are set askew. If Dom Juan is right, then Heaven does not exist and the arguments of such as Dom Louis and Elvire, not to mention Sganarelle, look absurd; if Dom Juan is wrong the laugh is on him as he is dragged off to Hell by the Commander. Given that Ulysses' postulates in his speech on 'degree', or Hector's in his enunciation of the 'laws of nature and of nations' are correct, then the whole action of *Troilus and Cressida* illustrates the tragic falling-off from these principles. But there is equally Ulysses' alternative view of life as a meaningless race against time, or the *reductio ad absurdum* of Thersites, to jostle and question the idealists' standpoint. Yet it is doubtful if any theatre audience at any period could quite hold all of this together and see it as comic. At the end of Chaucer's *Troilus and Criseyde*, Troilus after his death ascends to the eighth sphere and looks down on all the absurd antics of his fellows. Both *Dom Juan* and *Troilus and Cressida* present images which have their unified focal points for spectators on some such eighth sphere. For an earth-bound audience, however, the disparate refracted rays are always likely to make up a blurred pattern, or only accidentally a clear outline when seen from the arbitrary angle of a particular period in time.

9 Conflicting Contracts

Inflexibility Bergson thought to be the basic, the essential, comic sin. His book *Le Rire* isolates the origin of laughter in a central antithesis between the mechanical, the rigid, and the systematic, on the one hand, and the organic, the flexible, the accidental, on the other. This central concept is attractive in that it seems to comprehend a very wide range of different comic patterns, and can be interpreted at a number of different levels. Those, for example, who assert their individual will to control are frequently subjected to comic mockery. The living instincts of an Agnès escape the arbitrary schooling of Arnolphe; the peremptory father figures of comedy are perennially outwitted by the younger generation assisted by the infinitely agile tricky slave. The instance of Arnolphe, alternatively, might be related to the paradigm of theory against practice. Comedy is basically anti-theoretical. The whole comic tribe of doctors, pedants, learned ladies, is always falling into the pits dug for them by the actual. In the very broadest terms, comedy can be seen to be an assertion of life itself against all life-deniers. The *précieuses ridicules*, the King of Navarre's academy, are ridiculous in so far as they attempt to reject their own natural impulses. Jonson's Morose would shut out all noise, the audible evidence of vitality.

Anyone who sets out to change, reform, rebuke, or ignore the way of the world, for whatever reasons, we may expect to suffer comic humiliation and punishment. Of these, the zealot is frequently the hardest hit, the most unmercifully mocked. Those who insist fanatically on some ultimate ideal of behaviour are shown to be either hypocrites like Tartuffe, or fools like Orgon, and the more pretentious the ideal they represent the more we laugh at them. Comic humours characters who try to re-make the world to suit some idiosyncratic *idée fixe* of their own may be treated relatively indulgently, but those who claim a mission to re-make the world of others, above all to deny them their pleasures, are ruthlessly satirised. Writers who stress the festive origins of comedy would class such preachers and reformers as kill-joys trying to prevent the community from enjoying their holiday release. From another perspective, the zealots, like other theorists in comedy, would impose upon an imperfect human nature unreal standards of perfection. For a Christian audience there may be a lesson in humility in the spectacle of the arrogant fanatic whose principles are disproved by the reality of life. Rigid dogmatism may offend against an ideal of social flexibility, of the necessary compromises required by living in a human community; equally, from a spiritual point of view, it can be understood as the sin of pride, denying the fallen nature of man which makes charitable indulgence necessary.

The central Bergsonian idea can thus be extended and developed well beyond the terms in which he himself conceived it, and theories of comedy apparently remote from his are yet often related by means of this fundamental antithesis of the organic and inorganic. [1] The main argument of this study, however, has been to question whether comedy has any such single fixed pattern of ideas, any one universal tendency which can be extrapolated from its structure. It is certainly true that Bergson's thesis may be used to explain a number of different types of comic contract, though there are others that it fits less well. It seems to apply excellently to much of romantic comedy and social comedy of manners but with satiric comedy it is hardly very illuminating. No-one could be more flexible than Mosca yet *Volpone* is scarcely a celebration of the parasite's art; Tartuffe may be satirised as a life-denier, a kill-joy, but this is only a mask used to conceal a policy of opportunistic self-interest which is anything but rigid. Dom Juan, though a Houdini of escape, disguise, and evasion, is finally defeated by a very symbol of rigidity. However, rather than proposing negative examples of the sort of comedy which the Bergsonian concept excludes, the purpose of this final chapter is to examine two plays which seem almost text-book models of his theory in some respects, and which have nevertheless provoked centuries of controversy as to whether they are comedies at all. *Measure for Measure* and *Le Misanthrope* can both be categorised as comedies of zeal, illustrating the shortcomings of perfectionism, the failure of individual attempts to shape reality to an ideal pattern. Described in outline they can easily be assimilated to this model, but the actual experience of either play by readers or audiences tends to show that they are much more ambiguous and less clearly comic than the outline pattern would suggest. They can be used, therefore, as two last test-cases in our analysis of the comic contract and the circumstances in which it may break down.

LE MISANTHROPE

Le Misanthrope has by now almost ceased to be a controversial play. The nineteenth century view which questioned its status as a comedy and saw in Alceste a tragic portrait of Molière himself seems to have been definitively ousted, and a comic Alceste is now critically orthodox. Even the two most eloquent modern exponents of an autobiographical *Misanthrope*, Ramon Fernandez and René Jasinski, argue that in the play Molière ultimately controlled and distanced his own emotions by means of comic technique.[2] Where critical debate on *Dom Juan* has blossomed in all directions since the war, opinion on *Le Misanthrope*, among critics if not among actors and producers, has tended to solidify.[3] Earlier romantic misinterpretations, eighteenth and nineteenth century failure to understand Molière's terms of reference, the evidence we have of Molière's own style of acting in the part, have all been used to confirm the idea that Alceste was intended to be funny. A great deal of this reasoning has been extremely useful in eliminating the myths about the play and taking us closer to the text as a seventeenth century audience might have experienced it. However, without wishing to revive the image of the tortured Alceste/Molière or the tormenting Célimène/Armande, it is still possible to see strains within the play which work against a simple comic interpretation. Let us examine, first of all, the basic pattern of comedy in *Le Misanthrope*, the attitudes that pattern suggests, and then consider if a part of our response to the play may not be left out of that account.

From the very start it is clear that the comic action of *Le Misanthrope* will be to test Alceste's theory of life. The play opens with a conversation between Alceste and Philinte which, like that between Arnolphe and Chrysalde at the opening of *L'Ecole des Femmes*, prepares the terms in which we are to find the comic hero funny. Where Arnolphe's theory had to do with the training of a wife, Alceste's is an ideal of plain-speaking:

Je veux qu'on soit sincère, et qu'en homme d'honneur,
On ne lâche aucun mot qui ne parte du coeur.   I i 35—6

Philinte argues that this is impracticable and produces instances in which sincerity would be socially unthinkable. It is his function, as it is that of all Molière's *raisonneurs*, to draw out the ridiculousness of the comic protagonist and his obsession. Here he pushes Alceste to claim that he would tell the most unpalatable truths to such as the old coquette Emilie or the boastful snob Dorilas. We can tell in advance that Alceste's practice will betray his theory and so it is no surprise, though no less funny, when in the following scene the apostle of plain-speaking is reduced to the most obvious of social devices to avoid expressing his opinion of Oronte's sonnet. Instead of bold and forthright truth-telling, we have the patently fictitious anecdote of the nameless verse-writing friend. It is the technique which is later used in the most disingenuous of scenes between Arsinoé and Célimène. Although eventually Alceste is driven to condemnation of Oronte's sonnet plain and direct enough, just as Arsinoé and Célimène end up speaking their real minds, the comic point is made that absolute sincerity in cold blood is just not possible for social human beings, not even for an anti-social Alceste. There is, however, a far greater instance of inconsistency between Alceste's theory and practice which Philinte also points out to him in the first scene. If he is indeed as radically opposed to contemporary manners and as dedicated to misanthropy as he says, how has he come to fall in love, and to love someone as representative of her age and time as Célimène, rather than 'la sincère Eliante' or 'la prude Arsinoé'? Alceste's reply is a virtual admission of failure.

> J'ai beau voir ses défauts, et j'ai beau l'en blâmer,
> En dépit qu'on en ait, elle se fait aimer.   I i 231–2

What from anyone else would be an empty truism, must cost Alceste a lot to confess — 'la raison n'est pas ce qui règle l'amour', reason is not what rules love. Indeed it is not, and by the end of the play Alceste's passion for Célimène will have left his theories in tatters. The innate inconsistency of the misanthropic Alceste's love for the coquette was focussed as the play's central motif in the original sub-title, *L'Atrabilaire Amoureux*. The man governed by 'black bile' or melancholy should naturally be the opposite of the sanguine temperament of the lover. Although in the Renaissance a despairing lover was often portrayed as melancholy, in itself melancholy was the humour most unlike blood, the principle of sex and life. *L'Atrabilaire Amoureux* was an oxymoron of incompatibles like *Le Bourgeois Gentilhomme*, and it promised an audience the inherently comic spectacle of someone in a situation for which his temperament least suited him, a man out of his humour in a rather different sense to the Jonsonian.

The theorist in comedy, however, may not only be shown up for the impracticability of his theories, but also for his underlying dishonesty. In looking at *L'Ecole des Femmes* we saw how Arnolphe's ideals of marital honour were exposed by the reductive comedy of Alain and Georgette. In *Les Précieuses Ridicules* and *Love's Labour's Lost* the rejection of love and marriage turned out to be in fact a form of coquetry. It is easy to detect not only inconsistencies in Alceste's theory, but a basic taint of egoism which relates him to other comic characters. He fulminates against the dishonesty of the age, but the main example he produces is significantly a rogue who is his opponent in a law-suit. Rousseau quite rightly saw how much this damaged Alceste's claim to disinterested misanthropy, and condemned it as another instance of Molière's vilification of the character.[4] Several critics have suggested that Oronte's sonnet would have been addressed to Célimène — Oronte is described in the dramatis personae as 'amant de Célimène' — and that this consideration adds bitterness to Alceste's denunciation of it. The misanthrope's dogmatism is perhaps comic not only because it is ludicrously rigid and inflexible, but because it masks less theoretical and more self-interested motives.

It is not hard to align Alceste with Molière's other comic monomaniacs.[5] What they all have in common is a single obsession which is in fact a form of intense egoism. Harpagon's gold or Jourdain's image of aristocracy represent projections of themselves out into the world which is re-created to centre around these images. Their extreme anger and desolation is aroused when reality challenges their egocentric illusions. What we see on stage are overgrown children who have not learned the central principle of adulthood, that they must share their world with others. We laugh as grown-ups at their violent but constantly frustrated attempts to embody a dream of perpetual self-satisfaction. Alceste, too, is this sort of child. He has two instincts, as Guicharnaud has pointed out,[6] to run away and hide himself in some 'dark little corner', or to turn and attack those who will not leave him in peace. But are these not alternative versions of the child's exhibitionism, claiming attention by one form of singularity or another? Célimène places Alceste neatly in the portrait scene: 'ne faut-il pas bien que Monsieur contredise?' He asserts himself by contradicting everyone else, and his self-justification for this apparent perversity is a moment of absurd comic revelation: 'C'est que, jamais, morbleu! les hommes n'ont raison' — he is the only one who is ever right. To prove his point, to prove the universal infamy of everyone but himself, Alceste will lose his lawsuit practically on purpose. 'J'aurai le *plaisir* de perdre mon procès'. Throughout *Le Misanthrope* there is a strain of childish masochism in Alceste, cutting his nose off to spite his face.

Even his love for Célimène can be seen to have the same essentially egoistic character. He assures Philinte that of course he would not love her unless he were confident that he was loved in return. He believes that his love will reform her —

> sans doute, ma flamme
> De ces vices du temps pourra purger son âme. I i 233–4

Alceste is incapable of seeing the irony of Célimène's retort when he exclaims on his misfortune in loving her:

> *Alceste.* Morbleu! faut-il que je vous aime!
> Ah! que si de vos mains je rattrape mon coeur,

> Je bénirai le Ciel de ce rare bonheur!
> Je ne le cèle pas, je fais tout mon possible
> A rompre de ce coeur l'attachement terrible;
> Mais mes plus grands efforts n'ont rien fait jusqu'ici,
> Et c'est pour mes péchés que je vous aime ainsi.
> *Célimène.* Il est vrai, votre ardeur est pour moi sans seconde.
> II. i 514−21

The terms which he offers her finally, retreat with him to his 'désert', are the terms of a conqueror (magnanimous in his own view) to a defeated enemy. Alceste never really recognises Célimène's autonomy, any more than Arnolphe recognises that of Agnès. Whether it is authentic or not, contrast the passage in the pamphlet called *La Fameuse Comedienne* written some years after Molière's death in which he is imagined speaking of his jealous love for Armande:

> Ma passion est veneue à un tel point, qu'elle va jusqu'à entrer avec compassion dans ses interests; et quand je considère combien il m'est impossible de vaincre ce que je sens pour elle, je me dis en mesme temps qu'elle a peut-estre la mesme difficulté à détruire le penchant qu'elle a d'estre coquete, et je me trouve plus de disposition de la plaindre qu'à la blasmer. [7]

Just this degree of imagination of another's feelings on the basis of his own is what Alceste is incapable of experiencing.

The case for a comic Alceste has been made so often and so well in these terms in recent criticism that there may seem little to oppose it. To say that Alceste appears more attractive than other Molière comic heroes would only look like a return to earlier sentimental misreadings of the part. Yet there is evidence that Alceste did in fact win more sympathy than other Molière comic characters. Both Boileau and the Duc de Montausier were happy to accept identification as the misanthrope. [8] Which of Molière's contemporaries would have been proud to have been pointed out as the original of Arnolphe, Sganarelle, or Tartuffe? In all of his other plays Molière played characters of his own age — middle-aged men who are mocked when they plan to marry young women. It is noticeable that there is no such suggestion of a ridiculous disparity of age between Alceste and the 20 year old Célimène, and it may well have been to make himself appear younger that in this play, and in this play only, Molière acted without a large and ludicrous moustache. [9]

How old is Alceste? the question may sound like 'How many children had Lady Macbeth?', but it is curiously important to an interpretation of the play. The childish behaviour of most of Molière's comic figures is ridiculous because they are grown men, often fathers of families and heads of households, who should obviously know better. Orgon or Argan, reduced to chasing their servants round the stage, are funny because this is the way frustrated children not dignified adults, much less dying invalids, are supposed to behave. If Alceste is thought of as a man of 44, Molière's age when he played the part, then much of his childishness would be just as clearly comic. At that age still to be as socially maladroit as he is with Oronte, still to be running off in sulks when his friend embraced a chance acquaintance in the street, still to imagine that lawsuits are to be won or lost on the strict basis of justice, can only be construed as ingrained foolishness or chronic delusion. But a younger Alceste may surely be regarded more indulgently. To think of his behaviour as that of delayed adolescence is rather different from regarding it as a comic regression to childhood. The comedy of Alceste may be in some respects closer to the absurdity of Lélic in *L'Etourdi*, or to Molière's other naive *jeunes premiers* than it is to the great comic parts of Jourdain, Harpagon, or Arnolphe.

Alceste's lack of self-awareness, the ridiculousness of his behaviour, often serves to endear him to us. When Oronte asks his opinion on the sonnet, it is of course funny that Alceste is forced to belie his own principles with the evasions of 'Je ne dis pas cela', but it is after all a basically humane impulse which makes it impossible for him to be directly rude. It seems doubtful that, as critics have suggested, it is the undeclared self-interest of his rivalry with Oronte which makes Alceste condemn the sonnet so vigorously. We have evidence later in the play that Oronte was the one of Célimène's suitors whom he feared least. (IV ii 1239–40). The sonnet in itself is so representative of the style and manner of the society which Alceste detests that there is no need for any further explanation for his vehemence, and the comedy stems rather from his awkward unwillingness to express his real opinion rather than any disingenuousness in that opinion itself. We noticed earlier the link between this sonnet scene and the scene between Arsinoé and Célimène, both starting in an atmosphere of effusive cordiality and ending in war to the knife. But the contrast is also striking. Célimène and Arsinoé are from the start playing a game they both acknowledge, and the progression towards naked hostility serves to show the total fictitiousness of the rhetoric of friendship initially used on both sides. Alceste, however, refuses to play Oronte's game, will not give him the ardent professions of friendship, the flattering praise, which the social exchange demands, and his refusal in the context leaves him looking awkward and foolish. As Jules Brody puts it incisively, 'the sonnet scene tells us only one thing clearly: whether or not it is advisable to speak one's mind freely, it is devilishly difficult to do it gracefully'.[10] But grace is not a consistent criterion of value in the play, as Brody tends to suggest, and Alceste's human awkwardness exposes the emptiness of Oronte's social language as much as his own absurdity.

Alceste's refusal to play social games, his ignorance at times that a game is being played, tends often thus to satirise the games and the players. Arsinoé tries to draw him away from Célimène by a form of flattery which any other member of their society would appreciate, and which seems appropriate to Alceste's role of isolated idealist:

> Je voudrois que la cour, par un regard propice,
> A ce que vous valez rendît plus de justice:
> Vous avez à vous plaindre, et je suis en courroux,
> Quand je vois chaque jour qu'on ne fait rien pour vous.
>
> III v 1049−52

But Alceste will not rise to the bait of this image of himself as a signal example of merit unrewarded by society.

> Moi, Madame! Et sur quoi pourrois-je en rien prétendre?
> Quel service a l'Etat est-ce qu'on m'a vu rendre?
> Qu'ai-je fait, s'il vous plaît, de si brillant de soi,
> Pour me plaindre à la cour qu'on ne fait rien pour moi?
>
> III v 1053−6

Whether one sees Alceste here as genuinely modest, or too scornful of the promiscuous honours the Court offers to value them − 'Ce n'est plus un honneur de se voir loué' − he unintentionally sabotages Arsinoé's flattering strategy. Part of the comedy of this scene is one of ironic cross-purposes; Alceste cannot see where Arsinoé is heading, as we in the audience can. In one sense, perhaps, Alceste is as self-preoccupied as she is, but it is a much larger self. When she starts to abuse Célimène, the dignity of his replies exposes the maliciousness of her motives:

> *Arsinoé* . . . Je souhaiterois fort vos ardeurs mieux placées.
>   Vous méritez, sans doute, un sort beaucoup plus doux,
>   Et celle que vous charme est indigne de vous.
> *Alceste.* Mais, en disant cela, songez-vouz, je vous prie,
>   Que cette personne est, Madame, votre amie?

Arsinoé. Oui, toute mon amie, elle est et je la nomme
Indigne d'asservir le coeur d'un galant homme;
Et le sien n'a pour vous que de feintes douceurs.
Alceste. Cela se peut, Madame: on ne voit pas les coeurs;
Mais votre charité se seroit bien passée
De jeter dans le mien une telle pensée.   II v 1102—18

In this context, Alceste's simplicity and directness, so comic elsewhere in the play, serves as a withering rebuke to the petty-mindedness and self-interest of Arsinoé.

Alceste represents throughout a spirit of total seriousness and in a comedy those who cannot see a joke, especially against themselves, may be expected to be the comic butts. Again and again Alceste provides not only the audience in the theatre, but an audience on stage, with a source of laughter. From Philinte in the first scene laughing at his bouts of temper, through the *petits marquis* and Célimène in the portrait scene, to Eliante enjoying Philinte's account of the outcome of the confrontation with Oronte in Act IV, nearly everyone in the play finds Alceste funny. Yet there are moments of disjunction between the laughter on stage and our laughter in the audience. At the end of the second act when Alceste is storming out insisting that he will never back down on his opinion of Oronte's sonnet short of a direct order from the King, he turns upon Acaste and Clitandre who are laughing:

Par la sangbleu! Messieurs, je ne croyois pas être
Si plaisant que je suis.   II vi 773—4

His humourlessness here ought to make him still funnier, yet paradoxically these lines may rather tend to quell an audience's laughter. Do we, after all, want to be included in a group which has the inane marquises as its stage representatives?

Alceste *cares* in a society that cares for little beyond its amusements, and this makes him a spectacle of comedy. Oronte's poem is too unimportant to make the amount of fuss about it that Alceste does, but Alceste has made it a point of principle and hence his ludicrous indignation. In the portrait scene, Célimène's malicious caricatures appa! Alceste, not because they are unjust — Philinte points out that Alceste himself condemns the characters attacked — but because they are undertaken as an idle entertainment. And just because they are undertaken in that spirit, the witty Célimène can instantly place Alceste himself in the portrait gallery as the epitome of contradictory perversity. Once again the laugh is against him.

> Les rieurs sont pour vous, Madame, c'est tout dire,
> Et vous pouvez pousser contre moi la satire.   II iv 681—2

Guicharnaud is right to compare Célimène to Dom Juan in her ability always to evade attack, and to see a similarity between Alceste and Sganarelle handicapped by their very commitment to an argument in which they actually believe, where their opponents believe in nothing.[11] But Sganarelle's position is in itself ridiculous, his argument a pastiche of serious ideals; Alceste's viewpoint is constantly made to look ridiculous, yet represents a perfectly genuine if impracticable ideal.

We suggested earlier that Alceste was more likeable than other Molière comic characters. This is not merely a matter of an audience's or reader's impression. Though laughed at by so many of the characters in the play, he is also much better thought of by his fellow characters than any other Molière protagonist. The comic paterfamilias, M. Jourdain, Orgon, Argan, commands the duty and respect owing to his position, but there is little sense of personal esteem for him. Arnolphe's long and tried friendship with Oronte, the father of Horace, is a donné of the plot rather than something which his character as we see it serves to justify. Alceste, by contrast, is sought in friendship by Oronte, loved by Arsinoé and Eliante, treated with real if amused affection by Philinte, and even arguably wins more feeling from Célimène than any other of her suitors.

> En vérité, les gens d'un mérite sublime
> Entraînent de chacun et l'amour et l'estime   III v 1045—6

No doubt Arsinoé's words have to be taken in their proper ironical context, and her 'en verité', like Célimène's 'sans mentir', is the comic signal of its opposite. Yet however absurd he may be, the characters in *Le Misanthrope* do tend to recognise the 'mérite' of Alceste. Whether or not it is his merits which attract such as Oronte or Arsinoé, the attitude of Eliante is surely intended to be central and exemplary:

> Dans ses façons d'agir, il est fort singulier;
> Mais j'en fais, je l'avoue, un cas particulier,
> Et la sincerité dont son âme se pique
> A quelque chose, en soi, de noble et d'héroique.
> C'est une vertu rare au siècle d'aujourd'hui,
> Et je la voudrois voir partout comme chez lui.   IV i 1163—8

These are the lines which the advocates of a comic Alceste must necessarily find hardest to explain away, the lines which establish him, in spite of his ridiculousness, as the representative of an ideal against which contemporary society is judged and found wanting. Donneau de Visé in his *Lettre écrite sur la comédie du Misanthrope* was in no doubt as to Molière's purpose in the play:

Il n'a point voulu faire une comédie pleine d'incidents, mais une pièce seulement où il pût parler contre les moeurs du siècle.[12]

This pamphlet has come to be taken very seriously by modern criticism, and it has been strongly argued that it may have some of the authority of Molière's own opinion.[13] Even, however, if we allow for oversimplification on Donneau's part, this testimony to the broad satiric purpose of the play by a contemporary witness close to Molière must be considered important. Donneau goes on to admire Molière's skill in picking as joint protagonists a 'misanthrope' and a 'médisante' to fulfil his aim of castigating the manners of the time. This is not the way in which many of us think of the play, with Célimène contributing to a single effect of satiric commentary, but of course Célimène's caricatures are quite as devastating, if not much more so, than Alceste's indignant rages. If we add Philinte with his phlegmatic but equally disillusioned view, we have three alternative satirists who combine to expose the vacuous court society of the time. What we see of that society eminently justifies a satiric stance. Clitandre when he enters in Act II has just come from the 'levé' at the Louvre; at the end of the scene he reveals that his next engagement is to make an appearance at the 'petit couché'. Such are the arduous duties of a marquis. Acaste gives at the beginning of Act II the account of his reasons for self-satisfaction – 'les belles dents surtout, et la taille tout fine' – which in its very complacency is a marvellous comic indictment of the courtier. A final figure of the aristocracy, the 'grand flandrin de Vicomte', we only hear about in Célimène's letter:

depuis que je l'ai vu, trois quarts d'heure durant, cracher dans un puits pour faire des ronds, je n'ai pu jamais prendre bonne opinion de lui.   V iv
[1691]

In face of a society where the only diversions from idleness and boredom are malicious gossip and intrigue, what attitude does Molière expect his audience to take? Are we to join in the indignation of Alceste, grotesque though it may be, or does the amused participation of Célimène recommend itself as preferable by its sheer grace and wit?[14] Alternatively we may see things with the La Rochefoucauld eyes of Philinte, who opposes Alceste's fury with a philosophical pessimism:

> je vois ces défauts dont votre âme murmure
> Comme vices unis à l'humaine nature;
> Et mon esprit enfin n'est pas plus offensé
> De voir un homme fourbe, injuste, intéressé,
> Que de voir des vautours affamés de carnage,
> Des singes malfaisants, et des loups pleins de rage.   I i 173−8

We seem here to be back in the world of *Volpone*. It is almost as though Molière with Alceste had written a central role for Jonson's minor character Bonario whose outrage at the wickedness of his society was undercut by its very obviousness. From Philinte's viewpoint Alceste's indignation, like Bonario's, is naive rather than unjustified.

If we return to the *Lettre* of Donneau de Visé, we find that he seems to think Philinte's stance recommended: 'L'ami du Misanthrope est si raisonnable, que tout le monde devroit l'imiter'.[15] And yet he also argues that the outrageous and aggressive idealism of Alceste is an important satiric device because one has to demand a great deal even to achieve a very little. Alceste in the play seems to have achieved almost nothing except the self-destruction which he at least partly wanted, but we experience his defeat in some sense as loss. Philinte and Célimène can see their society more clearly perhaps than Alceste can, and certainly can live in it more successfully, yet the passionate anger which they lack is not seen only as a product of Alceste's comic egoism. It is a quality, as Eliante suggests, rare in their world and which to some degree it badly lacks. Alceste rushes off to his 'désert', to 'un endroit où d'être homme d'honneur on ait la liberté', but Eliante and Philinte follow to try to stop him. No-one tries to stop Arnolphe dashing from the stage at the end of *L'Ecole des Femmes;* his disappearance is necessary to the triumphant happy ending. But the society of *Le Misanthrope* cannot afford to lose the few 'hommes d'honneur' it has, even if they do appear absurd.

This perhaps accounts for the emotional ambivalence of Alceste's final confrontation with Célimène. It is the perfect climax of the play, the event which the frustrated Alceste has seen deferred through four acts. It is, of course, profoundly funny, the final marvellous exposition of the comic incompatibility of the misanthrope and the coquette. Each is prepared to make one final, very considerable, concession. Alceste will forget and forgive the humiliation of Célimène's double-dealing letters; Célimène offers what she has presumably always put off before, a definite agreement to marry. Yet neither concession is good enough for the other. Célimène may (or may not) be struck by the generosity and fidelity of Alceste in comparison with her other suitors, but still, 'la solitude effraye une âme de vingt ans'. For all-or-nothing Alceste her refusal to agree immediately to his proposition of a *désert à deux* is a betrayal for which there can be no forgiveness. Each of them are what they are; like all of Molière's comic figures they can never change, and this final cross-talk of character works on the principle of all his comedy.

And yet there is a strain of emotion in our response to the dénouemènt which is not quite contained by this comic detachment. To say that we want the play to end with Célimène marrying Alceste and are disappointed when it doesn't, would be purely sentimental. It is the very law of their nature, centrally demonstrated by the play, which prevents such a 'happy ending'. Yet in some sort it is the hypothetical happy ending of the play, however impossible. If we think back to the agreement of Act IV scene i, in which Eliante said that she would consider Philinte only if marriages between Alceste and Célimène, or Alceste and herself, were definitely ruled out, then it is clear that the Philinte /Eliante marriage at the end is not just a second- but a third-best solution. It of course confirms the need for compromise which the whole play illustrates. Yet a Célimène /Alceste union does remain, strangely, as an ideal at some level of our imagination. What drew Célimène to Alceste — however far she may in fact have been drawn — was a better part of herself: Alceste's ambition to reform her was not *just* egoistic tyranny or delusion, there was in Célimène something to be rescued from the petty bitchiness of the salon. Alceste loses too. His love for Célimène was the link which held him to the real world, forced him to acknowledge a human reality outside his own solipsist misanthropy.

Rousseau was wrong to see *Le Misanthrope* as a play in which Molière wantonly mocked an honest man to flatter the complacency of his audience.The effect of the play is not such as to encourage an audience's complacency, but rather to disturb and puzzle them. There has been much speculation on the reasons for the comparative lack of success of the play's first production, and whether it was the ambiguity and subtlety of the comedy which made for its hesitant reception. We should not make too much of this; an audience at any time is an uncertain class of beast, and *L'Avare*, in no way as ambivalent a play as *Le Misanthrope*, was also a partial failure when first performed. Yet Ramon Fernandez is illuminating when he discusses the strain placed upon the comic form by *Le Misanthrope*: 'The audience, at a comedy, needs to dominate the subject, not to be pressed too close by it, nor to be thrown into doubts about their own convictions'.[16] Just this sort of doubt *Le Misanthrope* does seem to raise, and it may well have affected the first audiences. The doubt arises from a conflict between two comic contracts. Alceste is ridiculous, as we have seen, in so far as he is a dogmatic theorist, trying to re-make his society to suit his own grandiose and egoistic ideals. We laugh at his rigidity and his gracelessness in social situations where suppleness and grace are the qualities required above all. Yet the play also satirises that supple society as a vain and idle place of affected and meaningless surfaces; a main thrust of *Le Misanthrope* is satiric, demonstrating a universality of hypocrisy and deception comparable to that in *Tartuffe* or *Volpone*. In this context, Alceste's truth-telling, however exaggerated, has some weight of authority. The effect of the super-imposition of two different contracts is to make possible a degree of ambivalent emotional response to the individual character which comedy normally excludes. The debate over Alceste is not a purely factitious one originating with romantic misreading of the part; it derives from the central ambiguity of a comedy which exposes the ludicrousness of idealism and the barrenness of a society without ideals.

MEASURE FOR MEASURE

No-one is likely to need convincing that *Measure for Measure* is something other than pure comedy. By formal origin and theatrical design it is tragicomedy at its most hyphenated. It might indeed serve as an excellent illustration of John Fletcher's slightly later definition of the genre as a play which has no deaths in it, but brings some characters close to death.[17] At various points in the play, Claudio, Barnardine, Angelo, and Lucio all stand under imminent sentence of death, only to be tragicomically reprieved. Because of its sources in Italian *novelle*, Shakespearean comedy had always had a tragicomic strain; in *The Two Gentlemen of Verona* and *Much Ado*, for example, extreme perils are only narrowly escaped. But *Measure for Measure*, with its deliberate exploitation of apparently insoluble dramatic situations, does seem to be closer to a formal model of tragicomedy than any other of the plays before the late romances, and Mary Lascelles, in her excellent book on the play, is certainly right to stress its basis in the genre.[18]

And yet it is possible to see underlying *Measure for Measure* the ground-plan of a comic pattern, what we called earlier the comedy of zeal. In this Angelo and Isabella are join protagonists whose idealist, perfectionist theories about life are tested and found wanting in the situations of life itself. This is so obvious in the case of Angelo, that it scarcely needs stressing. The Duke in explaining one of his (all too many) purposes in withdrawing from his dukedom prepares the terms of our expectation:

> Lord Angelo is precise;
> Stands at a guard with Envy; scarce confesses
> That his blood flows; or that his appetite
> Is more to bread than stone. Hence shall we see
> If power change purpose, what our seemers be.   I iii 50–4

The ice-cold deputy – Lucio later picturesquely claims that 'when he makes water his urine is congealed ice' – who denies the appetites, will sooner or later be proved of the same flesh and blood as the rest of humanity. The test on Isabella, and her failure of that test, is more disputable; not everyone would agree that she does learn, as Angelo does, her own frailty but several critics have tried to make this case. When she turns in anger on her brother for the mere suggestion that she might sacrifice her chastity to save his life, it is, according to G. Wilson Knight, because she has discovered that 'she cannot sacrifice herself. Her sex inhibitions have been horribly shown her as they are, naked'.[19] For those who pair Angelo and Isabella in this way, the ending demonstrates their new-found humility, when Angelo acknowledges his sin repentantly, and Isabella is brought to plead for his life. 'Both suffer, both undergo a public penance in which their mistakes are purged, and both are, by implication at least, rehabilitated and redeemed for worldly use at the end of the play.'[20]

Clearly the moral rigidity of an Angelo or an Isabella is of a different order to that of Alceste. Apart from anything else they are conceived as characters who can change, who can learn from experience, whereas Molière's misanthrope, like all the rest of the Molièrean comic characters, is a perpetual prisoner of his temperament. This opportunity for change and development, above all for the redemption of past errors, is thought by many to be the defining feature of Shakespearean comedy, and its most profoundly Christian pattern. The allegorical interpretation of *Measure for Measure* in these terms, by which the play illustrates the substitution of Divine grace and mercy for the severity of Mosaic justice, is well-known and has by now often been criticised as inadequate. Yet even critics unsympathetic to this way of seeing the play may concede that the ending reveals 'a generic and forgivable culpability in all men'.[21] Whether or not the Duke is identified as a figure for Divine Providence, the universal pardons he dispenses do suggest the charity which all men must exercise in judging their fellows. The standards of judgement of Isabella, of Angelo, even perhaps of the Duke himself in the earlier part of the play, are too high for any human being to impose on others. They must all learn the humility necessary to forgiveness.

This level of interpretation of the play's central pattern, however, leaves many of its low comic scenes awkwardly unexplained. G. Wilson Knight, for instance, is driven to the lengths of calling Pompey 'with his rough humour and honest professional indecency' one of the 'pure in heart'.[22] If, on the other hand, we see in *Measure for Measure* a traditional comic pattern in which the claims of life itself over-ride attempts to control it, more of the play may be included. 'The law against lovers', as a later adaptation of *Measure for Measure* was to call it, is an archetypal obstacle to sexual fulfilment which we considered already in Chapter Five with reference to *Love's Labour's Lost*. The function of much of the low comedy in the play is to reinforce Pompey's point that unless the authorities 'mean to geld and splay all the youth of the city . . . they will to 't'. Angelo and Isabella deny their own sexuality, whether as ascetic magistrate or as sister of the strict order of St. Clare, but it resurfaces in alarmingly perverse ways. There is a streak of sadism in Angelo's attraction to the cold and virginal Isabella which emerges most appallingly in the final terms of the 'monstrous ransom':

> Redeem thy brother
> By yielding up thy body to my will;
> Or else he must not only die the death,
> But thy unkindness shall his death draw out
> To ling'ring sufferance.   II iv 162—6

But is there not a comparable masochism in Isabella's assertion of her chastity?

> were I under the terms of death,
> Th' impression of keen whips I'd wear as rubies,
> And strip myself to death as to a bed
> That longing have been sick for, ere I'd yield
> My body up to shame.   II iv 100—4

Without stigmatising Isabella as 'prurient', as one critic has, it is surely suggestive that the imagery she uses in rejecting defilement is the imagery of sexual desire.

Sex is an anarchic and blind life-force which cannot be coerced by rigid legislation whether social or individual; repression will result in corruption and perversity. This may seem a very Lawrentian moral, but it can be related to what have often been identified as basic patterns of comic action. The bed-trick, for example, has been found offensive, yet it is essential to a certain sort of comic dénouement. Throughout Roman comedies, casual rapes committed in drunkenness or during Saturnalian holidays are often used as a plot-device to bring about the happy ending; the young man turns out to have raped the girl he wants to marry (Plautus' *Aulularia*) or the woman who is already his wife (Terence's *Hecyra*). The unthinking impulse of sexual attraction finds itself, by a form of comic providence, channelled into the socially acceptable terms of marriage. The bed-trick, with pre-contract as in the case of Mariana, was no doubt more acceptable to the moral scruples of an English Renaissance audience than a rape, however Saturnalian the extenuating circumstances. Yet the comic pattern is the same, a final surprising identity of instinct and social form.

If the Duke is not a figure of Providence, he may nevertheless represent the agent of this comic form of providence without the capital. We looked in Chapter Three at two Shakespearean comic controllers, Theseus and Prospero, who might be related to Duke Vincentio as the figures of authority who finally guarantee the happy ending. It is Prospero to whom the Duke in *Measure for Measure* is closer, and with whom he has often been compared. If he has not Prospero's magical powers to help him control the action, he is, like Prospero, the only figure in the play in possession of all the available information all of the time. His watching of events unseen, his enigmatic interventions, the final discarding of his disguise, all foreshadow the role of Prospero. In *Measure for Measure* as in *The Tempest*, it seems as if events can only find their ultimate comic clarification if they are allowed to develop to an extreme state of confusion, a confusion which the order-figure himself at times seems to promote. It is virtually a systematic course of alienation which Prospero and Vincentio inflict upon their fellow characters in order to bring them to a new state of self-awareness.

In these terms, the ending of *Measure for Measure* can, and has been, compared to other Shakespearean comedies. 'The tone of this play', argues David Stevenson, 'as it descends from its climactic scenes between Isabella and Angelo and Isabella and Claudio, is as surely ameliorative as is that of *As You Like It* or . . . *The Tempest*'.[23] The multiple marriages can be set beside those of *As You Like It* illustrating a variety of union from the highest level — Rosalind/Orlando, Vincentio/Isabella — through to Touchstone/Audrey, Lucio/Kate Keepdown. If we are inclined to balk at the idea of a rapidly reformed Angelo living happily ever after with Mariana, is not Oliver converted from villainy with just as incredible rapidity and as unfairly rewarded with marriage to Celia? In neither play is marriage simply romanticised; the ill-assorted coupling of Touchstone and his shepherdess, the shotgun wedding of Lucio to a whore, remind us that marriage may be no more than a social rubber-stamp for sanctioning sexual relations. Yet it can be more than that, and whether it is or not, the whole rhythm of the comic action drives towards it as the only satisfying conclusion. Marriage represents what both society and life itself demand. It is in so far as the ending of *Measure for Measure* re-integrates Isabella and Angelo into this social celebration of marriage that it may be said to have completed their comic education, have taught them that their perfectionist ideals of saintliness are sterile and corrupt. And it is over this situation that the Duke as comic controller benevolently presides.

Yet this hypothesis of a clear and unified comic pattern in *Measure for Measure* only serves to show how little it corresponds to the actual experience of the play. However ingeniously the play may be related formally or structurally to *As You Like It* or *The Tempest*, its effect upon readers and spectators is likely always to be enormously different. There have been plenty of explanations of why this should be so. There is the old-fashioned biographical view of Shakespeare in a 'dark period' of personal despair, comparable to the Molière of 1666 writing *Le Misanthrope* in the anguish of disillusionment. Or there is the more sophisticated modern version of the 'dark period' as a time of formal experiment in which the great tragic themes were emerging and tended to override comic patterns. Certainly *Measure for Measure* is related in thematic concerns to the great tragedies closest to it, *Othello* and *Lear*. From the viewpoint of this study, it is worth noticing the elements in the play which most signally conflict with the comic design outlined so far and which prevent a normal comic contract from operating.

Among these, the characterisation of Isabella is one of the most outstanding. We first hear of her as described by Claudio to Lucio, explaining why he wants her to plead for him with Angelo:

> I have great hope in that. For in her youth
> There is a prone and speechless dialect
> Such as move men.   I ii 172 – 4

One critic at least has seen in these lines an early indication of the sexual attractiveness of Isabella,[24] and this view might be borne out by Lucio's injunction to her at the end of Act I:

> Go to Lord Angelo,
> And let him learn to know, when maidens sue,
> Men give like gods; but when they weep and kneel,
> All their petitions are as freely theirs
> As they themselves would owe them.   I iv 79 – 83

Lucio, we may be sure, can be relied on to get a leer out of this as out of most things. And yet, in spite of his characteristic greeting to Isabella before he learns who she is, 'Hail virgin — if you be', he appears to be entirely genuine in his professions of respect for her:

> I hold you as a thing enskied and sainted
> By your renouncement, an immortal spirit,
> And to be talk'd with in sincerity,
> As with a saint.   I iv 34—7

To win this degree of solemnity from Lucio is a measure of the dignity associated with Isabella's vows. The 'prone and speechless dialect', the image of man giving like gods to maidenly petitions, may prepare us for the effect Isabella will actually have on Angelo. Yet these passages also suggest the powers of intercession of virginity, if not of the Virgin herself. The tone of the scene between Isabella and Lucio seems to modulate uneasily between an ironic awareness of sex and a genuine reverence for chastity.

The effect of Isabella's pleas to Angelo is even more striking. The basic structure of the scene is ironic, with two observers, Lucio and the Provost, as well as the asides of Angelo himself, designed to make us aware of the complexity of what is happening between the protagonists. Here the asides of Lucio to Isabella certainly emphasise the sexual aspect of her pleading:

> To him again, entreat him,
> Kneel down before him, hang upon his gown;
> You are too cold. If you should need a pin,
> You could not with more tame a tongue desire it.   II ii 43—7

By contrast the Provost's aside supplies a higher view of her mission, 'Heaven give thee moving grace'. And when at last we hear the inner thoughts of Angelo, it is to discover that she has won him in a way beyond the imagination of either of the watchers.

> She speaks, and 'tis such sense
> That my sense breeds with it.   II ii 142—3

Her effect on Angelo is neither the moving grace the Provost wishes for her, nor the feminine rhetoric urged on her by Lucio, but ironically a combination of the two which is deeply corrupting. What we appear to have here is a scene of multiple irony comparable to the eavesdropping scene in Act V of *Troilus and Cressida* in which we are made aware of a whole range of conflicting and mutually incompatible responses to a single event.

And yet Isabella's great speeches in this scene transcend entirely their ironic setting. At the simple level of argument on the particular case, Isabella is defeated again and again by the logic of Angelo, and she has to be urged on by Lucio. But when her passion is aroused, the poetry soars away from the details of individuality:

> *Angelo.* Your brother is a forfeit of the law,
>   And you but waste your words.
> *Isabella.*   Alas, alas!
>   Why, all the souls that were, were forfeit once,
>   And He that might the vantage best have took
>   Found out the remedy. How would you be,
>   If He, which is the top of judgement, should
>   But judge you as you are? O, think on that,
>   And mercy then will breathe within your lips,
>   Like man new made.   II ii 71 – 9

There is here that 'drowning and breaking of the dykes that separate man from man' which Yeats defines as the essential tragic emotion, the dykes, he goes on to add, on which 'comedy keeps house'.[25] It is a metaphor with the characteristic awkwardness of Yeats' prose, yet also characteristically illuminating. The differences between an Isabella and an Angelo, a Lucio and a Provost, are those which would normally make this a scene of comic irony. Yet these differences are annihilated, for the audience in the theatre if not for the characters on stage, by the radical and universal image of

>   man, proud man,
>   Dress'd in a little brief authority,
>   Most ignorant of what he's most assur'd   II ii 118 – 20

The language of moral absolutes, which in the mouth of Celia or Bonario in *Volpone* was made to appear stilted and inappropriate by its ironic context, here in *Measure for Measure* is made to ring out as a higher form of truth.

It is impossible for the rest of the play satisfactorily to reduce Isabella once again to a place in an identifiably comic pattern. We may well find offensive her unhesitating choice – 'More than our brother is our chastity' – or her violent attack upon Claudio for suggesting she change her mind. Yet this fierce and passionate virginity is entirely consonant with the character whose words have aroused in us such powerful emotion and in Lucio the respect due to 'a thing enskied and sainted'. The comparison of Isabella to Antigone is surely just;[26] as Antigone travels to living tomb instead of marriage bed, so we might expect the absolutism of Isabella to end in disaster. Almost no-one has been entirely satisfied with what Shakespeare in fact does with Isabella, and her marriage to the Duke is so problematic that modern directors have contrived to suggest that it was rejected. [27] If the character of Isabella were to have illustrated the comedy of zeal, as we suggested earlier, we would need to have seen her change under the pressure of events. From the crucial point of the Duke's intervention in the middle of Act III, scene i, it is true she seems to behave very differently, but this seems to be due to the general (and very puzzling) change in the mode of dramatic representation rather than to an inner change of motivation. There is nothing to suggest how or why Isabella should have been converted from her virginal marriage to Christ to a worldly marriage to the Duke.

We discussed earlier the idea of sex as an irrepressible life-force in the play. The moving lines of Lucio might serve as text:

> Your brother and his lover have embrac'd;
> As those that feed grow full, as blossoming time
> That from the seedness the bare fallow brings
> To teeming foison, even so her plenteous womb
> Expresseth his full tilth and husbandry.   I iv 40 – 4

But where else in *Measure for Measure* would we look for lines like this? Sex through most of the play is evoked as a disease-carrier rather than a life-force. The jokes of Lucio and his friends about syphilis do not represent a detachable low vein of comedy; they are related to the images which the other characters use. The Duke, still as Friar Lodowick in the last scene, describes the condition of society he has found:

> My business in this state
> Made me a looker-on here in Vienna,
> Where I have seen corruption boil and bubble
> Till it o'errun the stew   V i 3 14 – 17

It is impossible to sentimentalise the seething stew (or stews) of sexual life in Vienna, the Pompeys and Mistresses Overdone, as the anarchic energy of vitality. And it is not only at this level of general promiscuity that sex is associated with corruption. Claudio is explicit in his self-condemnation at his first meeting with Lucio:

> *Lucio.* Why, how now, Claudio? Whence comes this restraint?
> *Claudio.* From too much liberty, my Lucio. Liberty,

> As surfeit, is the father of much fast;
> So every scope by the immoderate use
> Turns to restraint. Our natures do pursue,
> Like rats that ravin down their proper bane,
> A thirsty evil; and when we drink, we die.   I ii 117–22

The severity of this is the more surprising because, as Claudio goes on to explain, his act was a 'crime' on a technicality only. Yet it is impossible to read this speech, with David Stevenson, as a 'wry jest'.[28] It is as authentically repentant as Juliet's equivalent statement to the Duke:

> I do repent me as it is an evil,
> And take the shame with joy.   II iii 35–6

Measure for Measure, then, is a play in which sex is seen and felt as an evil, even when as in the case of Juliet and Claudio it is the expression of true love all but sanctioned by formal marriage. It is this as much as anything else which makes it difficult to class the play as a comedy in which life triumphs over death, marriage over celibacy, and a liberal humanity over the ascetic ideals of Puritanism.[29] Although we may now be wary of the Dark Lady and the biographical interpretation of Shakespeare's plays, there is no doubt that the horror of sex in *Measure for Measure* is related to a nearly obsessive strain in the works of this period of his career, a strain still visible in the last romances. However, we need not try to explain away this strain in *Measure for Measure* as an uncontrollable and unbalancing thematic intrusion upon the play. It is a part of a general satiric pattern in the play which runs counter to the comic rhythm. The Duke's visitation of his dukedom incognito is a device intended to expose the radical and basic corruption of the society, like Altofront's disguise as Malevole in *The Malcontent*. He finds what he is meant to find, a world so thoroughly tainted with vice that the problem of justice becomes virtually insoluble, for who is sufficiently innocent to judge the guilty? The gospel doctrine 'Judge not that ye be not judged' is finally evoked not in a spirit of loving Christian forgiveness, but in the purely negative light, 'with what measure ye mete, it shall be measured to you again'.

Measure for Measure has a satiric contract superimposed upon the comic design outlined earlier. This much it has in common with *Le Misanthrope*, where the comedy of the would-be reformer is likewise complicated by the real need for reform in the society satirically exposed. Yet we must differentiate between the degrees of artistic coherence produced by this combination in the two plays. *Le Misanthrope*, in its finely balanced and precisely controlled ambiguities, is a magnificently achieved work, although it escapes the normal frame of comedy. *Measure for Measure*, as Rosalind Miles concludes at the end of her book on the play, 'is not a fully satisfying emotional experience because it deprives us of the sense of harmony and completeness, even the harmony and completeness of a consistent ironic vision, which is the accompanying sensation of a great work'.[30] The central key to this failure is generally agreed to be the character of the Duke. Only those who allegorise the Duke entirely have professed to be quite satisfied with his role in the play. Even those, like Elizabeth Pope or Mary Lascelles, who trace in the Duke the features of 'a good ruler as subjects of a Tudor sovereign conceived him',[31] do not find his actions wholly defensible. And from more sceptical critics he has attracted downright abuse.

It may be that part of what is wrong with the figure of the Duke is that he has been given two quite distinct and mutually incompatible roles. When he retires from his dukedom to become a 'looker-on', he takes on the part of high satiric censor. His choric moralising, as in the strange gnomic lines which end Act III − 'He who the sword of heaven will bear' − is intended to provide distancing detachment. His very isolation, outside and apart from his dukedom, makes him a figure of true order and authority, an order and authority his state so noticeably lacks. It is at this level that he is given divine association; it is at this level that his marriage to Isabella, perfect Justice with perfect Mercy, is conceived as an ideal. But at the same time the Duke has to act as the Mr. Fixit of the comedy, pursuing unlikely and at times apparently disreputable means to achieve his ends. The justice who dispenses justice in odd unaccountable ways is a familiar figure in comedy; Jonson's Justice Clement in *Every Man in his Humour* is an example close to Shakespeare, Brecht's Azdak in *The Caucasian Chalk Circle* a more modern instance. With such comic controllers, we expect the abnormal, the apparently irrational, and in so far as the Duke in *Measure for Measure* belongs to this type it is not so surprising that he should indulge in the multiple intrigues and deceptions he does, even if they sometimes seem quite gratuitous. This is the tortuous way of comedy. Yet if the Duke must also represent an absolute standard of judgement as the ultimate arbiter of a corrupt society, he cannot be permitted the liberal interpretation of ways and means which might be accorded him in a different sort of comedy. If he approves in principle, as he appears to do, of the need for the rigorous legislation under which Claudio is sentenced, then he can hardly look well promoting the identical 'crime' between Angelo and Mariana, however much the technicality of the pre-contract is stressed. Critics hostile to the Duke have been quick to pounce on this and other inconsistencies.

The relationship with Lucio provides a striking example of the anomalous effects of the Duke's dual role. Lucio's slanderous remarks about the Duke may, at one level, be intended to be taken quite seriously. The way in which in his idle gossip he re-makes the Duke in his own image as a covert philanderer, and then brazenly attributes his slanders to the 'Friar' to incriminate him, leads us to wait expectantly for his punishment as an irresponsible and wanton liar, ironically caught out by the Duke's disguise. But when we get to the judgement scene, the Duke is acting Justice Clement, dispensing pardons to all and sundry, even the impenitent and unpardonable Barnadine. In this general amnesty it would seem natural for Lucio, a relatively harmless character, to be pardoned as well and the severity of his sentence of whipping and hanging, even though it is swiftly remitted, comes as an unpleasant surprise. It is useless to point out that slandering a Prince in Shakespeare's time was a major offence which merited severe punishment. The mode of the end of the play is that of an indulgent comic justice, not what a Jacobean audience would have expected from the Star Chamber. Yet here, as throughout the play, it is doubtful if Shakespeare intended the irony to bear as heavily upon the Duke as some critics have imagined who see in his punishment of Lucio the evidence of a personal vanity which can forgive anything but a slight to himself. If the Duke looks at times an inconsistent and unattractive character, it may be because he is pulled two ways by his dramatic function, rather than because he is designed to arouse laughter or contempt.

One of the remarkable features of *Measure for Measure* is the intense degree of emotional reaction which its characters evoke. Although it has been defined as an 'intellectual comedy', it has little of the alienating and distancing quality of *Troilus and Cressida*. The Duke is often attacked by critics with a degree of fury which suggests a thorough personal dislike. Isabella is no longer as often warmly admired as she was in the nineteenth century, but she is frequently detested with just as much strength. More than one critic has come to express considerable admiration for Angelo: 'there persists in Angelo, even through the usurpation of his own soul by lust fully revealed and irresistible, a kind of integrity'.[32] This degree of feeling, in a critical age which tends to avoid identification with character as old-fashioned and simple-minded, is in itself remarkable. If comedy demands some degree of emotional detachment, in this too, *Measure for Measure* breaks through the restraints of comic form. The comment about the integrity of Angelo is particularly striking, for it is, in a sense, the breakdown of Angelo's integrity which the comedy of zeal was designed to reveal. And yet this is not what happens in the play; Angelo's integrity does survive. He discovers that his nature contains impulses of corrupt desire which he cannot control, but he analyses those impulses with a bewildered honesty in soliloquy, and continues to see them for what they are, however much he gives in to them.

> I crave death more willingly than mercy;
> 'Tis my deserving, and I do entreat it.   V i 479–80

These are his last words in the play. It is because the actions of Isabella and the Duke seem to betray this sort of integrity, coming down to the level of comic compromise represented by the bed-trick, that many people find them ultimately so unsympathetic.

The conflict of audience contracts in both *Le Misanthrope* and *Measure for Measure* creates the possibility of individual emotional response beyond normal comic expectations. The two plays are controversial because the comic consensus is fragmented. We are prepared to agree with a view of society in which the individualist is always wrong, the theorist always disproved by experience. Yet what we are faced with is a world so empty of meaning, or so corrupt, that we are made to wonder whether the attempt, at least, to impose ideals upon it may not be admirable if unavailing. We should be able to laugh quite comfortably at Alceste as he rages against the ways of the world; we should await with satisfaction the revelation of Angelo's all too unangelic nature, or smile indulgently at the asceticism of an Isabella. But in context we cannot so certainly place these characters as zealots; their desire for perfection, their confusion in the face of events, comes to seem on the contrary more honest, more deeply human, than their compromising fellow characters. Who would actually want to be Philinte rather than Alceste, the Duke rather than Angelo? Once the security of the comic agreement is broken down, then reactions may go different ways — Isabella or Angelo may be admired or disliked, Alceste may seem an unjustly treated 'honnête homme' or an absurd comic figure. But the solidarity of a common opinion shared by an audience in the theatre on which the comic contract depends is no longer possible.

Conclusion

The meaning of comedy has in the past most frequently been sought in the meaning of laughter; theories of comedy have been theories of the comic. Although several literary critics have argued against this approach, insisting that we ought to be concerned with the artistic structure of comedy as of any other genre rather than merely its comic effects, [1] there continues to be an expectation that any general idea of comedy should explain why we laugh and what our laughter signifies. It is inevitable that it should be so. Laughter is such a basic effect of comedy that it seems reasonable to approach it by way of the whole class of things which are laughable, and that necessarily takes us away from the purely literary or theatrical. The most eminent modern theorists of the comic, still after seventy-five years extremely influential, are a psychiatrist and a philosopher, whose ideas on the subject originated as by-products of their psychiatry and philosophy. We turn eagerly to Freud or Bergson for illumination on the fundamental nature of the comic because this seems the key to the understanding of comedy. And so, an aesthetic of comedy most often ends up as a psychology of laughter. This study has been concerned with the analysis of laughter only tangentially, concentrating on the structure and attitudes of comedy rather than on comic techniques. However it seems appropriate in conclusion to consider some of the implications of the comic contract which we have been examining in Shakespeare, Jonson and Molière in the light of previous general theories of the comic.

Theorists have tended to concentrate on one of three different aspects of the comic: the fantastic, the ridiculous, or the absurd. Those who emphasise the element of fantasy most often see the effect of laughter as one of therapeutic release. Freud links the structure of jokes to the structure of dreams, and argues that in both psychic energies normally used for repression are released. The 'joke-work' is a socially acceptable means of evading the normal adult ban upon the expression of certain impulses of aggressiveness, sexuality, or anarchic pleasure. Freud suggests that the 'specific characteristic of the comic' is 'the awakening of the infantile' — 'the regained "lost laughter of childhood" '. [2] The Freudian analysis of jokes has been extended by several writers to a general interpretation of comedy. For

Charles Mauron, comedy exorcises unconscious anxieties by fantastic images of wish-fulfilment; it represents the revenge of the pleasure principle upon the reality principle.[3] A more recent follower of Freud, Morton Gurewitch, although he is concerned with a wide range of different constituents of comedy, concentrates finally on 'its ability to utilise and even glorify irrational freedom'.[4] What is thus, at the individual level, the expression of psychological energies normally repressed, can equally be seen, collectively, as the holiday escape from the tyranny of the usual exemplified by festive comedy. 'Through release to clarification' is C. L. Barber's phrase to suggest the movement of Shakespeare's festive comedy from saturnalian confusion to renewed and deepened order.[5] Ian Donaldson, in a book which has been often cited in the course of this study, has traced through a century of English comedy images of 'the world upside-down', the inversion of social norms of authority often associated with holiday license.[6] For almost all of those who concentrate on its fantastic aspects, comedy is a means of coming to terms with the irrational in man by allowing it free expression, by allowing it a temporary victory over the rational.

The ridiculous necessarily implies someone or something ridiculed or mocked, and to be a mocker one must fancy oneself superior to the object of mockery. In Hobbes's famous definition this is the very essence of the comic:

> Laughter is nothing else but sudden glory arising from some sudden conception of some eminency in ourselves, by comparison with the infirmity of others, or with our own formerly.[7]

From Aristotle on, this idea of the ridiculous, of laughing at what is worse than ourselves, was central to the classical theory of comedy. We were thought to laugh at what was mentally, morally, or physically deformed and by our laughter to re-affirm our own standards of normality. It is in this way that comedy was held to fulfil its true didactic purpose by teaching us to despise and condemn the 'common errors of mankind'. What we laughed at we would be careful not to imitate. Jonson is the outstanding spokesman in English for this view of comedy. As he puts it in his preface to *Every Man in his Humour* — 'you that have so graced monsters may like men'. The audience's ridicule of the monstrous folly of the comic characters may lead them on to a truer appreciation of ideals of better human behaviour. The aggressiveness of Hobbes's 'sudden glory' is thus transformed into a morally educative process, in which we do not merely congratulate ourselves on our superiority to those we laugh at, but are inspired to earn that position of superiority. The standards by which the ridiculous is mocked are often thought to be ideal standards of logic and truth. As James Feibleman put it,

'Comedy consists in the indirect affirmation of the ideal, logical order, by means of the derogation of the limited orders of actuality'.[8] If the purpose of the fantastic in comedy is in some sort to celebrate the irrational, the function of the ridiculous is to make us judge and condemn it by an implied principle of reason.

The absurd is to be distinguished from the ridiculous in that it involves a more neutral perception of incongruity; it depends upon a sense of ironic awareness rather than conscious superiority. Many theories of the comic, particularly in the modern period, have stressed the notion of absurdity, the mental contrast between two incompatible ideas or images. Bergson's concept of the mechanical encrusted upon the living is, as we have seen, one of the most influential. Arthur Koestler in *The Act of Creation* has argued that 'the pattern underlying all varieties of humour is "bisociative" – perceiving a situation in two habitually incompatible associative contexts'.[9] Such ideas, which emphasise a duality at the basis of the comic, have been termed 'intellectualist theories',[10] because in them laughter derives from the intellectual perception of a contrast which cannot be resolved by reason. The recognition of the absurd does not lead on, like the ridiculous, to an implicit re-instatement of principles of logic and reason. The absurd is irremediable, irreducible, cannot be changed or reformed and thus can only be met by laughter. If fantasy is central to festive or romantic comedy, ridicule to satiric or corrective comedy, then the absurd may be said to belong most properly to ironic comedy, in which we glory neither in our freedom from ordinary restraints nor in our superiority over the comic butts, but laugh rather at the ludicrous disparities between one view of our lives and another.

The object of this study has been to illustrate a range of different comic patterns, to challenge the idea that the form and meaning of comedy can be explained in terms of a single fundamental purpose. We have looked in turn at plays in which the fantastic, the ridiculous, or the absurd may be seen to predominate. In the holiday atmosphere of Bartholomew Fair the normal structure of society is broken down, the figures of authority humiliated, although the forces of anarchy released are by no means wholly and unreservedly celebrated. The triumph of nature in *As You Like It* and *L'Ecole des Femmes* represents a victory of the instinctive and the impulsive over the arbitrary principles of social order. Both plays depend upon an ultimate belief in the powers of irrational nature to contribute to the renewal and rebirth of a rational social harmony. The task of arbitrating over this renewed order is assigned in *A Midsummer Night's Dream* and *The Tempest* to a benevolent father-figure. But before he can take control the image of another more threatening and tyrannic father-figure must be dispelled, and an essential part must be played by the capricious power of a non-human agent. The world controlled by Theseus Duke of Athens, or Prospero Duke of Milan is complemented by a stranger world in which Oberon or Prospero the magician reign. All of the plays considered in the first three chapters of this book could be used as convincing examples of the basis of comedy in the fantastic.

Equally, however, in the following three chapters, we have been primarily concerned with the ridiculous, with comedies in which the audience is given a variety of vantage-points of superiority over the comic characters. We can see through the cant and professional nonsense of the doctors and the alchemists where the gulls and the fools can not. Watching the comedy of deceiver and dupe, we can congratulate ourselves on our rational commonsense and intelligence. With *Les Précieuses Ridicules* and *Love's Labour's Lost* we are (more or less) indulgent adults observing the adolescent antics of courtship. We can place the language games and the make-believe postures for what they are, and the end of each play re-affirms by contrast a solid and down-to-earth reality. In *Les Femmes Savantes* and *Epicoene* it is masculine women and effeminate men, shrews and hen-pecked husbands, whom we laugh at with the amused disdain of sophisticated urbanity. Whether or not medicine, alchemy, or preciosity would be habitual objects of ridicule to us or to the original audiences outside the theatre, we are so placed by the comedies themselves that they appear ridiculous.

The characters and situations in the plays considered in the rest of the book are not ridiculous in this same way. We watch them pinned down by a cross-fire of ironies rather than the one-way attack of satiric ridicule. We can see through the hypocrisy of Volpone and Tartuffe as clearly as we can the confidence-tricks of Subtle or the quackery of Diafoirus, but we see also the impotence of those who try to tell the truth about them. The constant interchange of appearance and reality is recognised in all its absurdity. The happy endings of these two plays do not represent the vindication of a principle of reason but an ironically arbitrary imposed solution. The dissonances between image and actuality, theory and practice, projection and event in *Dom Juan* and *Troilus and Cressida* are so far-reaching, so universal, as to take us beyond the comic genre as such, although both plays do exploit the absurd for comic effect. In *Le Misanthrope* and *Measure for Measure* it is specifically ideals of perfection, of perfect justice or perfect honesty, which are undermined by the facts of social life. Throughout all these plays we are in a world of moral incongruities in which it is precisely the awareness of ambiguity, the simultaneous apprehension of incompatibles, which make for the basic ironic vision.

There can be no doubt that all three, the fantastic, the ridiculous, and the absurd are deeply rooted in comedy and represent main streams within the comic tradition. But no one of the three can be said to be the defining characteristic of the comic as theorists have tended to maintain. The fantastic, the ridiculous, and the absurd are all equally available to the comedian to build into the contract with his audience. If there is a single aspect of the comic which does seem essential it is its shared character as a group experience. It has generally been agreed that the comic is always a social phenomenon. Even a three-line joke needs an audience to be enjoyed, and stage comedy depends upon the contagiousness of laughter in a theatre for its success. In laughing we share a point of view, an angle of vision on the object of our laughter; but it is not always the same point of view, it is very frequently not the way we look on the subject outside the theatre. The comedian may use any number of distorting lenses to alter our vision. For the duration of the comedy, however, we are prepared to accept the reality of the comically distorted images, whether the extraordinary shapes of the fantastic, the caricatures of the ridiculous, or the bifocal forms of the absurd. The comedian draws upon a range of psychological sources, the anarchic release of festive comedy, the aggressive superiority of 'sudden glory', the cynical detachment of irony, as well as the simple wish-fulfilment of the happy ending. These, however, are all contained and transmuted by the framework of the comedy. We laugh at the public enactment of our private fantasies, attitudes, ideas, and in sharing the experience of laughter we acknowledge the truth of these as patterns of human behaviour and at the same time transcend them.

Comedy is to tragedy as party-going is to church-going. The point of the analogy is not that tragedy is solemn whereas comedy is festive and gay, but that the tragic involves a shared spiritual or emotional experience, the comic a shared social event. Comedy addresses us as a community of social beings, tragedy as a community of individual souls. However, this does not mean that comedy always calls upon us to take one social attitude rather than another, for or against social authority, say, progressive or reactionary. The sociality of the comedy consists in the accord of the laughing audience rather than in any essential or archetypal pattern of social meaning in the action. It is when we reach areas where this accord cannot operate that we come to the limits of the comic genre, as this study has tried to illustrate at a number of points. In the ending of *The Tempest*, for example, we recognise a non-comic mode because Prospero's final speeches place us in a world of spiritual values to which we must respond accordingly. This is perhaps more important than the traditional distinction of follies rather than crimes as the appropriate subject for comedy. *Volpone* and *Tartuffe* both go beyond follies, but the author-audience contract in each case makes it possible to treat the crimes of the deceivers as laughing matters. The cosmic ironies of *Troilus and Cressida* and *Dom Juan*, on the other hand, cannot be completely controlled by an agreed audience perspective, and with the ambiguities of *Measure for Measure* and *Le Misanthrope* we are left emotionally and intellectually uncertain and undecided.

A basic semantic problem has bedevilled the discussion of comedy – the meaning of the word 'serious'. How can what is funny, that is not serious, be considered serious, that is of lasting or profound importance? By definition, it would seem, what we laugh at is not what we take seriously. It is partly perhaps in order to come at some fundamental meaning behind or beyond laughter that so many critics of comedy have turned to general psychological theories of the comic. Whereas tragedy is self-evidently about issues of the greatest significance for us as human beings, comedy is so taken up with the trivial and the superficial that it seems to need the justification of an unseen deep structure or ultimate function to make it something more than diversion or entertainment. Our uneasiness about the seriousness of comedy in its pure form has also tended to give greater value to those plays which go beyond the normal limitations of the genre. In the modern period, particularly, as we have seen, 'problem' plays such as *Dom Juan* or *Troilus and Cressida* have been appreciated because they are perplexing, disturbing, in a way which comedy is not normally taken to be. 'Disturbing' is, in fact, a characteristically twentieth century word of praise for aesthetic effect, and insofar as many great comedies seem to encourage an attitude of comfortable complacency the reverse of disturbing, their achievement has been found hard to define. In our confident expectation of a happy ending, in our immunity from real pain or suffering, in our amused detachment from folly and absurdity, in all of these comedy appears to allow us an unthinking escape from the issues of serious reality. But the certainty which the comedian looks for in his audience is not merely complacency, enabling us to relax in confidence in our moral or intellectual superiority or in the assurance of the providential happy ending. The agreement is only temporary, the attitudes understood to be for the duration of the comedy only. The seriousness of comedy consists in the degree to which we can confront the fantastic, ridiculous, or absurd aspects of our humanity, recognise and place them by our shared laughter.

Translations

CHAPTER TWO

p.32   An intelligent woman can betray her duty; but at least she must dare to want to do so; the stupid one can be unfaithful in the ordinary course of events, without any desire to be so, and without thinking she is. (I i 113–16)

p.33   I shall shape this mind as I want; she is like a piece of wax in my hands, and I can give her the form that pleases me. (III iii 809–11)

p.34   *Alain.* It's because this action makes him jealous.
Georgette. But how come he is taken with this notion?
Alain. It comes from . . . it comes from the fact that he is jealous.
Georgette. Yes, but why is he? and why this anger?
Alain. It's that jealousy . . . do you understand, Georgette, is something . . . well . . . that makes one anxious . . . and drives people from around the house. I'm going to give you a comparison so that you'll be able to understand it better. Tell me, isn't it true, that when you are sitting down to your soup, if someone starving came to try to eat it, you'd be angry and want to beat him off?
Georgette. Yes, I understand that.
Alain. It's just exactly the same: a woman is the soup of a man. (II iii 423–36).

People made like you do more than money can, and you are well built for making cuckolds. (I iv 301–2).

p.35   As for the man, I think he's called de la Zousse or Souche: I didn't pay much attention to the name; he's rich from what I'm told, but not of the brightest, and he's spoken of as a ridiculous fellow. (I iv 327–31).
He came in then – I couldn't see him, but I heard him walking about with long strides, without saying a word, letting out pitiable sighs from time to time, and sometimes banging hard on tables, hitting a dog that was sorry for him, and throwing down sharply the things that came in his way. (IV vi 1154–9).

p.36   He swore that he loved me with a love beyond compare, and said to me the nicest possible words, things which nothing could ever equal, whose sweetness, each time I hear him speak, delights me and excites within me a certain something which leaves me deeply moved. (II v 559–64).

pp.36–7 I want to write to you, but I am in difficulties as to how I should begin. I have thoughts that I would like you to know; but I cannot tell how to go about saying them to you, and I am mistrustful of my words. . . . Truly, I don't know what you have done to me; but I feel that I am mortally unhappy at what I have been made to do to you, and that it would be the hardest thing in the world for me to do without you, and I would be very happy to be yours. Maybe it is wrong to say this; but indeed I cannot prevent myself from saying it and I hope it may be possible to do so without there being any harm in it. I have been strongly warned that all young men are deceivers, that one mustn't listen to them, and that all you tell me is only to mislead me; but I assure you that I cannot imagine this of you, and I am so touched by your words that I cannot believe that they are untrue. Tell me honestly how things stand; for indeed, as I am quite sincere, you would be doing the greatest possible wrong if you deceived me; and I think that I would die of unhappiness if you did. (III iv [947]).

p.38   All her heart feels her hand knew how to put into it, but in touching terms and so filled with goodness, with innocent tenderness and naiveté, the way, indeed, that a pure nature expresses the first wound of love. (III iv 941−5).

Despite the cursed precautions of an unjust tyranny, could a finer nature be seen? And isn't it beyond a doubt a punishable crime wickedly to spoil the admirable substance of this soul, to want to smother in ignorance and stupidity the light of this mind. (III iv 950−5).

p.39   What, the fate which persists in driving me to despair will not give me the time to catch my breath? Time after time am I to see my prudent and watchful care defeated by their intelligence? At my age am I to be hoodwinked by an innocent girl and a young fool? (IV vii 1182−7).

The more, when I watched her, I found her serene, the more I grew hot with anger and those seething rages that inflamed my heart seemed to redouble its loving passion; I was embittered, angered, desperate against her: and yet I'd never seen her so beautiful. (IV i 1016−21).

Arnolphe. So you don't love, in that case?
Agnès. You?
Arnolphe. Yes.
Agnès. Alas, no.
Arnolphe. What, no!
Agnès. Do you want me to lie?
Arnolphe. Why not love me, Madam impudence?
Agnès. Goodness, it isn't me you ought to blame: why didn't you make yourself loved, as he did? I never stopped you, as far as I know. (V iv 1531−6).

p.40   I know that, in order to punish her libertine love, I have only to let her evil destiny take its course, that I shall be revenged on her by herself. (II v 990−2).

Through this piece of innocence, just consider to what she is exposed by that madman's egregious folly, and what terrible dangers she could have run, if I were now a man to cherish her less. But my soul burns with too pure a love; I would rather die than have betrayed her; I see in her charms worthy of another fate, and nothing can now separate me from her but death. (V ii 1412−19).

p.41   What − will he let himself be ruled by his son? Do you want a father to have the weakness not to be able to make youth obey? (V vii 1687−9).

CHAPTER FOUR

p.70   We are not the only ones, as you know, who try to take advantage of human weakness. It is to that end that most human endeavour is directed, and everyone attempts to catch men by their weaknesses to make some profit out of them. . . . Alchemists try to profit from the passion for riches, by promising mountains of gold to those who listen to them: and fortune-tellers, by their deceitful predictions, profit from the vanity and ambition of credulous minds. But men's greatest weakness is their love of life; and we in our turn profit from that by our ceremonious hocus-pocus, and know how to take advantage of the veneration which the fear of death gives them for our profession. (*L'Amour Médecin* III i).

p.72   *Sganarelle.* I shall have to make you out a prescription.
            Gorgibus. Quick, a table, paper, ink.
            Sganarelle. Is there someone here who can write?
            Gorgibus. Do you not know how to?
            Sganarelle. Oh, I cannot remember; I have so much on my mind that I forget the half of it. (*Le Médecin Volant* v).

p.73   It must be admitted that all those who excel in any science are worthy of great praise, and especially those of the medical profession, as much because of its usefulness, as because it contains within it several other sciences, which makes the complete understanding of it very difficult . . . You are not one of those doctors who rely only on what is known as rational or dogmatic medicine, and I am sure that you practise with great success all the time: experience is the mistress of all things. (*Le Médecin Volant* viii).
            Yes, it was like that formerly: but we've changed all that, and now we practice medicine by a quite new method. (II iv).

p.75   Without us everyone would become unhealthy, and it is we who are their great doctors.

p.76   'Plus, on the twenty-fourth, a little enema, insinuative, preparative, and emollient, to soften, moisten, and cool Monsieur's intestines'. What I like about Monsieur Fleurant, my apothecary, is that his bills are always so polite: 'Monsieur's intestines, thirty sous', Yes, but, Monsieur Fleurant, it's not everything to be polite, one must be reasonable too and not skin one's patients. Thirty sous an enema; your servant, if you please. You put them down to me at only twenty sous in other bills, and twenty sous in apothecaries' language, is ten sous; so there, ten sous. (I i).

p.77   So now this month I have taken . . . eight medecines and . . . twelve enemas; and last month there were twelve medicines and twenty enemas. I am not surprised I haven't been as well this month as last. (I i).

p.78   But above all else, what pleases me about him, and where he follows my example, is that he holds blindly to the opinions of the ancients, and that he has never wanted to understand nor to hear the arguments and evidence of the so-called discoveries of our time, with regard to the circulation of the blood, and other opinions of the same brand. (II v).

p.79   Nature, by itself, when we let it alone, pulls itself gently out of the disorder into which it has fallen. It is our anxiety, our impatience which spoils everything, and nearly everyone dies of the cure not the disease. (III iii).

The workings of the human machine are mysteries, into which, as yet, men cannot see at all, and . . . nature has put before our eyes veils which are too thick for us to understand anything of them. (III iii).

p.80   He has his reasons for not wanting any of them, and he maintains that they are allowable only for vigorous and robust people who have the extra strength to bear the remedies along with the disease; but that, for his part, he has only just strength enough to bear his illness. (III iii).

p.81   Death and damnation! if only I were a doctor, I'd avenge myself for his impertinence; and when he was sick, I'd let him die without help. He could do or say what he would, I wouldn't prescribe him the least little blood-letting, the least little enema, and I would say to him, 'Die! die! that will teach you not to mock the Faculty next time'. (III iv).

p.89   *M. Purgon.* But since you are unwilling to be cured at my hands.
Argan. It isn't my fault.
M. Purgon. Since you have failed in the obedience due to your doctor.
Toinette. That cries out for venegeance.
M. Purgon. Since you have declared yourself a rebel against the treatment I prescribed for you . . .
Argan. Oh, not at all.
M. Purgon. I say to you that I abandon you to your bad constitution, to the intemperance of your intestines, the impurity of your blood, the bitterness of your bile, and the sedimentation of your humours. (III vi).

CHAPTER FIVE

p.97   I think these good-for-nothing girls with their pommade want to ruin me. I see nothing anywhere but white of egg, blanching-cream and a thousand other flim-flams that I know nothing about. They have used up, since we have been here, the fat of at least a dozen pigs, and four footmen could easily live off the sheep's feet they use. (Sc. iii).

pp.97–8   Father, my cousin here will tell you, just as I do, that marriage should never take place until after other encounters. To be attractive, a lover must know how to express fine sentiments, to show gentleness, tenderness and passion, and his courtship must be in the proper form. (Sc. iv).

p.98   *Magdelon.* My dear, this is a delightful character.
Cathos. I can quite see that he is an Amilcar. (Sc. ix).

p.100   At a given moment one knows 'So-and-so has composed the prettiest imaginable play on such-and-such a subject, so-and-so has written words to such-and-such a tune . . .' That's what makes you well thought of in company; and if one doesn't know such things, I wouldn't give two pence for all the wit one might have. (Sc. ix).

CHAPTER SIX

p.112   They [men] have senates, academies, courts, diets, councils, to establish themselves; we only, unawakened, only we, on the point of seeing ourselves overwhelmed, never dream that it is time for us to band together.

p.119   In a wife, as in everything else, I want to follow my own fashion. I find myself rich enough to be able, as I think, to choose a partner who receives everything from me, and whose submissive and total dependence could have nothing to reproach me with on the score of birth or wealth. (I i 124–8).

p.125   Don't you feel, as soon as you hear it, the disgust such a word conveys to the mind, with what a peculiar picture it offends us, what a sordid sight it forces us to imagine? (I i 9–12).

The consequences of this word, when I consider them, make me see a husband, children, household, and if my thinking is right, I see nothing there to offend the mind or make me shudder. (I i 15–18).

p.126   Soaring upwards on a great and fine spirit, you may inhabit the high regions of philosophy, while my mind, keeping here below, will enjoy the earthly delights of matrimony. (I i 63–6).

And I want to avenge us, us all, as many as there are of us, for the unworthy rank in which men class us, for limiting our talents to trivialities and closing to us the door of the highest knowledge. (III ii 853–6).

p.127   It is she who rules, and in a tone that admits no opposition dictates as law what she has decided. (I iii 209–10).

I will soon show her to whose authority, of the two of us, the laws of right-thinking make all her wishes subject; and who should rule, her mother or her father, mind or body, form or matter. (IV ii 1127–30).

p.128   Oh, gently there, be careful not to open your heart to me too fully; if I have been able to place you in the rank of my lovers, be content with the eyes as your only interpreters, and do not express in any other language desires which must seem an outrage to me. (I iv 276–80).

Philaminte. Don't let such pressing desires languish.
Armande. Hurry.
Bélise. Quickly, speed on our pleasures. (III i 717–18).
Bélise. Oh, gently, allow me a chance to breathe.
Armande. Please give us the time to wonder.
Philaminte. With these verses, one feels a certain something flow right to the heart so that one is quite overcome. (III ii 776–8).

p.129   Alas, Madame, it's an infant quite new-born, its fate should certainly concern you, for it was in your salon that I just now gave birth to it. (III i 720–2). My respect for ladies is well known everywhere, and, if I pay tribute to the brightness of their eyes, I honour also the light of their minds. (III ii 863–5).

p.130   Such talk has nothing in it to make me change, a wise man is prepared for all events; cured by reason of vulgar weaknesses, he is above these sort of matters, and there is no likelihood of his taking the least shadow of offense at anything which does not depend on his control. (V i 1543–8).

The body, those rags, are they of enough importance, enough value to be worth thinking about?   (II vii 539–40).

Yes, my body is myself, and I want to take care of it; rags if you want, my rags are dear to me.   (II vii 541–2).

p.131   The learned are only good for preaching from the pulpit; and, and, for my part, I've said it a thousand times, I would never take a man of wit to husband. Wit's not at all what one needs in the home, and books jibe poorly with marriage; and I want, if anyone is ever to engage my affections, a husband who has no other book but me, who, without offense to Madame, doesn't know A from B, who, in a word, is learned only in his wife.   (V iii 1622–70).

p.132   I grant that a woman may have knowledge of everything; but I don't like to see in her this shocking urge to make herself learned for the sake of being learned; and I prefer that often, when questioned, she should be wise enough to appear ignorant of the things that she knew; I want her in fact to conceal her learning, and that she should have knowledge without wanting it to be known, without quoting from authors, without using long words and tacking wit on to her slightest remarks.   (I iii 218–26).

pp.132–3   I saw in the hotchpotch of writing he gives us what his pedantic personality makes apparent everywhere: the constant arrogance of his presumption, that unshakably good opinion, that lazy state of extreme confidence, which always makes him so pleased with himself.   (I iii 251–6).

p.133   It [the court] has enough intelligence to master every subject; . . . at court one can acquire good taste; and . . . frankly, the tone of society there is worth all the obscure learning of the pedants.   (IV iii 1344–7).

CHAPTER SEVEN

pp.153–4   Men, for the most part, are peculiarly made. You never see them keep within the just bounds of nature; the confines of reason are too narrow for them; they overstep them in every aspect of character; and they often spoil the noblest thing by seeking to overdo it or pushing it to extremes. All this by way of passing comment, my dear brother-in-law.   (I v 339–45).

p.154   Oh yes, you of course are a reverend sage, and all the wisdom of the world is gathered up in you.   (I v 346–7).

What will a match like this give you? What's the point, with a property like yours, in choosing a beggar for a son-in-law?   (II ii 482–4).

p.155   The love which binds us to eternal beauties does not stifle our love of temporal things . . .   (III iii 933–4).

p.156   No, no, Madame, this must go further. I was in this place where I could hear everything and Heaven's goodness seems to have led me here to dash the pride of my treacherous enemy.   (III iv 1021–4).

Yes, brother, I am a wicked guilty man, a miserable sinner, full of
iniquity . . .   (III vi 1076−7).

You traitor, how dare you with this falsehood seek to tarnish the purity
of his virtue?   (III vi 1087−8).

p.157   Is there a tenet of true piety which instructs us to rob a lawful heir?
(IV i 1237−8).

p.158   This language, Madame, is rather hard to understand, and not so long
ago you talked in another style.   (IV v 1409−10).

I will believe nothing, Madame, unless you can assure my passion with
actions.   (IV v 1465−6).

Between ourselves, he's a man one can lead by the nose; in all our
conversations he counts for nothing at all, and I've brought him to such
a pitch that he can see everything without believing anything.   (IV v
1524−6).

p.159   For a long time I've doubted whether all was right, and I always thought
there would be a change of tune.   (IV 1547−8).

CHAPTER EIGHT

p.176   Goodness me, how you spout on! It seems you've learned that by heart,
and you talk just like a book.   (I ii).

pp.176−7   Lord, I was going to say . . . I don't know what to say; for you've
turned things in such a way, that it seems as though you're right; and yet
the truth is that you're wrong. I had the best ideas in the world, and your
speeches got me all muddled. Let it be: another time I'll put my
arguments in writing to dispute with you.   (I ii).

p.177   All beauties have the right to charm us, and the advantage of having
been first met, does not take away from all the others the just claims they
all have to our hearts.   (I ii).

Why do you not arm your forehead with noble impudence? Why do
you not swear to me that your sentiments towards me are still the same,
that you love me still with unequalled ardour, and that nothing but
death can separate you from me? Why do you not tell me that business
of the utmost importance obliged you to leave without giving me
notice . . .   (I iii).

p.178   What have you done in the world to be a gentleman? Do you think that
it is enough to bear a gentleman's name and arms, and that it is a glory to
us to come from a noble line when we live an infamous life? No, no,
birth is nothing where virtue is lacking.   (IV v).

CHAPTER NINE

p.187   I wish that people should be sincere, and, as men of honour, should not
utter any word that does not spring from the heart.   (I i 35−6).

p.188   In vain do I see her faults, in vain do I blame her for them, however
much I dislike them, she makes me love her.   (I i 231−2).

p.189   Doubtless my passion will succeed in purging her soul of these vices of the times. (I i 233–4).

pp.189–90   *Alceste.* Good God! must I love you! Oh, if I get my heart back from your hands, how I shall bless heaven for that rare good fortune. I don't hide it, I am doing everything I can to break the terrible attachment of my heart, but my greatest efforts have so far achieved nothing, and it's for my sins I love you so.

    Célimène. It is true, your passion for me is unique (II i 514–21).

p.190   My passion has reached such a point that it even makes me sympathise with her point of view; and when I consider how impossible it is for me to overcome my feelings for her, at the same time I tell myself that she has perhaps the same difficulty in repressing her tendency to play the coquette, and I find myself more inclined to pity than to blame her.

p.192   I wish the court, by its favourable notice, would do your worth more justice. You have cause to complain, and I am indignant when every day I see nothing done for you. (III v 1049–52).

    Me, Madame! And what grounds would I have for any claim? What service to the state have I been seen to perform? What have I done, if you please, so illustrious in itself, to complain to the court that nothing has been done for me? (III v 1053–6).

pp.192 3   *Arsinoé.* . . . I would dearly wish your passion better placed. There is no doubt you deserve a much happier fate, and your charmer is unworthy of you.

    Alceste. But in saying that, consider, I beg you, that this lady, Madame, is your friend. . . .   .

    Arsinoé. Yes, though my friend, she is, and I will call her so, unworthy of the service of a true man's heart; and the tenderness of her's for you is just pretence.

    Alceste. It's possible, Madame; one cannot see the heart. But in kindness you might have spared mine such a thought. (III v 1102–18).

    By Heaven, Gentlemen, I did not think to be so amusing as you find me. (II vi 733–74).

p.194   The laughters are on your side, Madame, that's all there is to be said, and you can direct your satire against me. (II iv 681–2).

    In truth, people of sublime merit attract the love and esteem of everyone. (III v 1045–6).

    In his ways of behaving, he is very peculiar; but he is for me, I confess, a special case, and the sicerity in which his soul takes pride, has something noble and heroic in it. It's a virtue rare in our age, and I would like to see it everywhere as it is in him. (IV i 1163–8).

p.195   He did not want to write a comedy full of incident, but simply a play in which he could speak against the manners of the age.

    Since I saw him, for a whole three quarters of an hour, spitting into a well to make ripples, I have never been able to think highly of him. (V iv [1691]).

p.196   I see these faults at which your soul rebels as vices integral to human nature; and my mind, then, is no more shocked at seeing a man dishonest, unjust, self-interested, than at seeing vultures hungry for carrion, monkeys mischievous, or wolves angry. (I i 173–8).

Notes

INTRODUCTION

1. The idea of these termini for the main tradition of classic European comedy was suggested to me in discussion by Richard Andrews of the University of Kent.
2. The contrast is a traditional one, but for two modern articles along these lines see Peter G. Phialas 'Comic Truth in Shakespeare and Jonson', *South Atlantic Quarterly* 62 (1963), 78–91, and Robert Ornstein 'Shakespearean and Jonsonian Comedy', *Shakespeare Survey* 22 (1969), 43–6.
3. A partial exception is Michel Grivelet's essay on *Amphitryon* and *The Comedy of Errors*, 'Shakespeare, Molière, and the Comedy of Ambiguity', *Shakespeare Survey* 22 (1969), 15–26.
4. There is an unpublished doctoral dissertation by Bruce Louis Jay on *The Comic Art of Ben Jonson and Molière* (University of Connecticut 1974), see *Dissertation Abstracts* 35 (1974), 2942-A.
5. Northrop Frye, *A Natural Perspective* (N.Y. 1965).
6. C. L. Barber, *Shakespeare's Festive Comedy* (N.Y. 1959).
7. Thomas McFarland, *Shakespeare's Pastoral Comedy* (Chapel Hill, N. Carolina 1972), for example, develops this point of view at length.
8. Many critics of Shakespearean comedy have commented on this aspect of the plays: two recent books which stress its centrality are Ralph Berry, *Shakespeare's Comedies: Explorations in Form* (Princeton 1972), and Alexander Leggatt, *Shakespeare's Comedy of Love* (London 1974).
9. L. C. Knights, *Drama and Society in the Age of Jonson* (London 1937).
10. After Knights, notable critics in this line have been A. H. Sackton, *Rhetoric as a Dramatic Language in Ben Jonson* (N.Y. 1948). E. B. Partridge, *The Broken Compass* (London 1958).
11. Jonas Barish, *Ben Jonson and the Language of Prose Comedy* (Cambridge, Mass. 1960).
12. John J. Enck, *Jonson and the Comic Truth* (Madison, Wis. 1957).
13. It was Ferdinand Brunetière who first put forward this point of view in his famous essay 'La Philosophie de Molière' – *Etudes Critiques sur l'historie de la littérature française* 4c. série (Paris 1891).
14. Daniel Mornet, *Molière* (Paris 1943).
15. Paul Benichou, *Morales du Grand Siècle* (Paris 1948).
16. John Cairncross, *Molière Bourgeois et Libertin* (Paris 1963).
17. W. G. Moore, *Molière: a New Criticism* (Oxford 1949), René Bray, *Molière: homme de théâtre* (Paris 1954).
18. An attempt to combine the two traditions, the historical and the dramatic, may be seen in Robert McBride's recent book *The Sceptical Vision of Molière* (London & Basingstoke 1977).

19. Jacques Guicharnaud, *Molière: une aventure théâtrale* (Paris 1963).
20. George Meredith, *An Essay on Comedy* (London 1898). This book was first published in 1877, entitled *On the Idea of the Comic and the Uses of the Comic Spirit in Literature.*
21. Henri Bergson, *Le Rire* (Paris 1940 [1e ed. 1900]).
22. Northrop Frye, *The Anatomy of Criticism* (Princeton 1957).
23. See Bergson *Le Rire* p. 15.
24. See, for example, James Feibleman, *In Praise of Comedy* (London 1930) – 'Comedy is an adjunct of the revolutionary principle' p. 102.

CHAPTER ONE

1. Barish, *Ben Jonson and the Language of Prose Comedy*, p. 238. For a similar view of Jonson's career see also Barish's article 'Feasting and Judging in Jonsonian Comedy', *Renaissance Drama*, N.S. 5 (1972) 3–35.
2. See, in particular, Alan Dessen's long chapter on *Bartholomew Fair* in *Jonson's Moral Comedy* (Evanston, Ill. 1971).
3. See, For example, Freda L. Townsend, *Apologie for Bartholomew Fayre* (N.Y. & London 1947), and Wallace A. Bacon 'The Magnetic Field: the Structure of Jonson's comedies', *Huntingdon Library Quarterly* 19 (1956), 121–53.
4. This view is represented by James E. Robinson, '*Bartholomew Fair*: Comedy of Vapours', *Studies in English Literature 1500–1900*, (1961) I, 65–80, and by John M. Potter, 'Old Comedy in *Bartholomew Fair*', *Criticism* 10 (1968), 290–9.
5. The most influential article of this sort has been that of Ray L. Heffner Jnr. – 'Unifying Symbols in the Comedy of Ben Jonson', *English Stage Comedy* (English Institute Essays), ed. W. K. Wimsatt jnr. (N.Y. 1954), pp. 74–97.
6. 'Who would ha' thought anybody would ha' quarrelled so early?' asks Haggis in Act III scene i.
7. Ian Donaldson in his very interesting book *The World Upside-Down* (Oxford 1970) pursues variants of this pattern through several English comedies (including *Bartholomew Fair*) from Jonson to Fielding. He uses the phrase 'justice in the stocks' for the title of his opening chapter.
8. Richard Levin in his helpful article on 'The Structure of *Bartholomew Fair*', *PMLA* 80 (1965), 172–9, reprinted in revised form in his book *The Multiple Plot in English Renaissance Drama* (Chicago 1971), gives a similar analysis and stresses the parallel structure of the Cokes and Littlewit group.
9. Eugene Waith speculates on the relative size of the booths in his reconstruction of the original staging. See Ben Jonson *Bartholomew Fair*, ed. Eugene M. Waith (New Haven and London 1963), Appendix II.
10. *Bartholomew Fair*, rather surprisingly, does not contain many opportunities for doubling except of very minor characters and extras. The final scene requires over twenty people on stage at once, and it is hard to see how the play could be performed with less than twenty-five actors.
11. See J. O. Bartley, *Teague, Shenkin and Sawney, being an historical survey of the earliest Irish, Welsh and Scottish characters in English plays* (Cork 1954), p. 19.
12. Levin, *The Multiple Plot in English Renaissance Drama*, p. 207.
13. J. A. Bryant Jnr., *The Compassionate Satirist* (Athens, Georgia 1972). See also

Guy Hamel 'Order and Judgement in *Bartholomew Fair*' *University of Toronto Quarterly* 43 (1973) 49–67.

14. Jackson I. Cope '*Bartholomew Fair* as Blasphemy', *Renaissance Drama* 8 (1965), 127–52.

15. Ian Donaldson, among others, invokes *King Lear* in this connection, *The World Upside-Down*, p. 71.

16. From Henry Morley's account, *Memoirs of Bartholomew Fair* (London 1857), it would seem that the fair was above all a citizen occasion, and members of the aristocracy would hardly have attended very often; this would fit in with the disdainful attitude of Grace, Quarlous and Winwife.

17. The disclaimer did not stop later writers from suggesting that Jonson intended his collaborator and rival Inigo Jones to be seen as the hobbyhorse man Lantern Leatherhead, or the poet Daniel in the idiotic Littlewit.

18. William Blissett 'Your Majesty is Welcome to a Fair' in *The Elizabethan Theatre* IV, ed. G. R. Hibbard (London and Basingstoke 1974), pp. 80–105.

19. Donaldson, *The World Upside-Down*, pp. 72–3.

20. *A Couter-blaste to Tobacco* (London 1954 [1604]), p. 36.

21. 'Ben Jonson, Dramatist', in *The Age of Shakespeare*, ed. Boris Ford (London 1955), pp. 302–17.

22. This same metaphor is used by W. D. Howarth in his Introduction to the anthology of essays on comedy which he has edited, *Comic Drama: The European Heritage* (London 1978), p. 5.

CHAPTER TWO

1. Suzanne Langer, *Feeling and Form* (London 1953), p. 331.

2. John Shaw has argued that the theme of the whole play is the conflict between Fortune and Nature 'Fortune and Nature in *As You Like It*', *Shakespeare Quarterly* 6 (1955), 45–50.

3. For example, W. H. Auden in an essay on 'Music in Shakespeare' remarks, 'In praising the Simple Life, the Duke is a bit of a humbug, since he was compelled by force to take to it'. *Encounter* IX, no. 6 (1957), 40.

4. As David Young remarks, 'the powerful descriptions of nature for which Shakespeare is admired do not exist in *As You Like It*. What we have instead is a stylised and sparsely pictured setting, whose literary and artificial character is kept always before us'. *The Heart's Forest: a study of Shakespeare's pastoral plays*, (New Haven and London 1972), p. 43.

5. In *John Lyly; the Courtier as Humanist* (London, 1962), p. 229.

6. Many critics, indeed, have found it hard to believe that Molière could be endorsing this attitude, and argue that Chrysalde is pulling Arnolphe's leg.

7. See P. H. Nurse 'The Role of Chrysalde in *L'Ecole des Femmes*', *Modern Language Review* 61 (1961), 167–71.

8. *The Country Wife*, IV ii.

9. See, for instance, Alvin Eustis *Molière as Ironic Contemplator* (The Hague, Paris 1973), p. 103.

10. Michael Taylor, '*As You Like It*: the Penalty of Adam', *Critical Quarterly* 15 (1973), 79.

CHAPTER THREE

1. See Geoffrey Bullough, *Narrative and Dramatic Sources of Shakespeare*, Volume I (London and N.Y. 1957), p. 368.
2. The text of *A Midsummer Night's Dream* used throughout is the New Penguin Shakespeare, edited by Stanley Wells (Harmondsworth 1967).
3. See 'Director in Interview: Peter Brook talks to Peter Ansorge', *Plays and Players* 18, no. 1 (October 1970), 18 – 19.
4. Paul A. Olson, '*A Midsummer Night's Dream* and the meaning of court marriage', ELH 24 (1957), 95 – 119.
5. See William A. Ringler Jnr. 'The Number of Actors in Shakespeare's Early Plays', in *The Seventeenth Century Stage*, ed. G. E. Bentley (Chicago 1968), p. 132, fig. 4.
6. Clifford Leech, 'Shakespeare's Comic Dukes', *A Review of English Literature* 5 (1964), 101 – 14.
7. Some of the principal critical expressions of the two points of view are summarised by D. J. Palmer in *Shakespeare* (Select Bibliographical Guides), ed. Stanley Wells (London 1973), pp. 69 – 70.
8. Olson, '*A Midsummer Night's Dream* and the meaning of court marriage'.
9. R. W. Dent, 'Imagination in *A Midsummer Night's Dream*', *Shakespeare Quarterly* 15 (1964), 124.
10. Stanley Wells, Introduction to *A Midsummer Night's Dream*, p. 33.
11. The only other Shakespearean use of the word 'discase', *Winter's Tale* IV iii 640, is also in the context of on-stage change of costume, and Poins promised Hal 'cases of buckram for the nonce, to inmask our noted outward garments' – *Henry IV* Part I, I ii 180 – 1.
12. *Coleridge's Shakespearean Criticism*, Vol. I, ed. M. Raysor (London 1930), p. 134.
13. Although many modern editions give this speech back to Miranda, as in the Folio, earlier editors, beginning with Dryden, felt that by its tone and language it had to be Prospero's.
14. The text *The Tempest* is short by Shakespearean standards, so short that critics have wondered whether it was abridged. But if the dances of the masque were in any way elaborate, as in the court-masque they frequently were, its running-time may not have been notably briefer than an average Elizabethan play – though still probably less than the four hours which the stage action takes.

CHAPTER FOUR

1. Harry Levin, 'Two Magian comedies: *The Tempest* and *The Alchemist*', *Shakespeare Survey* 22 (1969), 51.
2. See Edgar Hill Duncan 'Jonson's *Alchemist* and the literature of Alchemy', PMLA 61 (1946), 669 – 710.
·3. Bacon, *Sylva Sylvarum* (1626), p. 86. Quoted in Herford & Simpson X, p. 48.
4. Frances Yates, 'Did Newton connect his maths and alchemy?' *Times Higher Educational Supplement*, 18 March 1977.
5. Critics have conjectured that Molière may have had help with the details of this scene from his own doctor M. de Mauvillain, a graduate of Montpellier.

Certainly the evidence of the induction of a doctor in Montpellier witnessed by Locke in 1676, with its musical accompaniments, and the professor's long speech against innovation, suggests that Molière was not altogether exaggerating. See *Locke's Travels in France 1675–79* ed. John Lough (Cambridge U.P. 1953), p. 57.

6. *Letters de Mme. de Sévigné* 3 vols. (Paris 1953–6), Vol. 2, p. 203.
7. John Palmer, *Molière: his life and works* (London 1930), p. 348.
8. Cairncross, *Molière: bourgeois et libertin*, p. 24.
9. See Joseph Girard, *A propos de L'Amour Médecin, Molière et Louis-Henry Daquin* (Paris 1948).
10. A. Gill tried to restore the play definitely to the Molière canon in ' "The Doctor in the Farce" and Molière', *French Studies* 2 (1948), 101–28.
11. 'De la ressemblance des Enfans aux Peres', *Essais*, livre 2 (Paris 1969), pp. 421–48.
12. *Lettres*, 2, pp. 890–1.
13. The principle behind the frequent use of bleeding was the idea that the body created fresh new blood to replace the old stagnant blood removed, as a well produces all the more clean water the more dirty water is taken from it. See Francois Millepierres, *La Vie Quotidienne des Médecins au temps de Molière* (Paris 1964).
14. In his apology for medicine, G. de Bezançon was prepared to admit that there were any number of bad doctors for whom a crude routine of the Diafoirus variety did instead of the arduous and continuous study of different cases and different remedies which the good doctor undertook. *Les Médecins à la censure ou entretiens sur la médecine* (Paris 1677).
15. See L. Chauvois 'Molière, Boileau, La Fontaine et la circulation du sang', *La Presse Medicale* 62 (1954), 1219–20.
16. See René Jasinski 'Sur Molière et la médecine', *Mélanges de philologie, d'histoire et de littérature offerts à Joseph Vianey* (Paris 1934), pp. 249–54, and Guy Godlewski 'Les Médecins de Molière et leurs modèles', *La Semaine des Hôpitaux* 46 (1970), 3490–500.
17. Levin, 'Two Magian Comedies', 55.
18. See Herford & Simpson X, p. 81.
19. Salomon, King of Israel *Opus de arte magica, ab Honorio ordinatum*, a fourteenth century manuscript now in the British Museum which Herford and Simpson cite among the books in Jonson's library – Herford and Simpson I, Appendix IV.
20. See Duncan, 'Jonson's Alchemist and the Literature of Alchemy'.
21. Herford and Simpson II, p. 101.
22. See John Cairncross 'Impie en Médecine', *Cahiers de L'Association Internationales des Etudes Françaises* 16 (1965), 269–84.
23. J. D. Hubert, *Molière and the comedy of intellect* (Berkeley & Los Angeles 1962), p. 255. The same idea is pursued to absurd lengths by Carlo François who detects a parody of the nativity in the pastoral prologue to *Le Malade Imaginaire* – 'Médecine et religion chez Molière: deux facettes d'un même absurdité', *French Review* 42 (1969), 665–72.
24. Partridge, *The Broken Compass*, p. 127.

CHAPTER FIVE

1. The arguments have been most recently considered, in exhaustive detail, by Roger Lathuillère in *La Preciosité* (Paris 1966).
2. Benichou, *Morales du Grand Siècle*, p. 286.
3. Antoine Adam, 'La Genèse des *Précieuses Ridicules*', *Revue d'histoire de la philosophie et d'histoire generale de la civilisation* (Lille 1939), 14–46. The weaknesses of Adam's argument are well pointed out by Henri Cottez in an article in the same journal, 'Sur Molière et Mlle de Scudéry' (1943), 340–64.
4. A strong case based on the textual evidence has been made against the 'school of night' theory by E. A. Strathmann in 'The Textual Evidence for "The School of Night"' *Modern Language Notes* 56 (1941), 176–86.
5. M. C. Bradbrook, *The School of Night* (Cambridge 1936).
6. Ibid. p. 161.
7. A. N. Kaul, *The Action of English Comedy* (New Haven 1970), see particularly chapters on Shakespeare, Fielding, and Jane Austen.
8. R. David denies any resemblance to Lyly's style in Armado's speeches, see Introduction to New Arden edition of *Love's Labour's Lost* (London 1951), pp. xxx–xxxi.
9. Adam, 'La Genèse des *Précieuses Ridicules*', 16.
10. Benichou, *Morales du Grand Siècle*, p. 305.
11. The term 'antithesis' is borrowed from Eric Brene's *Games People Play* (London 1966).
12. It is M. C. Bradbrook who refers to the play's two shows as masque and antimasque *Shakespeare and Elizabethan Poetry* (London 1951), p. 218.
13. Bobbyann Roesen 'Love's Labour's Lost', *Shakespeare Quarterly* 4 (1953), 411–26.
14. See among others, Ralph Berry 'The Words of Mercury', *Shakespeare Survey* 22 (1969), 69–76.

CHAPTER SIX

1. Meredith, *An Essay on Comedy*, p. 8.
2. Samuel Chappuzeau, *L'Académie des Femmes* (1661), reprinted in *Les Contemporains de Molière*, ed. Victor Fournel (Paris 1875), Tome III, p. 237. *L'Académie des Femmes* is partly derived from Erasmus's *Senatulus* and has been suggested as one of Molière's sources for *Les Femmes Savantes*.
3. Antoine Adam, *Histoire de la Littérature Française au XVIIe Siècle* (Paris 1952), Tome III, p. 389.
4. Edward B. Partridge, 'The Allusiveness of *Epicoene*', ELH 22 (1955), 94. This article was later incorporated in Partridge's book *The Broken Compass*.
5. *Epicoene*, ed. E. B. Partridge, p. 174.
6. Jonas Barish in his article on 'Ovid, Juvenal, and *The Silent Woman*', PMLA 71 (1956), 213–24, though he does not comment on this particular speech, illustrates generally how Jonson tends to change the tone of the Ovid passages he is imitating.
7. The quotation is from Cotgrave's *Dictionary* of 1632. See Donaldson *The World Upside-Down*, p. 39.

8. See E. K. Chambers *The Mediaeval Stage* (Oxford 1903) i, p. 154, quoted by Donaldson, p. 40.

9. 7 January 1661. *The Diary of Samuel Pepys*, eds. Robert Latham and William Matthews (Berkeley and Los Angeles 1970), Vol. II, p. 7.

10. See, for instance, Michael Jamieson 'Shakespeare's Celibate Stage' included in *The Seventeenth Century Stage* ed. G. E. Bentley, pp. 70–93.

11. Partridge 'The Allusiveness of *Epicoene*', 106.

12. Barish, *Ben Jonson and the Language of Prose Comedy*, p. 179 .

13. Robert Knoll, *Ben Jonson's Plays: an Introduction* (Lincoln, Nebraska 1964), p. 114.

14. Partridge, *Epicoene*, Introduction, p. 19.

15. William W. E. Slights comments on the tradition of Renaissance prose paradox to which this speech belongs, '*Epicoene* and the Prose Paradox', *Philological Quarterly* 49 (1970), 178–87.

16. Donaldson, *The World Upside-Down*, p. 36.

17. L. G. Salingar 'Farce and Fashion in *The Silent Woman*', *Essays and Studies* 20 (1967), 29–46.

18. See Cairncross, *Molière Bourgeois et Libertin*, Annexe III, 'La Genèse des *Femmes Savantes*'.

19. Despois Mesnard, p. 49.

20. Despois and Mesnard quote from *Le Mercure Galant*, 1685, on the occasion of Hubert's retirement: 'Jamais acteur n'a porté si loin les rôles d'homme en femme', p. 49.

21. Despois Mesnard, p. 49.

22. Vaclav Cerny 'Le "je ne sais quoi" de Trissotin', *Revue des Sciences Humaines* (1961), 367–78.

23. Jacques-Henri Perivier suggests that Trissotin's sonnet itself involves a series of sexual *double-entendres* in 'Equivoques molièresques: le sonnet de Trissotin', *Revue des Sciences Humaines* 38 (1973), 543–54.

24. The letter of Bussy-Rabutin to P. Rapin (11 April 1673) is quoted by Georges Mongrédien *Recueil des Textes et des Documents du XVII Siècle Relatifs à Molière* (Paris 1965) II, pp. 409–10.

25. See Benichou, *Morales du Grand Siècle*, p. 288, n. 1.

26. Ibid.

CHAPTER SEVEN

1. Partridge, *The Broken Compass*, p. 70.

2. Ferdinand Brunetière, *Les Epoques du Théâtre Français (1636–1850)* (Paris 1901 – 5e édit.), p. 147.

3. See Partridge, *The Broken Compass*.

4. Ibid. p. 80.

5. H. Levin 'Jonson's Metempsychosis', *Philological Quarterly* 22 (1943), 231–9.

6. Jonas A. Barish, 'The Double Plot in *Volpone*', *Modern Philology* 51 (1953), 83–92.

7. See Alvin Kernan (ed.) *Volpone* (New Haven and London 1962), p. 214.

8. Richard Perkinson '*Volpone* and the reputation of Venetian justice', *Modern Language Review* 35 (1940), 11–18.

9. Ian Donaldson '*Volpone*: Quick and Dead', *Essays in Criticism* 21 (1971), 121–34.
10. John Creaser makes much of this point in his article 'Volpone's Mortification' *Essays in Criticism* 25 (1975), 329–56, and there is further discussion of this article in 'The Critical Forum', *Essays in Criticism* 26 (1976), 274–8.
11. Guicharnaud, *Molière: une aventure théâtrale*, p. 24.
12. Emanuel S. Chill, '*Tartuffe*, Religion, and Courtly Culture', *French Historical Studies* 3 (1963), 176.
13. Jacques Schérer, *Structures de Tartuffe* (Paris 1966), p. 186.
14. See Mongrédien, *Recueil* I, p. 292.
15. John Cairncross, *New Light on Molière* (Geneva and Paris 1956) and also *Molière Bourgeois et Libertin*.
16. Schérer, *Structures de Tartuffe*, p. 186.
17. Guicharnaud, *Molière: une aventure théâtrale*, p. 146.
18. Georges Pholien, 'Une défense de *Tartuffe*', *Marche Romane* 17 (1967), 183.
19. Jules Brody 'Esthétique et Société chez Molière' in *Dramaturgie et Société* ed. Jean Jacquot (Paris 1968) I, pp. 307–26.
20. See particularly Benichou, *Morales du Grand Siècle*, Chill '*Tartuffe*, Religion and Courtly Culture' and Jean Calvet, *Molière est-il chrétien?* (Paris 1950).
21. Lionel Gossman, 'Molière and *Tartuffe*: Law and Order in the Seventeenth Century', *French Review* 43 (1970), 910.
22. Raymond Picard, '*Tartuffe* "Production impie"?' in *Mélanges d'histoire littéraire offerts à Raymond Lebèque* (Paris 1969), pp. 227–39.
23. Benichou, *Morales du Grand Siècle*, p. 344.
24. Bossuet, *Maximes et réflexions sur la Comédie* 1694, quoted in Mongrédien *Recueil* II, p. 680.

CHAPTER EIGHT

1. There is, in fact, a useful casebook on *Troilus and Cressida*, edited by Priscilla Martin (London and Basingstoke 1976).
2. Daniel Seltzer ed. *Troilus and Cressida* (Signet Shakespeare, N.Y. 1963), pp. xxv–xxvi.
3. Richard D. Fly ' "Suited in Like Conditions as our Argument": Imitative form in Shakespeare's *Troilus and Cressida*' *Studies in English Literature* 15 (1975), 281.
4. Jacques Schérer, *Sur le Dom Juan de Molière* (Paris 1967), p. 27.
5. See, for example, Oscar J. Campbell, *Comicall Satyre and Shakespeare's Troilus and Cressida* (San Marino, Calif. 1938).
6. T. J. B. Spencer illustrates the Elizabethan bad reputation of the Greeks in ' "Greeks" and "Merrygreeks": a background to *Timon of Athens* and *Troilus and Cressida*' in *Essays on Shakespeare and Elizabethan Drama in honour of Hardin Craig*, ed. Richard Hosley (London 1963), pp. 223–33.
7. Robert Kimbrough, *Shakespeare's Troilus and Cressida and its Setting* (Cambridge, Mass. 1964), p. 45.
8. The case has been interestingly, but it would seem inconclusively, argued out between T. McAlindon and Mark Sacharoff in a critical discussion on 'Language, Style and Meaning in *Troilus and Cressida*', PMLA 87 (1972), 90–9.

232 _Shakespeare, Jonson, Molière: The Comic Contract_

9. Patricia Thomson 'Rant and Cant in _Troilus and Cressida_' _Essays and Studies_ 22 (1969), 42.
10. Extract from Gervinus in Martin, _Troilus and Cressida Casebook_, p. 49.
11. G. Wilson Knight, _The Wheel of Fire_ (London 4th rev. ed. 1949), pp. 47–8.
12. See Robert Kimbrough 'The Problem of Thersites' _Modern Language Review_ 59 (1964), 173–6.
13. Philip Edwards, _Shakespeare and the Confines of Art_ (London 1968), p. 97.
14. See Thomson 'Rant and Cant in _Troilus and Cressida_'.
15. John Bayley, 'Time and the Trojans' _Essays in Criticism_ 25 (1975), 55–73.
16. W. D. Howarth in his edition of the play claims that only the M. Dimanche scene appears to be wholly invented – _Dom Juan ou Le Festin du Pierre_ (Oxford 1958), p. xxi.
17. The 'Marché de décors pour _Dom Juan_' has been published by Madelene Jurgens and Elizabeth Maxfield-Miller, _Cent Ans de Recherches sur Molière, sur sa famille et sur les comédiens de sa troupe_ (Paris 1963), 399–401.
18. Guicharnaud, _Molière: une aventure théâtrale_, p. 193.
19. See particularly Nathan Gross 'The Dialectic of Obligation in Molière's _Dom Juan_', _Romanic Review_ 65 (1974), 175–200.
20. The idea of debt and credit in the play has been pursued by several critics, perhaps most interestingly by Michel Pruner 'La notion de dette dans le _Dom Juan_ de Molière' _Revue d'histoire du théâtre_ 26 (1974), 254–71.
21. Jules Brody, '_Dom Juan_ and _Le Misanthrope_, or the Esthetics of Individualism in Molière' _PMLA_, 84 (1969), 559–76.
22. Richard Coe has a convincing analysis of this scene in an admirable article on 'The Ambiguity of Dom Juan', _Australian Journal of French Studies_ I (1964), 23–35.
23. Jacques Morel points out interestingly the emphasis which contemporary preachers placed upon this doctrine of almsgiving – 'A propos de la "scène du pauvre" dans _Dom Juan_', _Revue de l'histoire littéraire de la France_ 72 (1972), 939–44.
24. This general point of view may be said to originate with W. G. Moore in _Molière: a New Criticism_ but it has been developed both in Moore's own later article '_Dom Juan_ Reconsidered', _Modern Language Review_ 52 (1957), 510–17, and in two articles of Gaston Hall, 'A Comic Dom Juan', _Yale French Studies_ 23 (1959), 77–84, and 'Molière, _Dom Juan_: "la scène du pauvre"', in _The Art of Criticism_, ed. Peter H. Nurse (Edinburgh 1969), pp. 69–87.
25. Guicharnaud, _Molière: une aventure théâtrale_, p. 207.
26. Jean Onimus sees Dom Juan as a scapegoat figure, at once threatening and liberating – 'Le Mystère de Dom Juan', _Annales du Centre Universitaire Méditeranéen_ 26 (1973), 55–9.
27. B. A. Sieur de Rochemont, _Observations sur une comédie de Molière intitulée Le Festin de Pierre_ included in Despois and Mesnard, V, Appendice à Dom Juan.
28. Roger Bellet, 'Le Dom Juan de Molière: un cavalier de l'entendement' _Europe_, nov.-déc. 1972, 127.
29. Extract from 'The Universe of _Troilus and Cressida_' in Martin, _Troilus and Cressida Casebook_, p. 71.
30. Joseph Pineau 'Dom Juan "mauvais élève"', _Revue des Sciences Humaines_ 38 (1973), 586.
31. Neville Coghill, _Shakespeare's Professional Skills_ (Cambridge 1964), p. 97.

32. Jean Rousset 'Dom Juan et le Baroque' *Diogène* 14 (1956), 3–21.
33. Kimbrough, *Shakespeare's Troilus and Cressida and its Setting*.
34. *Troilus and Cressida* (New Cambridge Shakespeare, Cambridge 1957), Introduction.

CHAPTER NINE

1. Suzanne Langer's chapter on comedy in *Feeling and Form*, pp. 326–50, is a good example.
2. Ramon Fernandez, *La Vie de Molière* (Paris 1929), René Jasinski, *Molière et Le Misanthrope* (Paris 1951).
3. Nearly all the most authoritative critics on Molière since 1945, Paul Benichou, W. G. Moore, Antoine Adam, Jacques Guicharnaud, have lent support to a comic view of Alceste. There have, of course remained some dissenters: Gerard Defaux, for instance, in an interesting article, suggests that there are elements of bitter self-mockery in the laughter which Molière shows Alceste arousing – 'Alceste et les rieurs', *Revue de l'histoire littéraire de la France* 74 (1974), 579–99.
4. Jean-Jacques Rousseau, *Lettre à D'Alembert sur les spectacles* (Paris 1935).
5. Betty Rotjman, in particular, argues the similarity of Alceste's position and character to those of Sganarelle in *L'Ecole des Maris* and Arnolphe in *L'Ecole des Femmes* – 'Alceste dans le théâtre de Molière', *Revue de l'histoire littéraire de la France* 73 (1973), 963–81.
6. Guicharnaud, *Molière: une aventure théâtrale*, p. 353.
7. *La Fameuse Comédienne ou histoire de La Guérin auparavant femme et veuve de Molière*, ed. Jules Bonnassies (Paris 1870 [1e ed. Francfort 1688]), p. 21.
8. See Mongrédien, *Recueil* I, pp. 261–6.
9. The point is made by Adam, *Histoire de la littérature française au XVIIe siècle* III, p. 245. The frontispiece of the first edition of *Le Misanthrope* shows a young clean-shaven Alceste listening to Philinte, where in all the other frontispieces to the plays the comic character played by Molière seems to be shown wearing a large drooping moustache, which it is said Molière imitated from Scaramouche.
10. Brody, '*Dom Juan* and *Le Misanthrope*', 571.
11. Guicharnaud, *Molière: une aventure théâtrale*, p. 394.
12. Donneau de Visé, *Lettre écrite sur la comédie du Misanthrope* in Despois and Mesnard V, p. 430.
13. See René Robert, 'Des commentaires de première main sur les chefs-d'oeuvre les plus discutés de Molière', *Revue des Sciences Humaines* 30 (1956), 19–49.
14. The latter view is that of Jules Brody, '*Dom Juan* and *Le Misanthrope*'.
15. Despois and Mesnard V, p. 441.
16. Fernandez, *La Vie de Molière*, p. 198.
17. 'A tragi-comedie is not so called in respect of mirth and killing, but in respect it wants deaths, which is inough to make it no tragedie, yet brings some mirth it, which is inough to make it no comedie'. *The Dramatic Works of the Beaumont and Fletcher Canon* ed. Fredson Bowers (Cambridge 1973), Vol. 3, p. 497.
18. Mary Lascelles, *Shakespeare's Measure for Measure* (London 1953).
19. Knight, *The Wheel of Fire*, p. 93.
20. Rosalind Miles, *The Problem of Measure for Measure* (London 1976), p. 229.
21. David L. Stevenson, *The Achievement of Measure for Measure* (Ithaca, N.Y.

1966), p. 128. Stevenson devotes a whole chapter of his book to the demonstration of the weaknesses of the allegorical interpretation of the play.

22. Knight, *The Wheel of Fire*, p. 95.

23. Stevenson, *The Achievement of Measure for Measure*, p. 58.

24. Marvin Rosenberg, 'Shakespeare's Fantastic Trick: *Measure for Measure*', *Sewanee Review* 80 (1972), 51–72.

25. *Essays and Introductions* (London 1961), p. 241.

26. Harriett Hawkins, *Likenesses of Truth* (Oxford 1972), p. 54.

27. For example, John Barton in his 1970 production of the play with the Royal Shakespeare Company at Stratford.

28. David L. Stevenson 'Design and Structure in *Measure for Measure*', ELH 23 (1956), 256–278, reprinted in *Measure for Measure Casebook*, ed. C. K. Stead (London and Basingstoke 1971), p. 215.

29. The most convincing argument for this point of view is that of Lawrence W. Hyman in 'The Unity of *Measure for Measure*', *Modern Language Quarterly* 36 (1975), 3–20. He claims that in the play 'we see sexuality as the source of life, whereas its absence, chastity, leads to death. Neither the sexuality nor the life to which it leads is necessarily good or desirable, and hardly ever do we see sexuality or its results as anything but sinful or shameful. But sexuality is the only force for life. Virtue, on the other hand, arising from chastity and being enforced by Justice, may often seem heroic and desirable, but it always results in death'.

30. Miles, *The Problem of Measure for Measure*, p. 287.

31. Lascelles, *Shakespeare's Measure for Measure*, p. 101. See also the helpful article of Elizabeth Marie Pope 'The Renaissance Background of *Measure for Measure*', *Shakespeare Survey* 2 (1949), 66–82.

32. A. D. Nuttall '*Measure for Measure*: Quid Pro Quo?' *Shakespeare Studies* 4 (1968), 231–51.

CONCLUSION

1. See, for example, Kaul, *The Action of English Comedy*, Introduction.

2. Sigmund Freud, *Jokes and their relation to the unconscious*, trans. James Strachey (London 1960), p. 224.

3. Charles Mauron, *Psychocritique du Genre Comique* (Paris 1964).

4. Morton Gurewitch, *Comedy: the irrational vision* (Ithaca, N.Y. and London 1975).

5. Barber, *Shakespeare's Festive Comedy*.

6. Donaldson, *The World Upside-Down*.

7. Hobbes, *Human Nature* IX, 9.

8. Feibleman, *In Praise of Comedy*, pp. 178–9.

9. Arthur Koestler, *The Act of Creation* (London 1976), p. 95.

10. Marcel Gutwirth, 'Réflexions sur le comique', *Revue d'Esthétique* 17 (1964), 10.

Bibliography

(General note: from the mass of material available only those items actually cited in this book or most frequently used been listed).

A. TEXTS

The following texts have been used for quotation throughout:

Shakespeare

> *As You Like It*, ed. Agnes Latham (New Arden, London 1975).
> *A Midsummer Night's Dream*, ed. Stanley Wells (New Penguin, Harmondsworth 1967).
> *The Tempest*, ed. Frank Kermode (New Arden, London 1954).
> *Love's Labour's Lost*, ed. Richard David (New Arden, London 1951).
> *Troilus and Cressida*, ed. Alice Walker (Cambridge 1957).
> *Measure for Measure*, ed. J. W. Lever (New Arden, London 1965).

Jonson

> *Bartholomew Fair*, ed. Eugene M. Waith (Yale Ben Jonson, New Haven 1963).
> *The Alchemist*, ed. Alvin B. Kernan (Yale Ben Jonson, New Haven 1974).
> *Epicoene*, ed. Edward Partridge (Yale Ben Jonson, New Haven 1971).
> *Volpone*, ed. Alvin B. Kernan (Yale Ben Jonson, New Haven 1962).

Molière

> *Oeuvres Complètes de Molière*, ed. Robert Jouanny (Paris 1962) 2 vols.

Other texts referred to include:

Shakespeare

> *Troilus and Cressida*, ed. Daniel Seltzer (Signet, N.Y. 1963).

Jonson

> *Ben Jonson*, ed. C. H. Herford and Percy and Evelyn Simpson (Oxford 1925–52) 11 vols (Brief reference – Herford & Simpson).
> *The Alchemist*, ed. F. H. Mares (Revels Plays, London 1967).

Molière

> *Oeuvres Complètes*, eds. Despois et Mesnard (Grands Écrivains de la France, Paris 1873–93). (Brief reference Despois Mesnard). *Dom Juan*, ed. W. D. Howarth (Oxford 1958).

B. SECONDARY SOURCES

I. Comedy: general and comparative

Bergson, Henri	*Le Rire: Essai sur le signification du comique* (Paris 1940).
Feibleman, James,	*In Praise of Comedy* (London 1939).
Freud, Sigmund	*Jokes and their relation to the unconscious*, trans. James Strachey (London 1960).
Frye, Northrop	*The Anatomy of Criticism* (Princeton 1957).
Grivelet, Michel	'Shakespeare, Molière, and the Comedy of Ambiguity', *Shakespeare Survey* 22 (1969), 15–26.
Gurewitch, Morton	*Comedy: the irrational vision* (Ithaca, N.Y. & London 1975).
Gutwirth, Marcel	'Réflexions sur le comique', *Revue d'Esthétique* 17 (janvier-juillet 1964), 7–39.
Hobbes, Thomas	*Hobbes' Tripos in three Discourses: Human Nature; De Corpore Politico; of Liberty and Necessity* (London 1840).
Howarth, W. D. (ed.)	*Comic Drama: the European Heritage* (London 1978).
Jay, Bruce Louis	*The Comic Art of Ben Jonson and Molière* (unpublished dissertation University of Conneticut 1974) — *Dissertation Abstracts* 35 (Nov. 1974), 2942-A.
Kaul, A. N.	*The Action of English Comedy* (New Haven 1970).
Koestler, Arthur	*The Act of Creation* (London 1976).
Langer, Suzanne	*Feeling and Form* (London 1953).
Levin, Harry	'Two Magian Comedies: *The Tempest* and *The Alchemist*', *Shakespeare Survey* 22 (1969), 47–58.
Mauron, Charles	*Psychocritique du Genre Comique* (Paris 1964).
Meredith, George	*An Essay on Comedy* (London 1898).
Ornstein, Robert	'Shakespearean and Jonsonian Comedy', *Shakespeare Survey* 22 (1969), 43–6.
Phialas, Peter G.	'Comic Truth in Shakespeare and Jonson', *South Atlantic Quarterly* 62 (1963), 78–91.

II. Shakespeare criticism

Auden, W. H.	'Music in Shakespeare', *Encounter* IX, 6 (1957), 40.
Barber, C. L.	*Shakespeare's Festive Comedy* (Princeton 1959).
Bayley, John	'Time and the Trojans', *Essays in Criticism* 25 (1975) 55–73.

Berry, Ralph — 'The Words of Mercury', *Shakespeare Survey* 22 (1969), 69–76.

Berry, Ralph — *Shakespeare's Comedies: Explorations in Form* (Princeton 1972).

Bradbrook, M. C. — *The School of Night: a study in the literary relationships of Sir Walter Ralegh* (Cambridge 1936).

Bradbrook, M. C. — *Shakespeare and Elizabethan Poetry* (London 1951).

Brook, Peter — 'Director in Interview: Peter Brook talks to Peter Ansorge', *Plays and Players* 18, 1 (Oct. 1970), 18–19.

Bullough, Geoffrey — *Narrative and Dramatic Sources of Shakespeare*, Vol. 1 (London 1957).

Campbell, Oscar J. — *Comicall Satyre and Shakespeare's Troilus and Cressida* (San Marino, Calif. 1938).

Coghill, Nevill — *Shakespeare's Professional Skills* (Cambridge 1964).

Dent, R. W. — 'Imagination in *A Midsummer Night's Dream*', *Shakespeare Quarterly* 15 (1964), 115–29.

Edwards, Philip — *Shakespeare and the Confines of Art* (London 1968).

Fly, Richard D. — '"Suited in Like Conditions as our Argument": Imitative Form in Shakespeare's *Troilus and Cressida*', *Studies in English Literature* 15 (1975), 273–92.

Frye, Northrop — *A Natural Perspective* (N.Y. 1965).

Hawkins, Harriett — *Likenesses of Truth* (Oxford 1972).

Hyman, Lawrence W. — 'The Unity of *Measure for Measure*', *Modern Language Quarterly* 36 (1975), 3–20.

Jamieson, Michael — 'Shakespeare's Celibate Stage' in *The Seventeenth Century Stage*, ed. G. E. Bentley (London & Chicago 1968), pp. 70–93.

Kimbrough, Robert — *Shakespeare's Troilus and Cressida and its Setting* (Cambridge, Mass. 1964).

Kimbrough, Robert — 'The Problem of Thersites', *Modern Language Review* 59 (1964), 173–6.

Knight, G. Wilson — *The Wheel of Fire* (London, 4th rev. ed., 1949).

Lascelles, Mary — *Shakespeare's Measure for Measure* (London 1953).

Leech, Clifford — 'Shakespeare's Comic Dukes', *A Review of English Literature* 5 (1964), 101–14.

Leggatt, Alexander — *Shakespeare's Comedy of Love* (London 1974).

McAlindon, T. & Sacharoff, Mark — 'Language, Style, and Meaning in *Troilus and Cressida*', *PMLA* 87 (1972), 90–9.

McFarland, Thomas — *Shakespeare's Pastoral Comedy* (Chapel Hill, N. Carolina 1972).

Martin, Priscilla (ed.) — *Troilus and Cressida: a Casebook* (London & Basingstoke 1976).

Miles, Rosalind — *The Problem of Measure for Measure* (London 1976).

Nuttall, A. P. — '*Measure for Measure*: Quid Pro Quo?', *Shakespeare Studies* 4 (1968), 231–51.

Olson, Paul A. — '*A Midsummer Night's Dream* and the Meaning of Court Marriage, *ELH* 24 (1957), 95–119.

Pope, Elizabeth Marie — 'The Renaissance Background of *Measure for Measure*, *Shakespeare Survey* 2 (1949), 66–82.

Raysor, T. M. (ed.)   *Coleridge's Shakespeare Criticism*, Vol. 1 (London 1930).
Ringler, William A. Jr.   'The Number of Actors in Shakespeare's Early Plays' in
                            The Seventeenth Century Stage, ed. G. E. Bentley
                            (London & Chicago 1968), pp. 110–34.
Roesen, Bobbyann   '*Love's Labour's Lost*', *Shakespeare Quarterly* 4 (1953),
                            411–26.
Rosenberg, Marvin   'Shakespeare's Fantastic Trick: *Measure for Measure*',
                            Sewance Review 80 (1972), 51–72.
Salingar, Leo   *Shakespeare and the Traditions of Comedy* (Cambridge
                            1974).
Shaw, John   'Fortune and Nature in *As You Like It*', *Shakespeare
                            Quarterly* 6 (1955), 45–50
Spencer, T. J. B.   ' "Greeks" and "Merrygreeks": a background to *Timon
                            of Athens* and *Troilus and Cressida*', in *Essays on
                            Shakespeare and Elizabethan Drama in honour of Hardin
                            Craig*, ed. Richard Hosley (London 1963), pp. 223–
                            33.
Stead, C. K.   *Measure for Measure: a Casebook* (London & Bas-
                            ingstoke 1971).
Stevenson, David L.   'Design and Structure in *Measure for Measure*', ELH 23
                            (1956), 256–78.
Stevenson, David L.   *The Achievement of Shakespeare's Measure for Measure*
                            (Ithaca, N.Y. 1966).
Strathmann, E. A.   'The Textual Evidence for "The School of Night" ',
                            Modern Language Notes 56 (1941), 176–86.
Taylor, Michael   '*As You Like It*: the Penalty of Adam', *Critical Quarterly*
                            15 (1973), 76–80.
Thomson, Patricia   'Rant and Cant in *Troilus and Cressida*', *Essays and
                            Studies* 22 (1969), 33–56.
Young, David   *The Heart's Forest: a study of Shakespeare's pastoral plays*
                            (New Haven 1972).
Wells, Stanley (ed.)   *Shakespeare* Select Bibliographical Guides (Oxford
                            1973).

III. Jonson Criticism

Bacon, Wallace A.   'The Magnetic Field: the structure of Jonson's com-
                            edies', *Huntingdon Library Quarterly* 19 (1956), 121–
                            53.
Barish, Jonas A.   'The Double Plot in *Volpone*', *Modern Philology* 51
                            (1953), 83–92.
Barish, Jonas A.   'Ovid, Juvenal, and *The Silent Woman*', PMLA 71
                            (1956), 213–24.
Barish, Jonas A.   *Ben Jonson and the Language of Prose Comedy*
                            (Cambridge, Mass. 1960).
Barish, Jonas A.   'Feasting and Judging in Jonsonian Comedy',
                            Renaissance Drama 5 N.S. (1972), 3–35.
Bartley, J. D.   *Teague, Shenkin and Sawney, Being an Historical Survey*

	of the earliest Irish, Welsh and Scottish characters in English plays (Cork 1954).
Blissett, William	'Your Majesty is Welcome to a Fair', in *The Elizabethan Theatre* IV, ed. G. R. Hibbard (London & Basingstoke 1974), pp. 80–105.
Bryant, J. A. Jr.	*The Compassionate Satirist: Ben Jonson and His Imperfect World* (Athens, Georgia 1972).
Cope, Jackson I.	'*Bartholomew Fair* as Blasphemy', *Renaissance Drama* 8 (1965), 127–52.
Creaser, John	'Volpone: the mortifying of the fox', *Essays in Criticism* 25 (1975), 329–56.
Dessen, Alan C.	*Jonson's Moral Comedy* (Evanston, Ill. 1971).
Donaldson, Ian	*The World Upside-Down: Comedy from Jonson to Fielding* (Oxford 1970).
Donaldson, Ian	'*Volpone*: Quick and Dead', *Essays in Criticism* 21 (1971) 121–34.
Duncan, Edgar Hill	'Jonson's *Alchemist* and the literature of Alchemy', *PMLA* 61 (1946), 699–710.
Enck, John J.	*Jonson and the Comic Truth* (Madison, Wis. 1957).
Goldberg, S. L.	'Folly into Crime: the Catastrophe of *Volpone*', *Modern Language Quarterly* 20 (1959), 233–42.
Hamel, Guy	'Order and Judgement in *Bartholomew Fair*', *University of Toronto Quarterly* 42 (1973), 46–87.
Knights, L. C.	*Drama and Society in the Age of Jonson* (London 1937).
Knights, L. C.	'Ben Jonson, Dramatist', in *The Age of Shakespeare*, ed. Boris Ford (London 1955), pp. 302–17.
Knoll, Robert	*Ben Jonson's Plays: an Introduction* (Lincoln, Nebraska 1964).
Leggatt, Alexander	*Citizen Comedy in the Age of Shakespeare* (Toronto 1973).
Levin, Harry	'Jonson's Metempsychosis', *Philological Quarterly* 22 (1943), 231–9.
Levin, Richard	'The Structure of *Bartholomew Fair*', *PMLA* 80 (1965), 172–9.
Levin, Richard	*The Multiple Plot in English Renaissance Drama* (Chicago 1971).
Morley, Henry	*Memoirs of Bartholomew Fair* (London 1874 [1st ed. 1857]).
Orgel, Stephen	*The Jonsonian Masque* (Cambridge, Mass. 1965).
Partridge, Edward B.	*The Broken Compass: a study of the major comedies of Ben Jonson* (London 1958).
Partridge, Edward B.	'The Allusiveness of *Epicoene*', *ELH* 22 (1955), 93–107.
Perkinson, Richard H.	'*Volpone* and the reputation of Venetian justice', *Modern Language Review* 35 (1940), 11–18.
Potter, John M.	'Old Comedy in *Bartholomew Fair*', *Criticism* 10 (1968), 290–9.
Robinson, James E.	'*Bartholomew Fair*: Comedy of Vapours', *Studies in English Literature* 1 (1961), 65–80.

Sackton, A. H.	*Rhetoric as a Dramatič Language in Ben Jonson* (N.Y. 1948).
Salingar, L. G.	'Farce and Fashion in *The Silent Woman*', *Essays and Studies* 20, N.S. (1967), 29–46.
Slights, William W. E.	'*Epicoene* and the Prose Paradox', *Philological Quarterly* 49 (1970), 178–87.
Townsend, Freda L.	*Apologie for Bartholomew Fayre* (N.Y. & London 1947).

IV. Molière Criticism

Adam, Antoine	*Histoire de la Littérature Francaise au XVIIe Siècle*, Tome III (Paris 1952).
Adam, Antoine	'La Genèse des *Précieuses Ridicules*', *Revue d'histoire de la philosophie et d'histoire générale de la civilisation* (jan.-mars 1939), 14–46.
Bellet, Roger	'Le Dom Juan de Molière: un cavalier de l'entendement' *Europe* (nov.-déc. 1972), 121–7.
Benichou, Paul	*Morales du grand siècle* (Paris 1948).
Bray, René	*Molière: homme de théâtre* (Paris 1954).
Brody, Jules	'Esthétique et Societé Chez Molière', in *Dramaturgie et Societé*, ed. Jean Jacquot (Paris 1968), Tome I, pp. 307–26.
Brody, Jules	'*Dom Juan* and *Le Misanthrope*, or the Esthetics of Individualism in Molière', PMLA 84 (1969), 559–76.
Brunetière, Ferdinand	*Etudes Critiques sur l'histoire de la littérature francaise*, 4e. série (Paris 1891).
Brunetière, Ferdinand	*Les époques du théâtre français 1636–1850* (Paris 1901).
Cairncross, John	*New Light on Molière: Tartuffe; Elomire Hypocondre* (Geneva & Paris 1956).
Cairncross, John	*Molière Bourgeois et Libertin* (Paris 1963).
Cairncross, John	'Impie en médecine', *Cahiers de l'association internationales des études françaises* 16 (1965), 269–84.
Calvet, Jean	*Molière est-il chrétien?* (Paris [1950]).
Cerny, Vaclav	'Le "je ne sais quoi" de Trissotin', *Revue des sciences humaines* (juillet-sept. 1961), 367–78.
Chauvois, L.	'Molière, Boileau, La Fontaine et la circulation du sang', *La Presse Medicale* 62 (1954), 1219–20.
Chill, Emanuel S.	'*Tartuffe, Religion, and Courtly Culture*', *French Historical Studies* 3 (1963), 151–83.
Coe, Richard N.	'The Ambiguity of *Dom Juan*', *Australian Journal of French Studies* 1 (1964), 23–35.
Cottez, Henri	'Sur Molière et Mademoiselle de Scudéry', *Revue d' Histoire de la philosophie et d'histoire générale de la civilisation* (1943), 340–64.
Defaux, Gerard	'Alceste et les rieurs' *Revue d'histoire littéraire de la France* 74 (1974), 579–99.

Donneau de Visé *Lettre écrite sur la comédie du Misanthrope* in Despois Mesnard, V, pp. 430–41.

Eustis, Alvin *Molière as Ironic Contemplator* (The Hague & Paris 1973).

La Fameuse Comédienne ou histoire de la Guerin auparavant femme et veuve de Molière, ed. Jules Bonnassies (Paris 1870 [1e. ed. Francfort 1688]).

Fernandez, Ramon *La Vie de Molière* (Paris 1929).

Francois, Carlo 'Médecine et religion chez Molière: deux facettes d'une méme absurdité', *French Review* 42 (1969), 665–72.

Gill, A. ' "The Doctor in the Farce" and Molière', *French Studies* 2 (1948), 101–28.

Girard, Joseph *A propos de L'Amour Médecin, Molière et Louis-Henry Daquin* (Paris 1948).

Godlewski, Guy 'Les médecins de Molière et leurs modèles', *La Semaine des Hôpitaux* 46 (1970), 3490–500.

Gossman, Lionel 'Molière and *Tartuffe*: Law and Order in the Seventeenth Century', *French Review* 43 (1970), 901–12.

Gross, Nathan 'The Dialectic of Obligation in Molière's Dom Juan', *Romanic Review* 65 (1974), 175–200.

Guicharnaud, Jacques *Molière: une aventure théâtrale* (Paris 1963).

Hall, H. Gaston 'A Comic Dom Juan', *Yale French Studies* 23 (1959), 77–84.

Hall, H. Gaston 'Molière, *Dom Juan:* "la scène du Pauvre" ', in *The Art of Criticism*, ed. Peter H. Nurse (Edinburgh 1969), pp. 69–87.

Hubert, J. D. *Molière and the Comedy of Intellect* (Berkeley & Los Angeles 1962).

Jasinski, René 'Sur Molière et la médecine', in *Mélanges de philologie, d'histoire et de littérature offerts à Joseph Vianey* (Paris 1934), pp. 249–54.

Jasinski, René *Molière et Le Misanthrope* (Paris 1951).

Jurgens Madeleine & Maxfield-Miller, Elizabeth *Cent Ans de recherches sur Molière, sur sa famille et sur les comédiens de sa troupe* (Paris 1963).

McBride, Robert *The Sceptical Vision of Molière* (London & Basingstoke 1977).

Millepierres, François *La Vie Quotidienne des Médecins au temps de Molière* (Paris 1964).

Mongrédien, Georges *Recueil des textes et des documents du XVIIe siècle relatifs Molière*, 2 vols. (Paris 1965).

Moore, W. G. *Molière: a New Criticism* (Oxford 1949).

Moore, W. G. 'Dom Juan Reconsidered', *Modern Language Review* 52 (1957), 510–17.

Morel, Jacques 'A propos de la "scène du pauvre" dans Dom Juan', *Revue d'histoire littéraire de la France* 72 (1972), 939–44.

Mornet, Daniel *Molière* (Paris, 5e édit., 1958).

Nurse, P. H.   'The Role of Chrysalde in *L'Ecole des Femmes*', *Modern Language Review* 56 (1961), 167–71.

Onimus, Jean   'Le Mystère de Dom Juan', *Annales du centre universitaire méditerranéen* 26 (1973), 55–9.

Palmer, John   *Molière: his life and work* (London 1930).

Perivier, Jacques-Henri   'Equivoques molièresques: le sonnet de Trissotin', *Revue des sciences humaines* 38 (1973), 543–54.

Pholien, Georges   'Une défense du *Tartuffe*', *Marche Romane* 17 (1967), 179–96.

Picard, Raymond   '*Tartuffe* "Production impie"?', in *Mélanges d'histoire littéraire offerts à Raymond Lebèque* (Paris 1969), pp. 227–39.

Pruner, Michel   'La notion de dette dans le *Dom Juan* de Molière', *Revue d'histoire du théâtre* 26 (1974), 254–71.

Robert, René   'Des commentaires de première main sur les chefs-d'oeuvre lesplus discutés de Molière', *Revue des sciences humaines* 30 (1956), 19–49.

Rotjman, Betty   'Alceste dans le théâtre de Molière', *Revue d'histoire littéraire de la France* 73 (1973) 963–81.

Rousseau, Jean-Jacques   *Lettre à D'Alembert sur les spectacles* (Paris 1935).

Rousset, Jean   'Dom Juan et le baroque', *Diogène* 14 (1956), 3–21.

Schérer, Jacques   *Structures de Tartuffe* (Paris, 1966).

Schérer, Jacques   *Sur le Dom Juan de Molière* (Paris 1967).

V. Other Works Cited

Berne, Eric   *Games People Play* (London 1966).

Bezancon, G. de   *Les médecins à la censure ou entretiens sur la médecine* (Paris 1677).

Bowers, Fredson (ed.)   *The Dramatic Works of the Beaumont and Fletcher Canon*, Vol. 3, (Cambridge 1973).

Chappuzeau, Samuel   *L'Académie des Femmes* in *Les Contemporains de Molière*, ed. Victor Fournel (Paris 1875), Tome III.

Haydn, Hiram   *The Counter-Renaissance* (N.Y. 1950).

Hunter, G. K.   *John Lyly: the Courtier as Humanist* (London 1962).

James I   *A Counter-blaste to Tobacco* (London 1954).

Lathuillère, Roger   *La Préciosité* (Paris 1966).

Lough, John (ed.)   *Locke's Travels in France 1675–1679* (Cambridge 1953).

Montaigne, Michel de   *Essais*, 3 vols. (Paris 1969).

Pepys, Samuel   *The Diary of Samuel Pepys*, eds. Robert Latham and William Matthews (Berkeley & Los Angeles 1970), Vol. II.

Sevigné, Mme. de   *Lettres de Madame de Sevigné*, 3 vols (Paris 1953–63).

Yates, Frances   'Did Newton connect his maths and alchemy?', THES, 18 March 1977.

Index